Henri Mignet and his FLYING FLEAS

Henri Mignet and his FLYING FLEAS

KEN ELLIS
&
GEOFF JONES

Foulis

Haynes

A **FOULIS** Aviation Book

First published 1990
© Ken Ellis & Geoffrey P. Jones 1990

Published by:
Haynes Publishing Group
Sparkford, Nr. Yeovil, Somerset
BA22 7JJ, England.

Haynes Publications Inc.
861 Lawrence Drive, Newbury Park,
California 91320, USA.

British Library Cataloguing in Publication Data
Ellis, Ken, *1953* –
    Henri Mignet and his flying fleas.
    1. Aircraft. Home built. French, history
    I. Title
    629.133'340422
    ISBN .i.0-85429-765-0

Library of Congress catalog card number 89-84706

Editor: Mansur Darlington
Design: Chris Hull
Layout: Tim Rose
Cover illustration: Ralph Pointer
Printed in England by: J.H. Haynes & Co. Ltd
Typeset in 11/12pt Rockwell Light Condensed

Frontispiece: **A photomontage by Henri Mignet which encapsulates his world: himself, the Flying Flea, his family, and his work.**

CONTENTS

FOREWORD

by Pierre Mignet

Pierre Mignet, Henri Mignet's son, autographs a copy of *Le Sport de l'Air* in the shade of a HM.1000 at Moulins in July 1988.
(Geoffrey P. Jones)

ADER TO ROGALLO – the list of aviation pioneers is endless. To these must be added the less well known; those who, often at the cost of their own lives, have been fundamental in the establishment of aviation as we know it today.

Very early on in aviation's history, the Bleriot used in the first Channel crossing in 1909 embodied the principles of control that have been extensively used in most types of aircraft, from the smallest to the largest, ever since. The fuselage is supported in flight by a fixed wing and a tail of which control surfaces move and determine the height and direction of the aircraft's flight. As it is, the classical design of aircraft would be perfect if it were not prone to one serious flaw: in certain flight conditions the pilot can lose control and, without the correct recovery action, the aircraft can fall to the ground. This is a spin or autorotation.

In the 1920s in a country house in the south west of France lived the son of an old local family. He was not very wealthy, but was gifted with a quick mind, plenty of manual skill, and above all else, imagination. Being the son of an artist, and an artist and aviation enthusiast himself, he could not come to terms with the dire effects of this sudden loss of control experienced in conventional aircraft.

He carried out extensive research in his own way; research that took him away from the beaten track. In 1933 he test flew his fourteenth prototype. A new aerodynamic formula had been born.

The aircraft was the POU DU CIEL or FLYING FLEA.

The man was HENRI MIGNET.

Although he was a genius, this pure and modest man never became wealthy as a result of his contribution to safety in aviation. He designed and built many other prototypes, all of them extremely safe. Establishment pilots chose either to ignore or to fight this man who was trying to bring about changes in their traditional thinking.

Many enthusiasts world-wide understood his ideas and, as this book reveals, hundreds of Flying Fleas have been built. A kind of mystique built up, a combination of admiration and friendly veneration, and on Henri Mignet the nickname 'Patron Saint of Homebuilders' was bestowed.

Some of these early amateur builders went on to form or to play significant roles in commercial aircraft manufacturing companies, sometimes unwittingly subsidised by the State, to design and build conventional aircraft. This is how France's light aircraft industry was reborn after the Second World War.

Today the descendants of the 'Patron Saint' are proving the enduring quality of the Flying Flea's principles, constructing the type commercially albeit in the Microlight/Ultralight category.

I am honoured to be Henri Mignet's son and to continue in my father's footsteps. It is in this dual capacity that I warmly congratulate Ken Ellis and Geoffrey P. Jones for evoking for you in the following pages the life of this truly exceptional Frenchman.

Pierre Mignet
Saintes, France

AUTHORS' INTRODUCTION

HENRI MIGNET'S NAME APPEARS PROMINENTLY in the annals of aviation history. A place in the history books need not, however, be an enviable position. History is littered with people who have become well known for the worst or most unfortunate of reasons.

To the great sadness of the authors, Mignet's just position in the aeronautical roll of honour is only truly appreciated by those who have been touched by his character and genius, or by those who have become his ardent followers.

To far too many, Mignet is at best a well-meaning but misguided individual, to others a crank or a maverick, to others a perpetrator of lethal design ideas.

This book serves, we hope, to place the man and his thoughts, and the products of those who have followed, into their correct historical context. Mignet's contribution was not an interesting, but fruitless, diversion in the path of aeronautical history. Mignet was in every sense of the word a pioneer. He hacked out a path of his own; a path down which tens of thousands have since trod, either adopting his design philosophy or taking up his notion of an aircraft built by and operated by the man-in-the street.

Through his endeavours, Henri Mignet took on the powers-that-be and had them accepting homebuilt aircraft where before they had not. Through his vision, Henri Mignet helped to spur the development of light aircraft design, aero-engine development and the formulation of organised homebuilding movements across the planet.

The ripples created by Mignet and his notion of *'Le Sport de l'Air'* have travelled right around the Earth and have seeped into almost every facet of light aviation. And today, his philosophy of aviation, if not his control theories, continue to be manifested physically in homebuilt aircraft, many of them true successors of the original *Pou du Ciel*. In France they call him the 'Patron Saint of Homebuilders'. In this book we aim to honour a great man who richly deserves that title and his rightful place in the history of aviation.

**Geoffrey P. Jones
Ken Ellis**

ACKNOWLEDGEMENTS

Naturally with a work of this size and scope, the authors have many people to thank for their contributions, guidance and advice.

In particular thanks must go to Pierre Mignet and his family for access to family records and photographs, and his enthusiasm and support during the gestation of this book.

In Britain particularly we wish to acknowledge the pioneering work of Peter Schofield for his initial researches into the Flea movement in the UK and for his unstinting search for records, memories and even airframes that has contributed considerably to the amount of knowledge on the HM.14.

Argentina: Ildefonso Durana, President of EAA Argentina; Jean de la Farge, French and Latin American Flea pioneer; Daniel Gomez; Francisco Halbritter.

Australasia: Bob Cornwell, antipodean Flea-researcher and builder, and Jim Jensz.

France: O. Coutrot; Raymond Dohet; Pierre Gaillard; Emmanuel Lerin, HM.8 builder; *Réseau du Sport de l'Air,* in particular Jacques Avril.

Great Britain: The late Stephen Villiers Appleby, Flea pioneer, for his comments and memories; John Bateman for much help on motorcycle engines and their aerial application; the late Harold Best-Devereux for his memories of Luton Aircraft and other Flea concerns of the mid-1930s; Roy Bonser; Alan Curry; Malcolm Fillmore; Alistair Goodrum; Peter Green; Mike Grigson, former Editor of *Popular Flying;* Roger Jackson for access to the A.J. Jackson photographic collection; Philip Jarrett of *Flight International;* George Jenks; Key Publishing, particularly Duncan Cubitt; Steve Langfield of Yeadon Aeroplanes; Nigel Ponsford, Flea sleuth and owner; Richard Riding, Editor of *Aeroplane Monthly;* Brian R. Robinson; Frank Sergeant, Flea builder; David Shrimpton, for access to his father's collection; John Stubbs, Flea builder; Peter Underhill, Editor of *Popular Flying;* Mike Vaisey; Peter West of Lincoln Graphics, for his illustrations; John Walls, Flea sleuth.

Netherlands: Dick Siebelink, Flea builder; Henk Wadman.

North America: Harry Adams, who dug deep into pre-war records on the American Mignet Corporation; Elton Barnum; Fred Bishop; Louis Dagne; Laurent Duval; Jake van Dyke; Frank Easton; The Experimental Aircraft Association at Oshkosh, Wisconsin, and especially to Pat Packard for his help on the Crosley Flea and promoting 1980s Flea interest in the USA; Chris Falconar, founder of Falconar Aviation; *Kitplanes* magazine; Leo Kohn; Bill Larkins for his extensive researches; Jack McNulty; Jack McWhorter, HM.360 builder; National Air & Space Museum Library; Albert Osterman; Norm Regnier; Harold Sherman, Director of the Yankee Air Force; Brian Sportsman; Bill Sterling; Robert Taylor, President of the Antique Airplane Association; Joseph Travis; John Underwood.

Also to numerous other people who have lent photo sources; these are credited below the relevant photograph.

For splendid efforts involved in translating a wealth of documentation from an assortment of languages: Colin Giles, Malcolm Ridge and Yvon Thoz.

Lastly, but most importantly, Geoff would like to thank his wife, Val, for her tireless support throughout the researching and writing of this work, and Ken would like to acknowledge his cat, who is genuinely called *Fleas!*

Chapter 1

FROM THE MEADOWS OF CHARENTE

THE MIGNET FAMILY HOME WAS NEAR Saintes in the *département* of Charente-Maritime in western France. In rural setting amid fields and woods, the house was relatively large, but represented a moderate family standard of living. Animals and landscapes were the particular specialities of Henri's father, who was an extremely talented painter although he was almost unknown outside this region of France. The family income was supplemented by breeding retrievers. The Mignet family enjoyed the outdoor life of hunting, animals and the countryside.

Henri Mignet was born at the family home on 19 October 1893. Not unnaturally, Henri's upbringing was heavily influenced by his family and home environment. In later years he recalled his first memories being of animals and the shadows and shapes of the woods and forests near his home. Mignet's father soon had his son involved in hunting expeditions, even though he was dwarfed by the six big retrievers he had been trained to handle. Henri did not really enjoy hunting and would forgo catching rabbits and hares to sit or lie in the meadow watching the big birds circling around overhead.

He counted the seconds between the flaps of the birds' wings, and his father used to tell him 'they are sailing' when bombarded with questions about bird flight. Mignet longed to be able to speak to these creatures to find out the secret of their flight.

At the age of eight, Henri left home to become a boarder at the church school of Notre Dame de Recouvrance, about eight miles from Saintes. From here he went on to study at the grammar school in Nantes. School life was a mixture of learning, comradeship, self-expression and mischievousness; in short, he was no different from thousands of other boys thrown together in a boarding school.

Henri's interest in flight was still very much with him. It received further encouragement when Orville Wright flew his aircraft at Le Mans in 1909. Pictures of this event and France's Antoinette over Betheny, near Reims in August 1909, when the world's first air race attracted 38 entrants, meant that aircraft were plastered over the front pages of all the newspapers. Mignet copied their silhouettes and shapes onto the covers of his school books, a skill he would use in years to come in the illustration of his articles and books.

During his school days his inventiveness and determination were to find many outlets. Like a prisoner he managed to file his own key. He did not want to escape, however, but to get access to the school's darkroom. The darkroom was used for only eight days a year and it seemed the ideal location for a secret and private workshop. Here Henri reigned, undisputed as he feigned sickness during French, history and book-keeping lessons, sneaking away to the solitude of the darkroom to work on his first electronic radio receiver.

His aerial was clipped onto the headmaster's telephone line. He was able to pick up the weather forecasts that were regularly broadcast from the Eiffel Tower.

As well as his dabblings with radio, the darkroom also saw him creating first his kite and then a camera. The camera was made of cardboard and rubber and was blackened with burnt cork, the lens coming from a pair of opera glasses. The whole item weighed only a couple of ounces.

With the camera mounted on the kite, he devised a method of aerial photography. Some of the first photographs he took were of the family house near Saintes. Upon showing them to his mother she is reputed to have remarked, when seeing the large expanse of roofing for the first time, that it was no wonder there were so many gutters and rainwater pipes!

All of Henri's savings went on buying books and magazines about aviation and new and better tools for his workshop. He used to give the day boys money and instructions on what he wanted. They would smuggle the goods into school on Monday mornings. The workshop soon became more like a small factory. Kites were joined by model aeroplanes, including one with flapping wings which Mignet claimed flew with some success.

At the age of eighteen Mignet started corresponding with Gustav Lilienthal, the German glider pioneer. During the summer holidays of 1912 at Saintes, Mignet built a full-size Lilienthal-type glider from bamboo canes and brown wrapping paper reinforced with string. Although not designated at the time, this was the HM.1 – the first of a long line of designs bearing the 'HM' prefix, a line still proudly continued by the family.

Having built the HM.1, Mignet was naturally anxious to test it. One of the meadows surrounding his parents' house had a favourable down-gradient, even though it was surrounded by trees. Much like a modern-day hang-glider pilot, Mignet strapped on the HM.1 and ran down the field at speed. Sometimes he would take off, sometimes not. When he did achieve take-off, winds and downdraughts would bring him crashing to the ground, scaring the living daylights out of this ambitious teenager.

This partial success gave him encouragement for his next project. Using similar methods and materials, he built a biplane hang-glider on the lines of the aircraft built by Octave Chanute. Again, this was undesignated, but we shall call this the HM.1.2. With Henri's family as worried rather than curious spectators, one windy day their aviator son carried out some trial hops.

While Henri effected some minor repairs, Henri asked his father to hold the HM.1.2 at the front while he went around to the tail. With a lull in the proceedings, Henri's father decided to light a cigarette. He slackened his grip just as a gust of wind caught the biplane. It took off, did a half-loop and crashed down – upon the head of Henri's sister! She was unhurt, but the wing fabric was badly damaged and Henri conceded that this was a lucky escape. That cigarette was to be cursed even many years later!

School days over, Henri Mignet was enrolled at the Bordeaux *École Philomatique* (School of Electro-Physics). Here he had to work somewhat harder, reading industrial design as well as completing his studies in electricity. Aviation and flying machines were put to one side in favour of radio and wireless telegraphy.

His first job was also in Bordeaux, at the Motobloc factory. He was soon surprising his supervisors, given his age and relative inexperience, by the quality of his work. On the outbreak of the First World War in August 1914, Henri hid some of his valuable radio equipment in the loft of a nearby church.

The war enabled Mignet to pursue his career in radio, serving as a radio-telephonist. He seems to have been an independent person, putting on the headphones at the start of his duty and removing them when he'd finished, hoping in the meantime that there had been a delivery of mail so that having eaten his meal, he could return to his quarters to read and write.

Serving at first on the Champagne front with an artillery unit, he practised drawing a bead on reconnaissance aircraft. Here he renewed his interest in flight, using the range-finder to study the flight of buzzards. He got his first real taste of flying when he used his off-duty time to chat to and befriend the mechanics at a nearby squadron airfield. Here, he could witness the comings and goings of Nieuports, SPADs, Breguets, Salmsons and the like.

Putting on the blue overalls of the mechanics he would sneak out onto the airfield and helped to start engines, remove wheel chocks and walk the aircraft back to the flight line after a landing. All the while he was getting to know the more intimate details of the aircraft he was handling. With the help of an amiable sergeant pilot, Mignet managed to get a flight in a SPAD. The aircraft ended up upside down in a wheat field, the sergeant sustaining three broken ribs. Mignet left the scene hurriedly, returning to the relative safety of his wireless van to resume his proper duties.

He was posted to the Balkan Front to Stroumica on the River Vardar in Macedonia. Here he studied, in between radio-telegraphy duties, bird flight. He was particularly taken with the migratory flights of storks and vultures, avidly recording his observations in copious notes. In 1918 he contracted malaria and returned to his parents' house in Charente for a lengthy period of convalescence. He used this time to design and construct radio valves, learning how to blow glass, create vacuums and to handle mercury. He then caught yellow fever, possibly transmitted by the same mosquito that gave him the malaria. Rest with no exercise whatsoever was the therapy, so he sat in an armchair, dreaming. Mignet reflected on those notes from Macedonia and Champagne on bird flight.

Mignet described his home as the oasis to meet all the needs of daily life. His workshop was well equipped with lathes, grindstones, drills and suchlike. The stable served as his laboratory and his library of papers, magazines and books was in the attic.

Nineteen twenty was to be the turning point in his aviation work as the product of his thoughts, writings, designs and manual effort resulted in the completion of his first powered aeroplane, the HM.2. A monoplane, looking akin to a Bleriot from the front, it had a wingspan of 32 ft 9 in (9.9 m) and had pivoting wings, as pioneered by Willi Messerschmitt.

'Roll out' came in March 1920, Mignet taking the HM.2 into the meadow. Using all his acquired knowledge from reading, talking and flying the HM.1s and the SPAD, he started to teach himself to fly. 'Aviation started to become a reality,' he said. Yet hopes and aspirations were for nothing: the HM.2 could not, or would not, fly. All it did was make a tremendous noise.

A collection of bits and pieces, some poached, some fabricated in the workshop, the HM.2 featured basic flying instruments and a home-made carburettor. Everything worked well, but never simultaneously!

Describing the HM.2 as cumbersome, Mignet dismantled it and used many of the parts in the new HM.3. It was his sister who nicknamed the HM.3 *Le Dromadaire* (Camel) because it had a very obvious hump to the fuselage. Power came from a 30 hp engine, the power of which scared Mignet and it was never run much above idle speed. Even so the little machine sped across the field between the

The large HM.3, which was nicknamed *Le Dromadaire* (Camel) by Mignet's sister. It did not fly. (RSA, via Jacques Avril).

cows and the sheep causing much consternation. Like those before it, the HM.3 did not fly.

Mignet travelled to the first Congress of Motorless Flight, held at Combergrasse in 1922. He wanted to glean a better insight into the latest in flying machines. Strange that at a motorless flight congress he should find out about the latest aero-engines, but it was here that he was told of the 10 hp Anzani, a motorcycle engine made by the French motorcycle manufacturer, and took immediate steps to acquire one. This engine and the

The HM.4 of 1923, rudderless, like the HM.3, but now exhibiting the low-slung parasol configuration that was to epitomise Mignet's designs.
(RSA, via Jacques Avril).

Above: The HM.5 hang glider which made quite a name for itself in French gliding circles.
(Geoffrey P. Jones Collection).

Left: General arrangement of the HM.4.

Congress were to inspire his next two designs, the HM.4 and the HM.5 glider. The glider was made from the left-overs of the Anzani-powered, rudderless, monoplane.

Mignet took both the HM.4 and HM.5 to an aviation meeting at Orly, near Paris, by train in 1922. When they arrived, still intact, they

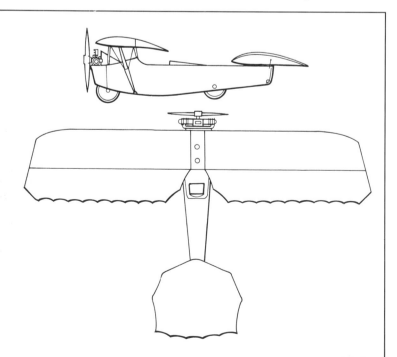

were pushed by hand along the road to the aerodrome. The HM.4 made several hops, never more than 32 feet high. Resembling a modern hang-glider, the HM.5 was tested in the wash of the propellers of the aircraft from the Richard Flying School.

Les Ailes (Wings), the French aeronautical magazine then under the helm of Georges Houard, reported on the event, and in its issue dated 14 June 1923 the British weekly *Flight* described the HM.4 as 'this experimental light plane of unorthodox design'. In the article, *Flight* talked of Mignet's fear of 'the greatest danger to the ordinary aeroplane, *perte de vitesse*, or stalling'. *Flight* was happy to agree with Mignet's analysis of the stall, but not with his method of solving the problem.

Mignet earned a meagre living running a small business from home making and selling wireless sets, but he always preferred to work on his aeroplanes. The second Congress of Motorless Flight was held in 1923 at Vauville, near the Cap de la Hague on the west coast of the Cherbourg peninsula – still the site of a small airfield. He and his friend Bonnet, who had built a glider similar to Mignet's HM.5, packed up their aircraft so that they were no larger than big packing cases and set off by train for Cherbourg with their 'luggage'. Some of the other competitors with non-foldable machines had to pay as much as 2,000 francs to the railway for the transport of their aircraft.

At last Mignet seemed to be achieving some success with the HM.5. At Vauville he would continue to fly hanging beneath the HM.5 even when strengthening winds prevented the others from flying. This delighted the crowd of spectators even though the HM.5 was tethered to a rope with a maximum height of around six or seven feet being achieved. Nessler, another friend of Mignet, recorded the event with his camera by lying flat with the HM.5 hovering above him.

At Vauville Mignet won one of the prizes and received much in the way of encouragement. The prize wasn't even enough to pay his hotel bill and although Mignet was keen to try out further developments of the HM.4 and the HM.5, his resources were sadly depleted and for a while he had to concentrate on establishing a business of some sort.

He had read books about the new American method of chicken farming, the forerunner of the modern-day battery hen system. This was a moderate success, not from the production of eggs, but from the sale of chicken meat. The books said that one man should be able to farm 1,000 hens per hectare, Mignet's method was half a man farming 500 hens on half a hectare! The other half of the chicken-farmer was busy in his workshop building the HM.6, financed by his hens.

This design was a complete revision of previous layouts, with the pilot seated right at the front, with a high pivoting wing above the pilot's head and a pusher engine mounted behind him. An open framework extended back to support the tail and tail skid. The HM.6's tail would take off easily, but never the heavier nose. 'This was sport but not aviation,' he later wrote, and undertook a redesign.

Next Mignet turned his attentions to vertical take-off. The HM.7 was a helicopter. Substantiating his ideas and researching the HM.7 had involved Mignet in many months of reading and sifting through piles of papers, books and journals. He came across details of experiments by the Cornu brothers and so Mignet devised a way to make the 10 hp Anzani drive a 19 ft 6 in (5.9 m) diameter rotor via a series of pulleys and belts. It succeeded in lifting the machine and pilot, but the Anzani was past its prime.

The radical HM.6, a major departure from previous Mignet design thinking.
(RSA, via Jacques Avril).

Trouble with the variable pitch control gave problems with the big pulley causing the belt to stick: the HM.7 crashed. Mignet decided it was time to give up such ventures. There were too many bits and pieces involved, he didn't have enough experience with this form of flying and was beginning to lose his patience.

All his documents, notes, drawings and results from his work on the HM.7 were collated together as a record of the experiments. Mignet hoped to have the time to come back to them one day and continue where he had left off.

In 1926, aged 33, Henri married Annette and they moved to Paris where he worked in the publicity department of Société Philips. His interest in radio had led him in this direction, sets were now much more compact than those available when he first dabbled with them. On the 40 metre waveband Mignet could pick up transmissions from up to 1,250 miles (2,012 km) away. In 1927, François, their first son was born and the news was transmitted via other helpful amateurs to Henri's brother-in-law in Saigon, French Indo-China (now Vietnam). Return congratulations were received the following day as quickly as using cable, and of course, free.

By 1927 photography was an established science, but moving pictures and the cinema were entering an exciting period. Mignet took an interest for a while, building his own camera using the cogs and gears from an old alarm clock.

Despite these diversions, Mignet could not get the thought of aeroplanes and flying out of his mind. He still had the engine, wheels, fuselage and wings of the HM.6. Mignet could not exist without an aircraft to work on, even if it wouldn't fly. He asked journalists not to laugh at his predicament, even if they could not understand it: 'To fly is not the only thing that aviation is all about'.

The first aircraft for the amateur

Helped with finance and sponsorship from the Brissaud brothers, who specialised in the transportation of abnormally large loads, Mignet was able to continue his work on the next aeroplane design, the HM.8. This was a hybrid of bits and pieces from earlier projects combined with new ones.

Returning to Charente, in the meadows that had witnessed earlier failures, the overhauled Anzani made the HM.8 tear about in clouds of dust as Mignet began to get the feel of the new machine. The parasol wings which were a complete redesign were better centred, had quite a pronounced dihedral and, most significantly of all, did not have ailerons. The tailplane was of the all-flying kind and had a conventional fin and rudder.

For the first time Mignet saw 'the ground move away sideways as the wheels left the

The prototype HM.8, the start of Europe's homebuilding movement.
(RSA, via Jacques Avril).

ground'. With the Anzani giving out a healthy roar it was time for Mignet to learn the practicalities of piloting. For two months Mignet was thrilled at carrying out 'real aviation'. This aircraft was a significant step forward, Mignet having taken advice and arranged for the centre of gravity of the aircraft to fall just behind the centre of lift of the wing. The wing pivoted at its centre of lift, or thereabouts, and could be moved up or down to increase or decrease the angle of attack.

On the beach at Royon, where Mignet had taken the HM.8 for some more flying, he experienced his most serious crash to date. At quite low level the aircraft was caught by a sideways gust of wind while Mignet was reducing speed. The little aircraft spun into the ground and Mignet was lucky to escape with only minor injuries. The HM.8 was wrecked and Mignet's mind began to think back to his observations of bird flight. He swore then never to be found in the air at the controls of a conventional aeroplane.

Although frustrated and annoyed by the crash, Mignet had the satisfaction of knowing that he had designed and built his own aircraft, taught himself to fly it and enjoyed a couple of months accumulating many hours of flight experience. He wondered whether his ideas and experiments were unique because the pages of all the aviation journals of the time were full of stories and details about larger aircraft and gliders. There was, he claimed, virtually nothing being published about his kind of light aviation.

Before the crash at Royon, Mignet had painted an idyllic picture of life while test flying the HM.8. With the advantage of its easily folded wings he and Annette were able to wheel the aircraft along roads and tracks for about 1½ miles to a suitable, large, field. Annette would sit under a tree sewing baby clothes while Henri would attempt to fly the HM.8, a task that was largely governed by the moods of the Anzani engine. Field modifications would be made to the HM.8, but when they had had enough, the wings would be folded, the tools and Annette's sewing basket would be placed in the cockpit, and they would wheel the creation home.

In many people's minds this kind of flying is the epitome of what flying is about, even today. No interference, total freedom and pure fun in a light, small aeroplane that is easily transportable.

Mignet read avidly in both aviation and radio. Realising that there was a dearth of articles on the type of aviation now dearest to his heart, Mignet reasoned that he had nothing to lose by writing about his aerial exploits. The 22 March 1928 edition of *Les Ailes* published his first article: *L'Aviation de l'Amateur est-elle une Possibilité?* Mignet described how he had built the HM.8 for the same price as his radio receiver, about 3,500 francs. He wrote that he was not unique and that anybody with an average degree of skill could emulate his achievement.

Immediately, a hornets' nest was stirred up. There were the partisans who admired and applauded Mignet but there was an equally large and vociferous group who thought his ideas a joke. Among this latter group, Mignet sensed a degree of nervousness. Had he challenged the Establishment? Were the aircraft manufacturers of France smugly sitting by in their factories ignoring the kind of aviation the HM.8 stood for?

Some of the negative comments generated by the article in *Les Ailes* were in the following vein: 'Mignet is joking, he cannot have made his own propeller', or 'The aircraft will break up on take-off', or 'Assembly of an aircraft entails responsibilities, it is not just wood and nails thrown together', or 'The designer has to understand the theories of the strengths of materials'.

These criticisms had to be answered by Mignet and in the three months after publication, *Les Ailes* was full of letters, comments and counter comments. Whichever side the reader took, it was undeniable that Mignet had launched the word 'amateur' into the world of European aviation. While considerable clarification of the ideas and soothing of ruffled feathers in the Establishment was necessary, the time was right to capitalise on the ripples created in the pond. Mignet had to be the man for this, as Annette told her husband, 'It's for you to do, my old man'.

On 21 May 1929 Jean Joubert from Angouleme, near Saintes in western France, made the first flight in an amateur-built HM.8. It was not quite the floodtide of building that was to occur with the HM.14 *Pou du Ciel* five years later, but it was an epoch.

With the interest that Mignet's little HM.8 had stirred, he reflected for a while on why, to his

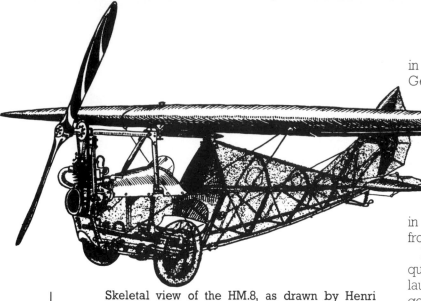

Skeletal view of the HM.8, as drawn by Henri Mignet.
(Musée de l'Air).

knowledge, he was the first serious promoter of the amateur-built aircraft outside the United States. At the same moment he accepted that in the world of gliding, and particularly in Germany, there was a strong amateur movement. He concluded that although France had light aircraft manufacturers, the designers and managers of these six or seven companies were not pilots. Light aircraft trials had been held almost simultaneously in France and Britain in late 1923 but little seemed to have stemmed from them.

Mignet asked himself two important questions: 'Aviation for the people; will it be launched by pilots?' and 'The rules which govern aviation; do they come from civilians?' The answer to the first question was yes, and to the second no. Now that he had shown that the air could also be a sports ground for people's aircraft, it did not matter about the aircraft the factories were building or the rules and regulations that governed flying – the future could look after itself.

In an infectious style that was rapidly becoming Mignet's trademark, he continued to eulogise his success with the HM.8. He admitted that the design was not perfect and he was fully aware of the many pundits who

Left: Many would-be fliers undertook the construction of HM.8s. This example of unknown origin has an unusual engine cowling arrangement. Note also the twin tailwheel – a feature to become standard on the HM.14. (Musée de l'Air).

Below: Advert for plans for the HM.8 as featured in the French magazine *Les Ailes.* (Musée de l'Air).

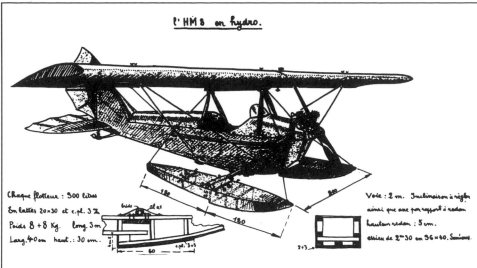

l' HM 8 on hydro.

Above: Mignet's workshop, November 1931. HM.8 in foreground, HM.9 at rear, with, probably, HM.11 in centre. (Musée de l'Air).

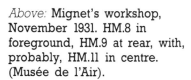

Above: Mignet's sketch of how to put the HM.8 on floats. (Musée de l'Air).

wrote off the HM.8 and the interest it had generated as a short-lived fad. Henri Mignet, former squadron radio operator, cockpit parasite and aviation spectator, without any major financial help or major discussions, without political intrigue or string pulling, had managed to inspire hundreds who had never flown before to start building and flying their own aircraft.

None of these HM.8s, mainly built in France, was officially registered. Most were flown from fields and unofficial aerodromes. These builders helped not only Mignet to continue his pursuit of an aircraft for the people but also to establish one of the first amateur aircraft movements in the world.

Between the publication of Mignet's article in *Les Ailes* in 1928 and 1931, he received a continuous stream of letters and photographs from all over the world on the subject of the HM.8 and what it represented. When all this material was assembled it weighed fourteen pounds.

Now sufficiently confident about the HM.8, Mignet felt that he could bring his thoughts together and reach an even wider audience. He would write a book. The first edition of *Le Sport de l'Air* was published in October 1931, a handwritten book in which Mignet described how to build one's own ultralight aeroplane for

around £50 plus the cost of the engine.

While he knew that his ideas were popular, Mignet estimated that around 200 or so copies might be sold, so he decided to publish it himself. As well as the meticulous Mignet longhand style for the text, Mignet did all the

General arrangement of the HM.8.

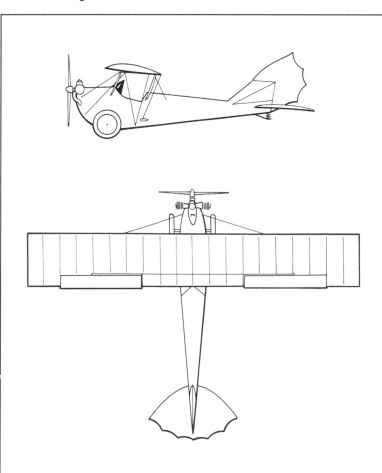

illustrations and then made his own negatives and offset printing plates.

A friend in the newspaper business loaned him a printing press and Henri and Annette laboriously bound each copy by hand. The entire print run was sold out in eight days and a second edition went just as quickly once prepared.

An anonymous HM.8B found in the hangars at Pont St-Vincent in July 1977.
(Henk Wadman).

The Dessenis AD-01, designed by Albert Dessenis for the Club-Aviation Valenciennes, was derived from the HM.8. It was powered by a 40 hp Salmson.
(Musée de l'Air).

As the numbers of HM.8 builders grew, their feedback and enthusiasm for Mignet's concepts continued to encourage him. Mignet's mail included such endorsements as: 'I have never doubted the attributes of your design; I am now extremely pleased – you have given us the "bug".' Or, 'I am one of your numerous followers who is now clocking up flying hours, very thrilled and I would like to thank you sincerely – I do not just skim the grass at low level in my aeroplane, I fly at many different heights – your book for me is a providence. . . .'

Another wrote, 'After months of hard labour, foregoing many things, surviving many ups and downs, we can now report on our HM.8. On behalf of all our group I would like to thank you for your book which has enabled us to live our dream'. And 'While I was away my parents read the book and you have managed to win them over to your cause even though they are hardened *bourgeois*!' And finally, leaving the class struggle aside: 'One of the best works of aeronautical explanation, we'd like to tell you that it is your book which not just lit the flame but kept it going, enabling us to stick the project out to the end'.

One of the first HM.8 builders in France to complete his aircraft following the instructions in the book was an ex-First World War pilot. He immediately set off on a 75 mile cross-country flight in his unlicensed, unregistered HM.8 and was fined 100 francs for landing such a craft on a public aerodrome.

Mignet made several visits to see HM.8s that

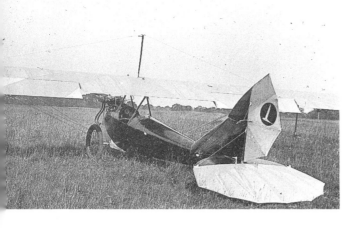

Emmanuel Lerin's first HM.8 (via Emmanuel Lerin).

other builders had completed; he commented, 'It was as though the same person had built them all, with very few differences, all somewhat basic, all well cared for, but none fragile. The building and the assembly of the main structure is correct and although my instructions are perhaps a little vague in places, they have all been sensibly interpreted – on this score there seems to be nothing to worry about!'

The year is 1933 and a young Emmanuel Lerin is at work on the 10 m wing of his first HM.8. (via Emmanuel Lerin).

Emmanuel Lerin's HM.8 makes its first flight in 1936, in the hands of a French Air Force pilot. (via Emmanuel Lerin).

On the Monday of Pentecost in 1931 and at the age of 18, Frenchman Emmanuel Lerin started the construction of an HM.8 at his home near Les Montils using a copy of the articles published in *Les Ailes* and then the hand-written book *Le Sport de l'Air*. It was completed and flown for the first time in 1936 by a military pilot friend. Lerin then flew it although he had no previous piloting experience. In October of

The year is 1983 and Emmanuel Lerin is again at work on an HM.8 this time his second version with a 8 m span. (via Emmanuel Lerin).

The Lerin HM.8 No 2 F-PYTA, in as many ways as possible but for the narrower span, is a faithful replica of his first HM.8 of 1936. Colour scheme is light blue trim with varnished wood fuselage. (via Emmanuel Lerin).

the same year overconfidence in the face of lack of experience got the better of him and he wrote the aircraft off when he hit the top of a tree; fortunately without serious injury to himself.

M Lerin kept certain parts of the original aircraft including the Ava engine and exactly fifty years to the day after he started work on his HM.8 No.1, and at the age of 68, he started work on HM.8 No.2. The 1980's version was identical to the original, following Mignet's plans faithfully with the exception that it had an 8 metre wingspan, 2 metres shorter than the original. No.2 was brought to the RSA rally at Brienne in 1985 by road to participate in the Fiftieth Anniversary celebrations of the publication of *Le Sport de l'Air,* Mignet's book about the HM.14. The following year in November the HM.8 No.2 was granted its CNRA certificate, given the registration F-PYTA and was flown for the first time at Le Breuil airfield, Blois. Asked about completion of the project, Lerin said, 'I have now achieved a fitting tribute to Henri Mignet. I'll only fly the aircraft a little as I want to preserve the HM.8 as a reminder for future generations of the early days of amateur aviation'.

Mignet admitted that the engines for the HM.8, as would be the case a few years later

with the HM.14, were one of its major problems. He felt that converted motorcycle engines – used by almost every builder – were only a temporary solution. Of the propeller, he said that although most had been carved at home by amateurs, this was really a job for a craftsman. Nonetheless, this had not proved an obstacle and, like the standards of writing, grammar and spelling in the letters he received, so it was with building and carving: some were better than others.

Through their active interest in the HM.8 many of the builders and partisans of the Mignet cause learnt that their 'leader' was continuing his development of the idea of amateur aviation, extending it to the totally safe, easy to fly, unstallable and unspinnable aeroplane. The HM.8 was the springboard from which Mignet would make further refinements. He designed a new wing for it, doing away with the three-axis controls that had contributed to his crash at Royon. He was aiming to build a craft with 'natural controls'.

This was the HM.9 which had pivoting wings of 42 ft 6 in (14.8 m) span that operated differentially in an attempt to achieve lateral control. Trials at Orly with the HM.9 were unsuccessful and the aeroplane was scrapped following an accident.

By 1930 the HM.10 was under development employing virtually the same control system but with a thick, fixed, wing. The engine was positioned behind the pilot in the fuselage, driving a tractor propeller through a chain reduction gear and transmission shaft.

It was at this stage of his researches that the ever-resourceful Mignet constructed his own wind tunnel, assisted by his two good friends and helpers, Albert and Pierre Brissaud. The wind tunnel utilised the faithful old Anzani, which was placed at one end of the tunnel to suck air through, whilst a scale model of the aircraft under test was positioned at the other end. With this device Mignet could ascertain the characteristics of the new wing for builders of the HM.8. The wing arrived at was of elliptical planform and was far more efficient than the original, constant chord one.

Mignet was determined to provide a degree of 'builder-support' and continued to improve the basic design. This level of concern for his customers is still lacking in some modern day homebuild aircraft marketers.

With as many as 200 HM.8s under construction, with Mignet's research continuing and the publication of *Le Sport de l'Air*, the word soon spread that his new ideal aircraft would have tandem wings. For the first time the French press referred to this project as *Le Pou du Ciel* –Flea of the Sky, Flying Flea, Sky Louse.

The HM.8 had been a success, but it was primitive and complicated. Mignet was set to take a new direction with his followers, an enthusiastic and active group who were ready to pursue him in the search for a smaller, easier, safer and cheaper version of the amateur aircraft.

The meadows of Charente had spawned the ideas. It was time for the woods of Bouleaux to help them mature.

The pivoting wing HM.9 fitted with a 500 cc Chaise motorcycle engine with chain drive to the propeller.
(RSA, via Jacques Avril).

Pioneers of the homebuild movement who built HM.8s

An estimated 200 HM.8s were built and many of these successfully flew in France and its colonies. It was the first true European homebuilt aircraft as we understand the term today. Researches have discovered the following pioneer builders:

Jean Joubert of Angoulême who called his HM.8 *Michele-Annie*
Robert Robineau who became one of Mignet's most loyal supporters
Albert Mouchet from Paris who also became a lifelong supporter
M Dessenis of Valenciennes
M Gaston Chenu
M Courrègelongue of Marmande
Jean Rul of Bougan (Herault)
Stephen Appleby who flew his HM.8 at Nice with first a 24 hp Harley-Davidson and then an ABC Scorpion engine of 35 hp before advancing to an HM.14 (see Chapter 4)
Leon Bare of Monthureux-sur-Saône
Charles Dumont of Troyes
M Lévy of Calais
J. Jaltel of Puy-Guillaume
Emmanuel Lerin of Les Montils Loir-et-Cher who first fitted a Harley-Davidson then a four-cylinder Ava engine. In 1983 he built another HM.8 to be at Brienne le Château for the 50th Anniversary of *Le Sport de l'Air* in 1985
M Henrotte who completed his HM.8 in 1931
Henri Gérard a shopkeeper of Leopoldville in the Belgian Congo
De Prieto and André Costa of Mostaganem in Algeria; their HM.8 first flew on 23 October 1933

Plus others from all walks of life, both young and old: mechanics, lawyers, carpenters, dentists, waiters, managers, postmen, farmers, market stall holders, painters, doctors, sculptors, students, builders, harvesters, a Spanish marquis, a docker from Marseilles, garage owners, millers, restaurateurs, photographers, a music teacher, gardener . . ..

As Mignet said: 'The enthusiasm of the air is universal – amateur aviation is not a problem of construction.'

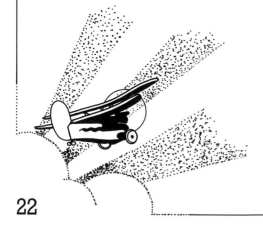

Chapter 2

THE FLEA IS BORN

Take ten young men, all interested in sport, full of life and strength. Assume that they have never seen an aeroplane. Pick out one of them haphazard, it doesn't matter which, and put him in an aeroplane. Say to him, 'The pedals are for steering; by moving the control column this way you re-establish your lateral balance; this way, you rise or you descend. With the throttle you regulate the power of the engine'. Start the propeller and leave him to his own devices. He will not have flown 100 yards before he is in a spin. What is more, the other nine young men will also spin. Quoted from the chapter 'Pourquoi' (Why?) by Henri Mignet in his book Le Sport de l'Air, 1934.

MIGNET'S SOMEWHAT UNCOMPLIMENTARY assessment of the average young man's ability to fly a conventional aeroplane may have been clouded by his statement a few lines further on: 'Je ne suis pas pilote' (I am not a pilot).

It was with his friend Pierre Colin, an instructor during the First World War, that Mignet tried to learn to fly a conventional aeroplane, the Potez 43.0 F-AMJS. In the summer of 1932, Mignet accumulated about thirty hours in the Potez, some in the pilot's seat, but many just as observer and navigator on trips around northern France and Belgium. 'A machine quite beyond me,' was Mignet's assessment of the Potez.

No matter what, these flying experiences were to have a major influence on Mignet's philosophy about flying and the mechanics of piloting a flying machine. In his flowery and prophetic style he grouped his experience of both types of aircraft into a comparison: 'Luck has so arranged – oh my guardian angel – that I should pilot the *Pou du Ciel* before taking in hand seriously the control of an aeroplane. My reactions were formed by sane instinct. All the

stuff learned in ten consecutive hours of flying an aeroplane vanished in 100 metres of flight on the Flea.'

His denigration of the conventional aeroplane, or perhaps just himself as a pilot of a 'normal' aeroplane, then comes to a monumental conclusion:

'What is it in fact, this learning to fly? To be precise, it is to learn NOT to fly wrong.'

Did the Flea come into existence because of Mignet's dissatisfaction at his skills in piloting a conventional aeroplane, or was it the Flea and its unconventional design and controls that caused Mignet, its creator, to crusade for it with the tunnel vision of a zealot? A classic chicken and egg argument. Whatever the origins of the venom, Mignet was not just disillusioned with the conventional aeroplane: 'The aeroplane is frightening,' he wrote.

This character assassination of the conventional aircraft was because throughout his design experience so far, Mignet had found the 'normal' aircraft to be wanting as an amateur-built, fun aeroplane. He was looking for a cheap, safe, easy-to-fly, lightweight aeroplane for the man in the street.

Mignet was quite content to accept the use of conventionally controlled aeroplanes for air transport but another system would be needed for true amateur aviation. The tenets Mignet listed for his concept still hold true today –and work just as well on today's designs, described in Chapter 15.

Mignet's criteria were:

Security of construction.
Security by means of a margin of speed.
Security by means of stability of shape.
Security by rational controls for flight.
Economy – of materials, dimensions, powerplant and running costs.
Lightness of the aircraft; which implies smallness, small powerplant and cheapness.

Mignet wrote at length about these in the French aviation magazine *Les Ailes* for 28 January 1932 in relation to aeroplanes of less than 220 lb (100 kilos) empty weight and concluded that it was possible to make such a craft that was no heavier than the average pilot (176 lb; 80 kg). 'To fly very cheaply one must make something very small.'

By combining the idea of a small lightweight aeroplane with Mignet's enthusiasm for the simplicity of piloting an aircraft the stage was set for the Flea to be born. But how did the unique Flea formula come about?

The Flea was the culmination of many years of research, study and experimentation. Even before the Wright brothers had flown in 1903, Mignet had concluded that birds were so free in the air because they could control directly the amount of lift employed at any moment. Model kites and aeroplanes towed behind a bicycle showed him that the kite remained stable, but the aeroplane was unstable, spinning around and around. Mignet concluded, rightly, that an aeroplane needed a pilot to control it, whereas a kite did not.

Mignet was openly hostile about the control of conventional aeroplanes in which aileron had to be corrected by rudder to achieve a balanced turn, and the fact that it was possible to cross these controls could lead to a spin and disaster. If one of these controls could be removed, he argued, it would be impossible to cross them and, *voilà*, the problem would be solved!

Mignet observed that a kite does not possess ailerons yet is perfectly stable, only needing to be controlled in altitude and direction. Thus he decided that it was ailerons that he could afford to do without on his new design.

Using his earlier design, the conventional HM.8, Mignet made a brief study of aerodynamics – the centre of pressure, balance and controls. He dismissed bombastically the follies that had accumulated in the design of aircraft to date: 'Leave aviation to the aviators – let us go off on our own voyage of discovery.'

In a conventional aeroplane the pilot alters lift by varying the angle of incidence of the wing, using the elevators at the tail. This system, Mignet believed, introduced a delay in the controls and, just as a horse rider can establish a direct feel, or control, between himself and the horse, Mignet wanted a control system that gave immediacy to the aircraft's control.

If the tail (elevators) were fixed, he argued, and the main wing detached from the fuselage and allowed to pivot through direct control linkage with the control column, this immediacy of control could be achieved. Mignet realised the importance of the centre of pressure (Cp) in his system; it could only work if the pivot point of the wing were placed so that in all flight conditions the centre of pressure was behind it. This would ensure that the trailing edge of the wing was always trying to lift, creating a continuous 'feeling' on the control column and automatically tending toward a condition where the angle of incidence, and therefore the lift, decreased.

Mignet realised also the importance of the aerofoil shape required to stabilise the movement of the Cp, and his new aerofoil had an upturned trailing edge. Any increase in incidence would increase the pull on the control column. This would be a force instantly recognisable to the pilot; in Mignet's terms: "He has a *living* wing'.

Landing with the new wing presented problems. The conventional arrangement of the HM.8 meant that, upon cutting the engine for a landing, the aircraft was still going too fast, necessitating a pull back on the stick to increase the wing's incidence. At 30 mph, still flying, Mignet pulled back still further with the aeroplane dropping alarmingly to the ground. The craft had run out of lift and stalled – displaying, in fact, the characteristics common to conventional aircraft when flown inaccurately.

Mignet considered the installation of a Handley Page Slot on the leading edge to overcome this condition. He eventually viewed this unfavourably because it worked best at an exaggerated angle of incidence – not a good attitude for a landing or take-off. His solution used the slot principle, but in such a way that it was unrecognisable.

One has to admire the Mignet solution to the design problem. It was simple and logical yet totally revolutionary. What would happen if a trailing edge of a wing from which the air was about to 'unstick' was positioned close to another wing that was in an unstalled state? Mignet figured that, given the pressure on the underside of the front wing and depression on the upper surface of the rear wing, air would rush between the gap. This gap would act as a venturi and would help further in pulling down the air leaving the front wing, delaying the breakaway and in so doing delaying the stall.

Mignet had arrived at a kind of biplane with wings of the utmost stagger, almost a tandem, but not really one or the other. Mignet claimed that this arrangement's major attribute was that if the rear wing lifted too much and the front wing would not lift at all, then the craft would fall forward and dive. A real stall would be impossible.

So the configuration of the HM.14 *Pou du Ciel* came to be. Mignet summed up his findings in *Le Sport de l'Air*: 'The slot or gap effect gives the rear wing progressive independence of the front. A tailplane becomes superfluous. Our tandem biplane, which is neither thing in fact, becomes a single wing with a gap . . . a tailless plane.'

This philosophy Mignet termed *'Aéro-technique'* in *Le Sport de l'Air,* going on to discuss fore-and-aft balance, sudden loads, lateral balance, lateral control, defects and finally the art of turning. To turn the Flea the pilot simply moved the control column to the side, the aeroplane taking up its own bank proportional to the amount of rudder. 'Whether one turns wide or short, whether one is a new or experienced pilot, one turns correctly because ONE CANNOT TURN OTHERWISE!' Pleased with his conclusions, Mignet often highlighted his final sentences with block capitals.

His progression through what must have been virgin territory for many of his readers was presented in an easily readable and understandable manner – though his conclusions were not always the result of classical logic. His style was infectious, bringing the reader to peaks at crucial conclusions and concreting ideas as he progressed through the book. He broke the barrier protecting the world of aviation from the man in the street with statements such as:

'. . . all the work of pilotage is entrusted to the hand.'
'The technique of flight control is that of a bird.'
'The Flea is a kite with an auxiliary engine. Isn't that another kind of flying?'

He cut through jargon and mystique with ease, making flying seem a natural extension of human exercise. His affable style and new ideas uncorked the champagne bottle. His formula for a lightweight 'aerial motorcycle' that anyone could fly was what many handymen with a latent interest in aviation had been waiting for.

Steps to the Flea

Having got the theories onto paper through *Les Ailes* and his book, it was time for Mignet to become practically involved, both in the new craft's design and its test flying. He described the Flea as the grown-up brother of the HM.8, the HM.14 using the same method of construction as the HM.8 for both the wings and the fuselage. The Flea benefitted from the considerable feedback from HM.8 builders and Mignet's own experiences.

The HM.14 design conformed to two chief principles:-

to be safe and easy to pilot
to be small, simple, solid and practical – it should be possible to build a Flea in a 13 foot (4 m) long room.

Wing span for each of the Flea's wings was initially 13 ft (4 m) but improved efficiency was sought and the forewing's span became 16 ft 5 in (5 m) and later 19 ft 6 in (6 m). Simplicity of construction without sacrificing strength was claimed for the wings. The wings were basically similar with a single box spar, and most of the same ribs, the whole being covered with varnished fabric. There were no ailerons, no slots, no elevators, no complicated movements, no hidden cables, levers or mechanisms. Mignet claimed that both of these very simple structures could be built in eight days. He did not, however, state how many working hours per day would have to be devoted to achieve this target.

The fuselage concept was identical – basically an empty box. His dislike of conventional aircraft and their enclosed cockpits, and the need for simplicity, gave rise to the 'flying armchair' style of cockpit, giving excellent visibility in all directions, including forward.

On to this structure was assembled the control column and linkages to the front wing and rudder, the axle and wheels and of course the engine and its accessories. With the exception of the lower portion of the control column, all mechanisms were readily accessible. Mignet anticipated a favourable reaction from airworthiness authorities because of this 'open' construction –no cowlings to hide the engine, no ailerons and their controls. If the wing covering were transparent this would be the final accolade!

The cardinal aspect of 'security of construction' was dealt with quickly, Mignet deducing that being of simple design it could be made so strong that only 'a real crash would smash it to pieces'. Mignet supports this analysis with the survival of his prototype Flea during his wintertime experimentations in the Bois de Bouleaux.

Materials were given little attention, wood and mild steel being readily accessible to the amateur. Today's guardians of the homebuilder, the Experimental Aircraft Association (USA), the Popular Flying Association (UK) and the Réseau du Sport de l'Air (France), would be horrified. All materials now have to come from approved suppliers whose stocks are regularly checked and inspected.

Though the concept of the 'Flea' was by now crystalized in Mignet's mind, there was still a long way, and a number of important intermediate designs, to go before its materialization as the HM.14.

Mignet's writings and theories were always the result of his own practical tests and experiments. He made his first 'expedition' into the wilds to test his notions with the HM.11 around 1931. With the aircraft in tow behind a Harley-Davidson motorcycle and sidecar borrowed from his friend Pierre Brissaud, and with his wife Annette in the sidecar surrounded by an assortment of luggage and packages, he

set off from Paris to the Bois de Bouleaux.

The HM.11 triplane of 1931; one of Mignet's steps to the HM.14 concept. It flew successfully. (Geoffrey P. Jones collection).

Barred from official landing grounds – the reason for this remains unclear – he described France as a vast aerodrome for the amateur camper. Travelling 70 or so miles to the north east of Paris, he found a wooded plateau to the east of Soissons, the plain of Beaurepaire where he established his campsite and open air 'workshop'. The HM.11 had a large trailing edge 'flap', a high tail, tapered fuselage and was very much in the style of what was to become the classic Flea layout. Engine was a two-cylinder 500cc Harrissard producing 15 hp at 4,000 rpm with a chain reduction drive fitted.

After many straight-line hops, Mignet decided the HM.11 needed many modifications. The 'flap' became almost a third wing, the tail was altered and the engine inverted. The HM.12 had come into being.

Although the HM.12 made a few half-hour flights, Mignet admitted that he was unable to get the craft to fly very well. He confessed to some hairy landings, one of which had him and the aeroplane bounce back into the air nearly 30 feet (9 metres) 'with the engine up in the sky'. A few days later Mignet escaped almost unhurt when the HM.12 dived into the ground and tumbled over and over. It was a complete write-off.

Next came the HM.13 with its small cabin and significantly poorer visibility. It returned to the tandem wings and a much larger rudder with

Above: Mignet (left) with Albert Mouchet and his wife at Soissons, August 1932. In the background is Mignet's HM.11 (left) and Mouchet's HM.8. (Musée de l'Air).

Right: Mignet seated in the HM.11. From this view it is clear that the HM.14 configuration is established, other than the pivoting wing. (Musée de l'Air).

Below: The HM.12, developed from the HM.11, was a complex aircraft. (RSA, via Jacques Avril).

Mignet camping in the Bois de Bouleaux with the HM.11 and Harley Davidson combination borrowed from friend Pierre Brissaud.
(RSA, via Jacques Avril).

a tail fillet atop the rear wing/fuselage.

These were the steps to the Flea, paving the way for the crystalization of Mignet's thoughts and ideas. On 10 August 1933 he started to build his prototype HM.14. Exactly one month later this first 'real' Flea took to the air from the Bois de Bouleaux on its maiden flight. From this moment on the frustrations and elations in

General arrangement of the HM.14.

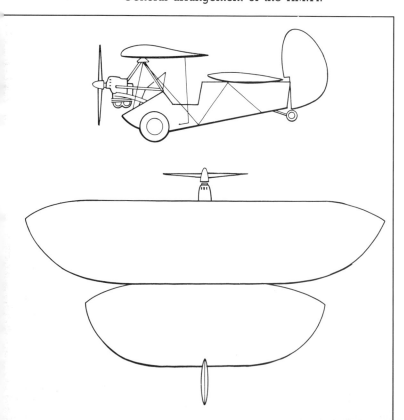

mastering the Flea, together with the fine-tuning of the basic design were recorded in Mignet's diary. Extracts from his flying diary appear separately.

Into print
'I have the right to write a book.' Mignet's construction diary closes with this claim. This book was to be his second book entitled *Le Sport de l'Air,* published in France in November 1934 a year after his experiments in the Bois de Bouleaux had been concluded and with some ten hours' flying under the HM.14's wheels.

Prior to this Mignet had gone into print in September 1934 in the French aviation magazine *Les Ailes*, writing an article entitled *Le Pou du Ciel.* Readers of *Les Ailes* were already familiar with the name Mignet as he had made several contributions to it, including the famous article *L'Aviation de l'Amateur – est-elle une Possibilité?*

No sooner had *Le Sport de l'Air* been published than further exposure of the Flea to the world of aviation was assured by its display at the *14ème Salon de l'Aéronautique au Grand Palais* held between 16 November and 2 December 1934. The real test came a week later when Mignet organised the first public flying demonstration of his HM.14 at Orly Airport, then an all-grass airfield.

Painted red and white and powered by a 17 hp Aubier et Dunne the HM.14 was 'hopped and flown all around the airfield'. These demonstration flights certainly helped to capture the public's imagination, and Mignet was carried shoulder high in triumph by one ecstatic group who witnessed his flying. The weather for this flying was very poor with winds of 20 mph, gusting to 40 mph. *Les Ailes* for 13 December reported the event, stating that Mignet was not put out by the conditions,

making one landing with the engine cut.

Both *Les Ailes* and *The Aeroplane* referred to 'the joke' that neither Mignet nor his aeroplanes were licensed by the French authorities. *The Aeroplane* had reported on the Flea a few months earlier in their Paris Salon edition noting that 'this machine warranted more serious attention than its obscure position in the Salon and curious appearance were likely to make for it'. Their edition of 13 March 1935 brought to the British aeronautical public their first detailed taste of the 'Sky-Louse' as the magazine christened the Flea.

The Book, the Salon and the Orly demonstration had further opened the flood gates. By March 1935 popular gossip put the total number of Fleas already under construction at 500. As with every new craze there were equal amounts of hard fact and fiction. With the craze gathering momentum in France, Britain was rife with reports of all-metal Fleas, retractable undercarriage Fleas, aerobatic Fleas, night-flying Fleas and family cabin versions of the Flea.

With so many Fleas under construction in France the *Réseau des Amateurs de l'Air* (RAA) was formed for Flea builders to have a central organisation to look after and promote their interests. Henri and Annette toured the country visiting regional groupings of the RAA. Pictures taken in 1935 already show gatherings of two, three and sometimes four Fleas. All would be basically similar, often with different powerplants, but all perpetuating 'the joke':

Mignet in his prototype HM.14 with its second engine, the three-cylinder Aubier et Dunne. (Pierre Mignet).

Master and the disciple. Mignet (right) greets Robineau and his Flea. (RSA, via Jacques Avril).

Early days of the RAA, a pleasant group with their aircraft in 1935. Included are de Roubaix, Dehove, Groene, André Thomas with (in the centre) Henri and Annette Mignet.
(RSA, via Jacques Avril).

Flying without licences for either aeroplane or pilot.

On 13 August 1935 'the joke' invaded Britain. Mignet, piloting his Flea powered by a 17 hp Aubier et Dunne, crossed the English Channel from St. Inglevort to Lympne in 52 minutes. The invasion of Britain was to be achieved with the help of The Air League, who adopted a rôle similar to that of the RAA.

Autumn 1935 saw *Les Ailes,* a long time supporter of Mignet's exploits, organising the first official Flea meet. This would be staged at Orly, where Mignet had already experienced triumph. The meeting was to be held under the patronage of General Denain, France's Minister of Air. This was a contradiction in terms. Here

The Orly meeting of Fleas, with the mighty Kohler and Baumann example in the air.
(Musée de l'Air).

Some of the nine Fleas lined up at Orly in October 1935 at the meet organised by *Les Ailes*. (Geoffrey P. Jones collection).

was the embodiment of French officialdom supporting a meeting of aircraft and aviators that were, strictly speaking, illegal.

Mignet had flown in the face of authority by launching amateur aviation on a wide scale in France with the HM.8 and was set for even bigger things with the HM.14. Few people believed such a movement was possible, least of all those in the French administration. Mignet had earlier recommended builders of his designs to make sure there were no *gendarmes* around when wanting to fly. If

Line up at Orly. The radical Salmson-powered Kohler and Baumann with two 'standard' Fleas beyond. (Musée de l'Air).

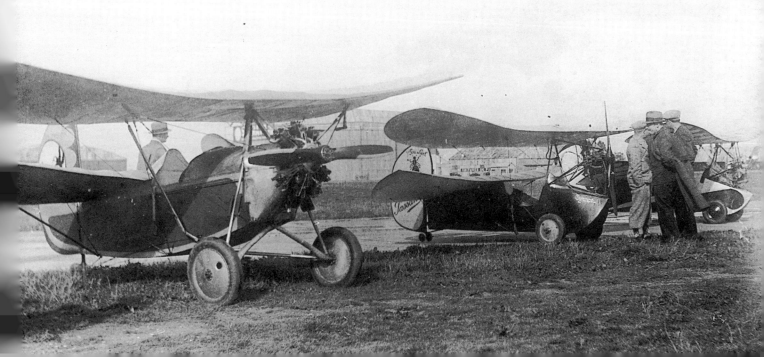

forced to land away from home there was a real possibility of the pilot ending up in court.

At Orly 'the joke' presented the authorities with a *fait accompli* and virtually forced them to change their attitudes. The Ministry of Air backed down, but not without considerable resentment from many quarters. Around 15,000 spectators turned up at Orly to see the Fleas, proof – if it were needed – of the wide public appeal that the Flea had created in such a relatively short period of time. Nine Fleas attended the event, including Mignet's

Edouard Joly, leaning into the cockpit, makes some adjustments to the controls of his Flea at Orly. Joly was to be half of the highly successful post-war Jodel concern.
(Geoffrey P. Jones collection).

Moving one of the nine Fleas in attendance at Orly out onto the apron.
(Musée de l'Air).

prototype, now fitted with a 27 hp Aubier et Dunne.

The Fleas present at Orly showed the idiosyncrasies of each builder and there was a variety of engines employed. Most distinctive was Flea No. 6, built by Francis Kohler and André Baumann. It had a lengthened and streamlined fuselage, considerable dihedral on its wings, a robust undercarriage with 2 ft (0.61 m) diameter pneumatic-tyred mainwheels that lifted the aircraft well clear of the ground. Most significantly, it had a nine-cylinder, 40 hp Salmson powerplant with which it performed outstandingly in the air.

Flea No.26 arrived from its birthplace in Beaune, Côte-d'Or, powered by a 25 hp Poinsard engine. Its builders were André Montoloy and Edouard Joly. Joly was to become famous in light aviation circles after the Second World War with his partner Jean Delmontez and their Jodel series of light aircraft, which were both homebuilt and also placed in series production. Two others at Orly were No.3, built by Etienne Passani from Deuil, with a 16 hp Clerget and No.15, built by René Coupez and Victor Lane from Verneuil, with a 25 hp Poinsard.

This *Rassemblement de l'Aviation Légère* witnessed the amazing sight of all nine Fleas in loose formation overhead Orly. Pilots for this memorable occasion were Robineau, de Roubaix, Kohler, Pic, Joly, Lamblin, Blanchet, Lane and, of course, the 'squadron leader', Henri Mignet himself. For his achievements and

Above: A Flea built in 1935 by Felix Louis at Pantin, with a 25 hp Poinsard engine. (RSA, via Jacques Avril).

Below: Mignet demonstrating the first HM.14. (Musée de l'Air).

HM.14 displayed at the Musée de l'Air, Le Bourget, Paris with Aubier et Dunne engine.
(Duncan Cubitt, *FlyPast* Magazine).

work Mignet was made a Knight of the Légion d'Honneur. General Denain concluded the event with the words: *Et maintenant, les gêneurs n'ont plus qu'à se taire* (Now the critics can only shut up).

Air-to-air of Flea No.3. Note the air speed indicator pitot ahead of the main wing. (Musée de l'Air).

Les Ailes celebrated the completion of 100 Fleas in France with the publication of the booklet *Cent Poux-du-Ciel*. This was a summary of all the information and articles they had published to date on the subject of Mignet and his Fleas.

Glory for *Le Pou du Ciel* was going to be short-lived, for even before the *Rassemblement* at Orly the first reported fatal accident occurred on 19 August 1935 when M. Marignan spun and crashed in Algiers. The following month the type was banned in Algeria. The headlines would soon turn from triumph to shock, and before long the Flying Flea was to be dealt a blow by the authorities that it had challenged almost from birth, and one from which it would never fully recover.

Extracts from Mignet's Flight Test Diary for the HM.14 prototype
(Taken from *The Flying Flea* by Henri Mignet, Chapter VI)

September 14

My machine is flying very badly, I cannot understand it. There does not seem to be any stability in any direction . . . My spirit is failing me; I would have been better off in Paris in my cool flat. It is too warm here. I did two straight flights by leaps and bounds; I flew badly and landed badly.

September 15

I took off the fabric from the middle of the back wing, cut out three feet of the main spar, joined it together, re-covered it and revarnished it. It works better.

September 16

I tried again in the evening; the wind had fallen. A friend came to see me from Lille, in order to photograph me flying 1,500 feet above the ground!

When I throttle back in order to land, there is a tendency for the tail to drop; the front wing is too high, and there is a tendency to stall. I seemed to glide down very well, but I misjudged my landing and landed in the road.

September 17

It is very warm; there is no wind, no air. I work in a bathing costume . . .

I lowered the wing four inches by cutting the tubes which supported it. It glides better now, but I always throttle back too late, and I find myself landing on the rough ground. I tried its control by pushing my hand to right and to left, which gave me the most extraordinary curves. Landing I let my hand go too soon, and dived into the ground from twenty feet up.

The fuselage actually struck the ground as the wheels came up to the full length of the shock absorber, and made a groove in the ground: both tips of the propeller were broken. I got back to earth after bouncing to thirty feet – somehow! The engine was vibrating; I stopped it.

. . . I return with a little spare airscrew; too small as a matter of fact. I bolt it on again, and start the screw going . . . The balance fore and aft seems to be perfectly correct; the lateral control seems to be too strong, but even then the machine doesn't seem to want to turn; it is too stable.

September 19

I think over my accident of yesterday. It was the same story as last year when I broke my old machine. This time the machine is stronger and has stood up to it. I think out the matter. Each time I had moved my hand too abruptly. I must be gentler with the controls . . .

November 8

On this day I telegraphed to my wife, 'I made my first circuit of twenty minutes at a height of 1,300 feet quite safely. Hurrah!' . . . At 3 o'clock in the afternoon I started the engine. . . . I take off towards the east correctly, and pull upon the joy-stick. Here I am at fifty feet. I can stop if I wish, there is still time. No, I am going on. . . . I feel myself surrounded with clear green air; the sun is low. I am surely high enough to turn? Let's try it. Stick to the left a little, push a little harder, and suddenly I see the ground apparently straight below. This startles me a little. . . . 'Do not think about empty space you fool.' The country moves past me transversely all right. One wing on the horizon, the other high in the sky, a turn in a semi-circle and following along the road towards the west, brings me within sight of Soissons.

. . . My Flying Flea does exactly what I want it to do, and I feel reassured. By the by, how high am I? My altimeter is in the pocket of my shirt; I wonder if I can get it out with my left hand, without moving my right? Gently? Ah! it is done. I am 1,300 feet up!

. . . I turn again on one wing like a master pilot! It is quite a smart turn! Hullo! Too much hand to the left. The Flying Flea comes back on a level keel easily. My wood comes before me, two miles away under my engine. I reduce my speed. . . . The glide goes on. I keep a little engine, because I am still rather short. I give a little more throttle. I come down a little too fast. I throttle off, and settle gently on the ground, almost touching my little wood. Solo for the first time! I have thoroughly deserved it . . .

November 21
A beautiful day without a breath of wind, and the Flying Flea is covered with frost. I hear the sound of an engine, and a large aeroplane comes and lands. It is my friend, Colin*, who has come to photograph my flight in the air. We take off. It is a new sensation for me to see this great yellow whale gliding along at my side, at one time covering me with its wing, at another zooming away at a giddy speed. When it dashes past me at about 140 mph it is rather startling. My friend waggles his wings three times – the photographic seance is finished. I go down and land. Colin lands beside me.

December 1
This was to be a duration test. There was a slight wind, and I had an easy take-off with the motor running beautifully. Holding the control stick with my left hand I wrote notes on a block. Suddenly I got a shock for the petrol was flowing out of the tank in a great stream; the petrol cock had come unsoldered. I stopped the engine and looked at the ground . . . I managed to put the machine down very slowly in the last furrows of a field, and hastened to block up the hole in the tank with my thumb. Some field labourers ran up. 'Give me a cork,' I cried out to them. I put the petrol cock into my pocket and fixed up the pipe with the cork.

In front of me I have a field 400 yards long with a small drain every forty yards. At the end of it there is a curtain of high poplars: on the left there is marsh land planted with little trees . . .

I open the throttle and leap towards the poplars. At the first ditch I pull quickly on the stick and run over it. The second I leap in a similar manner. By the time I reach the third I am in full flight . . .

After flying for an hour, and after a moment of panic when I cannot find Soissons, I land at my camp.

December 3
It is blowing hard from the north east, a freezing sort of wind. The sky is empty. Even the birds are not flying . . .

. . . I take off in twenty-five yards, and am buffeted about at once. Laterally my machine does not behave any better than an ordinary machine – fore-and-aft, that is another affair! We are flying quite steadily and are not afraid of anything.

. . . The spectators were startled. They looked at one another asking how this adventure would terminate. One of them was a doctor: had he got his bag with him? Another prepared his little car to pick up the pieces . . .

*Pierre Colin with his Potez 43

I am now facing the wind. At 300 feet above the ravine I find myself in the most violent storm with the maximum of turbulence. I make practically no progress. At 1,300 feet I cannot go forward at all . . .

In a moment or so I arrive above my camp. I turn and throttle down. At 300 feet above the ground disturbances are very violent, and I have plenty to do to keep control

. . . . I push down my nose a bit. I am going at seventy-five to eighty miles an hour, but am hardly making any progress. The stability seems to be very good, and I find it absolutely perfect fore and aft. The machine does not tire one at all, and I do not feel knocked about as I am in an ordinary aeroplane.

The ground gets closer. I rather wish that this was all over. I begin to think I have had enough. I have to open up the engine a bit because I am short, and I carry on for three or four hundred yards hedge-hopping. Not once am I lifted up or dropped. I find that with my stick I can avoid all change of altitude; this is the result of the *direct control of lift.* I land finally, rather foolishly, at the edge of the little wood, and hit the ground with one wheel doing an involuntary turn, which makes me run into the wood and break a few branches.

My Flying Flea is intact, and I am too. I unbuckle my belt and climb out of the machine with a pleasure which I cannot hide. I am absolutely delighted with this last test. Whatever happens the Flea flies. I shall go back to Paris content.

I have the right to write a book

Chapter 3

ANATOMY OF THE FLEA

RECIPE

Plywood	6 sheets 6 ft x 3 ft, 3 mm thick
	4 sheets 6 ft x 3 ft, 1.5 mm thick
Spruce Laths	6 lengths 5 m x 15 mm x 60 mm
	or 10 lengths 3.20 m x 15 mm x 60 mm
	10 lengths 4 m x 20 mm x 20 mm
	50 lengths 3 m x 6 mm x 12 mm
Linen Fabric	36 yards x 38 inches
	100 yards notched strip about 2 inches wide
Clear Dope	about four gallons
Wheels and Tyres	two, about 450 x 100 mm

Mild Steel Tubing	4 m of $\frac{5}{8}$ inch, 16 gauge
	2 m of $\frac{3}{4}$ inch, 14 gauge
	2 m of $\frac{3}{4}$ inch, 16 gauge
	2 m of $1\frac{5}{16}$ inch, 16 gauge
	0.5 m of $1\frac{1}{16}$ inch, 16 gauge
	1.2 m of $1\frac{3}{8}$ inch, 14 gauge
	1.2 m of $1\frac{9}{16}$ inch, 14 gauge
	0.2 m of $1\frac{3}{4}$ inch, 14 gauge
Mild Steel Sheet	about three square feet of 14 gauge small quantities of 16, 19 and 24 gauge
Mild Steel Drawn Rod	2 m each of $\frac{3}{16}, \frac{1}{4}, \frac{5}{16}$ and $\frac{3}{8}$ inch
Mild Steel Screwed Rod	3 m each of $\frac{3}{16}, \frac{1}{4}$ and $\frac{3}{8}$ inch
Bolts	50 2 BA x 1.6 inches
	30 2 BA x 2.4 inch
	20 2 BA x 1.6 inch
	plus plenty of nuts for the above and the screwed rod

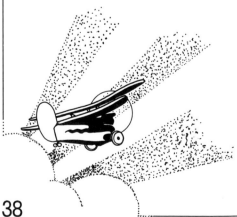

Aircraft Steel Cable	10 m for 4.5 mm for wing bracing with 20 or 25 cwt thimbles and twenty attachments for ends 15 m in 2.4 mm for wing controls with 15 or 10 cwt. Thimbles and fifteen attachments for ends. 10 m of 5 cwt for rudder controls with five thimbles and five attachments for ends. Turnbuckles for the above.
12 m of ½ inch Additionally	Shock Absorber Cord Casein Glue, piano wire, screws, nails, copper tacks (for fabric covering).
And	An engine and a propeller.

IN MIGNET'S BOOK THE TEN PAGES OF Chapter VIII are given over to 'Materials'. As can be seen from the above list of essentials the ever-present problem of mixed Imperial and metric units reared its head. The book included copious conversion tables in the hope of helping the would-be builder. At every step, suppliers or sources of advice were given as the Air League and the publishers were well aware of the risks if other materials of less-than-adequate quality found their way onto this 'shopping list'.

Through careful buying – making sure that quotes were acquired from several stockists – *The Flying Flea* estimated the materials should come to £25 [in 1935] – excluding the engine and proprietary items. First-grade materials should be used, though the book admitted that they need not be AID approved.

Through purchase of the book, or through instalments in *Newnes' Practical Mechanics,* was how Mignet 'marketed' the Flea. Royalties on the book and the part-works were his only revenue. It is interesting to compare the approach of present day designers of homebuilt aircraft who use a more controlled method. Information packs are generally the first step for a would-be builder. Through this purchase come performance figures, photographs of completed aircraft, notes from satisfied customers, breakdowns of costs or kit availability. More often than not, the purchase of the information pack is deducted from the purchase of a set of plans – in many cases full scale. Plan quality varies from the difficult to interpret to the immaculate; either way such plans represent a legal contract, or licence, to build just *one* aircraft from that particular set of plans. A sale of a set of plans to another builder *should* be accompanied by a royalty payment to the designer.

Being the first person in Europe to offer his creation to the general public for construction under their own discipline, Mignet's method seemed the most practical to him. The book approach had worked well with his previous model, the HM.8, and he saw no reason to change. His chosen method of distribution made him money, that is certain – but had he built the Flea today and sold the plans at the rates that homebuilts can now command, he would have been an appreciably richer gentleman. Of course, it is arguable that – setting aside Mignet's friendly, inspiring and seductive approach – because his method of conveying plans to the populace was through books or magazine inserts, he reached a market far bigger than the number of people who could have afforded plans. One library copy of *The Flying Flea* could spawn many Fleas, but for its creator only one royalty.

As well as the problems of conversion of metric units and the strange mixed use of Imperial and metric units, the plans that appeared in the book or in the magazines were, naturally, much reduced, and required much redrawing and interpretation by the builder. Doubtless many copies of *Newnes' Practical Mechanics* were ripped to shreds so that plans could be arranged on workshop walls and seen alongside one another. Few would want to do that to the book, however, as it included much more, the words of the man on how to fly the creation, for example.

'I am not designing for imbeciles.' Mignet was at pains not to underestimate the sort of person who he considered would be undertaking the construction of a Flea. In a note on boring holes he made the above statement when explaining that exact dimensions were not given as the design was deliberately elastic

HOW TO BUILD THE 'FLYING FLEA'!

NEWNES

PRACTICAL MECHANICS

OCTOBER

6D

Big Birthday Number!

Cover of *Newnes' Practical Mechanics* for October 1935, the first of three issues giving details of how to build the Flea.
(Ken Ellis Collection).

to take in local conditions, materials available and the innovative whims of the builder. In many cases, certainly of British-built Fleas, a more authoritarian approach by the author might have led to more Fleas taking to the air. Mignet, however, was not one to lead people by the hand.

Newnes' Practical Mechanics redrew and reappraised Mignet's own constructional sketches that appeared in his book. The October 1935 issue dealt with the construction of the fuselage and gave an extensive list of materials, November's issue the wings, and the December issue the rudder, engine mountings, instruments etc. Narrative instructions did not follow Mignet's style in total, although clearly based upon the subject-structure of *Flying Flea*. Better layout of constructional drawings may well have made the magazine version a

Cutaway drawing of the Flea, from *The Aeroplane*.
(*The Aeroplane*).

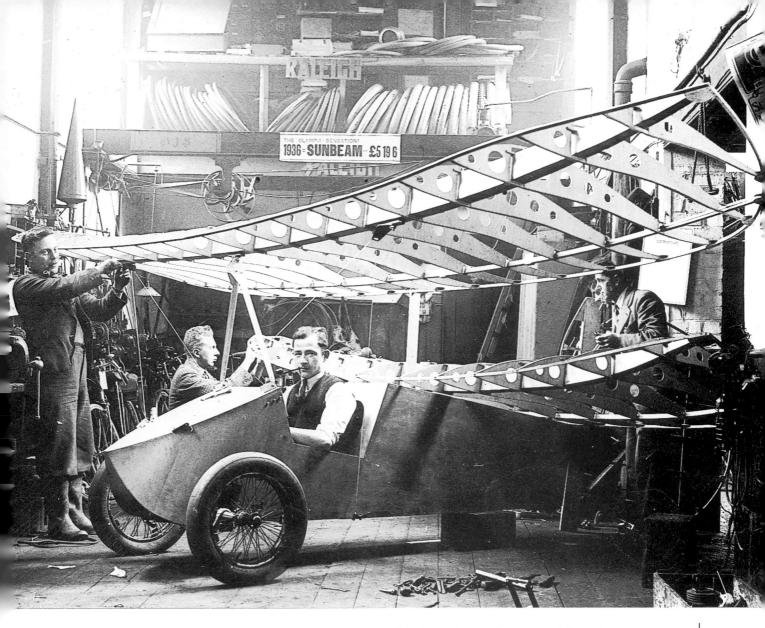

A.C. Dale, a garage proprietor from Warminster, Wilts, tries the cockpit of his Flea for size. A Bristol Cherub was the intended powerplant. Construction seemed to proceed at a leisurely pace as it was still 'under way' in 1939. (Wiltshire Times/Ken Ellis Collection).

favoured reference source, although it is comforting to note that, where traceable, most builders or relatives that were contacted in the research that produced this work refer to ownership, or possession at one time or another, of 'The Book'.

Fuselage

Not until page 113 of *The Flying Flea* does Mignet come around to the construction of the little aircraft. Before that is the Mignet philosophy on flight, design, the destiny of

mankind, and much more. Mignet's own frustrations of design, construction and flight, added to his increasing experience of homebuilders and their needs, put him in a unique position to assess the urges and demands of the nascent homebuilding movement.

Chapter IX dealt step-by-step with the fuselage. Knowing full well that many builders would want to crack straight on with the wings, he applied the handbrake immediately. Such builders 'would glue the feathers to the egg before the chicken comes out in order to go faster'!

It is here that Mignet likens the fuselage to a packing case, construction of the Flea fuselage being quite unlike that of any other aircraft. Essentially it is a complex box made of straight plywood sides glued and nailed to a wooden lath framework.

While the wings put the craft into the air, the little 'packing case' is the core of the HM.14, with every element carrying out a multitude of tasks. The basic shape, from which the remainder of the fuselage stems, is a wedge, lying on its side, coming to a point at the tail. At the nose is a flat 'plate' upon which the engine mounts will go. The apex of this flat area is the mounting point for the tripod-shaped wing support pylon.

The reverse of the bulkhead upon which the wing pivot is located holds the instrument panel. Behind and below this a box structure that will take the undercarriage axle and its suspension and immediately behind this the pivot for the flying controls, either going up to the forward wing, or running backwards to the rudder.

Aft of the undercarriage box is the space for the pilot, immediately behind which is a bulkhead which forms the seat back and is a major strengthening structure in the fuselage. Behind this run what might be called longerons

in more conventional aircraft, tapering to a point at the tail. From the bulkhead behind the pilot and the taper point another box-like structure is built up from laths, including the critical sternpost.

To the sternpost the rudder will be attached. The rudder's pivot is a mild steel tube structure, which at the base includes the horns to take control lines from the cockpit and the mounting for two small, all-metal wheels and immediately above this a simple rubber bungee to take some of the shock of landing. This inclusion of the tailwheel(s) as part of the rudder was a keynote feature in many of Mignet's subsequent designs and in the Mignet-inspired designs. The rudder itself follows the construction methods of the wings. Also attached to the sternpost is a small handle to aid manhandling the aircraft when dismantling for towing on a road. The tow bar

Cutaway drawing of the Flea, from *Aeroplane Monthly*.
(*Aeroplane Monthly*, courtesy Richard Riding).

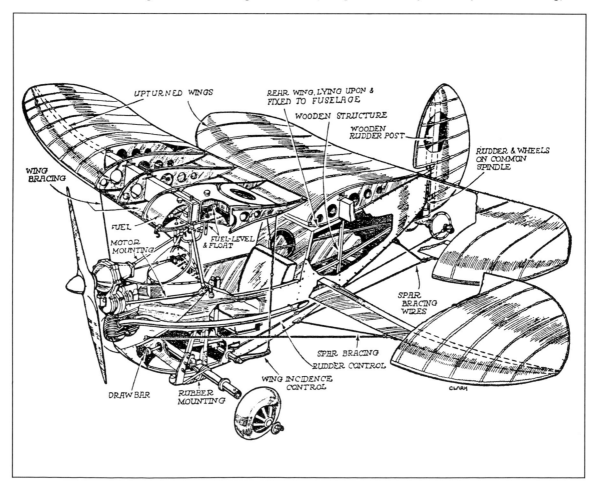

Above: Not the best use for a Flea fuselage, but this view well illustrates the simplicity of the structure. The Aeroplane Collection's BAPC.13, built by L.W. Taylor at Knutsford, Cheshire, circa September 1935, about to move to new premises in a snowy January 1985.
(Alan Curry).

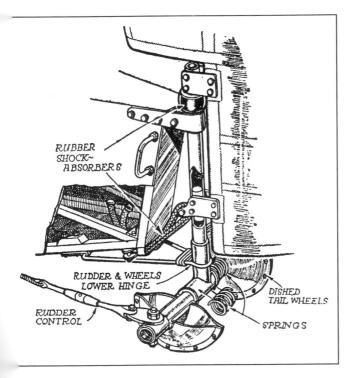

RUBBER SHOCK-ABSORBERS

RUDDER & WHEELS LOWER HINGE

DISHED TAIL WHEELS

RUDDER CONTROL

SPRINGS

for road towing attaches to a point under the mid-fuselage and to the base of the rudder post.

The main undercarriage unit boasts strength with simplicity, being mild steel tube within a mild steel tube, with a pneumatic-tyred wheel at each end. Below the axle, where it comes into contact with the lower 'longerons', is a substantial rubber pad. Wrapped around the axle, kept in tension, a series of rubber bungees supplies the suspension system. The 'box' within which the axle is mounted provides a goodly space for upward movement of the axle. Clearance of the fuselage bottom from the ground is minimal, Mignet putting this clearance at 14 cm ($7\frac{1}{2}$ in) without the pilot in place.

Left: Cutaway showing the sternpost area, with shock absorbers, rudder attachment and tail wheels well evident.
(*The Aeroplane*).

As with engine and propeller choice, Mignet left the selection of suitable wheels to the builder. Though noting that the size of the tyres was best as 450 x 100 mm a suitable source of lightweight wheels was not mentioned. Many British builders placed heavy, industrial or agricultural units on their already overweight

Rudder of Mr Thorpe's Flea, complete with family crest showing, in a slightly crumpled form, the 'standard' shape. There were variations to this theme.
(Ken Ellis Collection).

creations. Mignet suggested to manufacturers that someone should produce such wheels for this new aircraft market. With a weight of around 2 kg (4½ lb) he pronounced they would sell like hot cakes'!

All flight control derives from inputs to the control stick, an inverted 'T' made out of mild steel tube. Mignet, wherever possible, avoided the welding of tubular components and claimed that the recourse to such methods in his design was so limited that the builder could afford to take items to a local skilled in welding.

Detail of the main undercarriage axle, with bungee shock-absorbers.
(*The Aeroplane*).

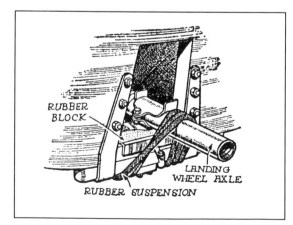

RUBBER BLOCK

LANDING WHEEL AXLE

RUBBER SUSPENSION

The control stick achieved its 'T' shape through the use of five bolts.

From the base of the 'T' comes the cable control for the rudder. This passes out of the fuselage sides and via the only two pulleys ('two pulleys too many' according to Mignet) in the design, down to the horns on the rudder pivot near the tailwheels. The base of the 'T' itself passes out through the fuselage and ends, each side, in a small rearward-facing arm. From here control wires run up to the wing, fore-and-aft movement of the stick moving the entire wing around the pivot point down or up.

Wings

Mignet's HM.14 was a truly adaptable design. The great man intended that the wings reflect this in that the builder could choose the span most suited to his flying needs and, indeed, to the room or workshop in which he was to build them.

Coming up with a figure for the average room or apartment of 3 metres (9 ft 9 in) by 4 metres (13 ft 1 in), Mignet was most adamant that a wing of 4 metres could indeed be made in such confines. His most successful tests were made with a 5½ metre wing. *The Flying Flea* offered the choice of 4, 5 or 6 metre main wing spans. A 4 metre span would give an earth-bound trainer, capable of only hopping, but nevertheless it would give its pilot all of the sensations of control that would be needed

Part of the excellent portfolio of photographs taken by Dr M.D.S. Armour of his Flea G-AEOJ before it was modified in the light of the 'ban'. Undercarriage was simple, but capable of taking a lot of punishment. A simple rubber bungee absorbed some of the shock.
(Ken Ellis Collection).

Brian Park's G-ADYO prior to covering and the fitting of its Scott A2S engine. It is seen in the yard of Clarington Forge, Wigan, Lancs, circa autumn 1935. The wing pivot point is clearly evident. (Ken Ellis Collection).

later. Indeed, the Flea builder, if he so wished, could build two sets of wings and exchange them as his confidence and skills grew.

Alan Troop's Flea in skeletal form at Wellingore, Lincs, 1936, giving a good insight into construction and the scale of the little aircraft. This aircraft is extant, with The Aviation Heritage Centre. (via Mike Hodgson).

Both wings were essentially the same in design and construction. The forward wing included two fuel tanks in its centre section, plus the mounting unit for the pivot and the bracing wires. The rear wing required mounting fixtures to attach it to the top of the rear fuselage and for bracing wires. Both featured a box spar behind the leading edge and a secondary spar in front of the trailing edge. The front wing containing eighteen ribs (lightened with drilled holes), the rear wing twelve ribs of similar manner.

The Mignet-developed aerofoil section was not rounded, mainly for reasons of ease of

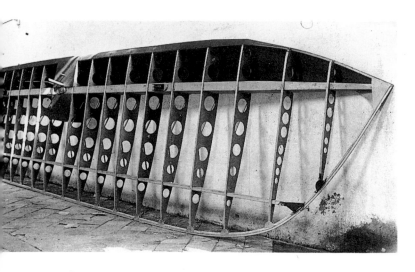

The main wing of Dr M.D.S. Armour's aircraft, prior to covering. The main box spar and trailing edge auxiliary spar are well evident, as is the fuel tank installation.
(Ken Ellis Collection).

construction, being decidedly pointed, rounding out over the main spar and decreasing in a gentle S-shape to the trailing edge, which ended in a very narrow taper. Mignet likened his aerofoil section (or profile as he termed it) to those to be found on 'the super-racing machines of the Schneider Trophy' although he admitted that the Flea was not in their league of performance, because his creation relied on 'rabbit-power'.

As the whole forward wing was also a control

Detail of the control column, showing simple bolt-together structure, pulley controls to the rudder and lever control to the main wing.
(*The Aeroplane*).

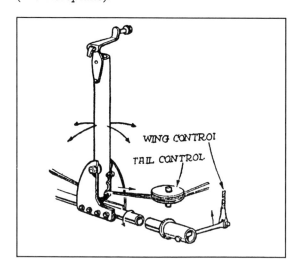

surface – it was all-moving – it is perhaps easier to envisage his aerofoil as an aileron or an elevator. Such devices frequently have more flat and pointed geometry.

Between the central ribs of the main wing went the two fuel tanks, one in front of the main space, with a capacity of 12 litres (2 gallons 5 pints) and the other behind the spar with a capacity of 15– 20 litres (roughly three to four gallons). The tanks rested on plywood planking and, once in place, became sealed units, inspection and repair requiring the removal of the fabric and the breaking open of the plywood box encasing them.

'Photograph the skeleton of the wing. It is the last time for a long time that you will see it in the open. It will be a good souvenir for you and you can also, as a mark of friendship, send a copy of it to the author of these lines, who will be delighted to receive it.' Many builders certainly took Mignet's advice, if the number of surviving sepia photographs of wing skeletons is anything to go by. One wonders how many such photographs went via the publishers to Mignet.

As well as the vee-shape wing pivot which, via its bolt joint to the main wing, not only held the wing on to the remainder of the aircraft, but allowed the derigged main wing to swing through ninety degrees to permit the craft to be towed home by road, the main wing was secured by two bracing wires to a point at mid-span on the main spar. These arose from a fixture on the engine-mounting 'plate' and from an attachment under the fuselage below the cockpit. The rear wing was attached to the upper fuselage box and by bracing wires running from underneath the fuselage near the tail and the same under-cockpit location that held the front wing. Again, they travelled to an attachment at mid-span on the rear wing's main spar.

Wires from the arms of the control column's 'T' travelled upwards to four positions on the forward wing's secondary spar, movements on the stick altering the angle of incidence of the wing. A shock-absorber kept the main wing in tension against these control wires and also stopped the trailing edge of the main wing braining the pilot when it was no longer receiving lift.

The Flying Flea gave detailed notes on such elements as engine mounting assemblies, engine accessories and instrumentation,

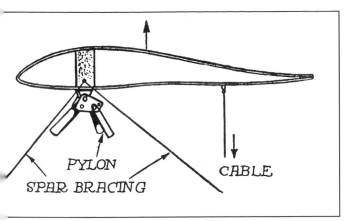

Sectional view of the main wing, showing location of the pivot point pylon, control cable and bracing wires.
(*The Aeroplane*).

chapters of his book dwell briefly on engine management and how to fly the little machine.

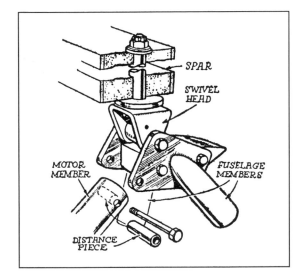

Close detail of the pivot point, showing method of attachment to the spar.
(*The Aeroplane*).

Right: The rear wing of Dr Armour's aircraft, essentially a scaled down version of the main wing. In February 1937 this wing was either discarded or rebuilt to enable G-AEOJ to have the pivoting rear wing modification required to overcome the Air Ministry's 'ban'.
(Ken Ellis Collection).

construction of a propeller and even how to make a map pocket. The author could only be precise about the airframe, that was his and all builders were expected to follow this to the letter. The engine and its ancillaries would all depend on the builder, his ambitions, whims and, above all else, his pocket. The remaining

Close up of the wing pivot joint and fuel line on the main wing of E. Claybourn and Company's G-AEKR. The pivot not only provided the axis of movement for the main wing, but could also swing through ninety degrees to allow the Flea to be taken by road.
(Ken Ellis Collection).

Mignet demoted piloting skills to 'merely an act of supervision' because:

'The Flea flies on its own
It cannot side slip
It cannot get into a spin
It cannot stall
It can fly at angles beyond the stall'

'To pilot the Flying Flea is infinitely easier than to drive a motor car.'

Left: View of the instrument panel on Dr Armour's G-AEOJ. Left to right revolution counter, air speed indicator with compass beneath, and altimeter. Below the ASI is a small compass and below that a cross-level. A small fuel tank has been rigged near the pivot point for ground running trials. (Ken Ellis Collection).

Through a step-by-step system of self-education – how else, there was no two-seater – Mignet encouraged his 'pupils' to take to the air in a series of what he called 'outings', each getting progressively more adventurous.

With his style, self-confidence could easily be built. More than a hint of male chauvinism crept in to his narrative as he encompassed the possibility of some of his remote-control 'students' being female:

'Your shadow follows you or precedes you . . . the horizon is very different seen from above than seen from below . . . and you have a smile on your face.'

'It is so simple that it is too simple. The control-stick, the air speed indicator, the throttle. That's all!'

'A sport for a woman!'

The woman?

'. . . Her light weight (don't make me say her small brain) invites her particularly to the sport of the air!'

Below: A view of Dr Armour's aircraft in completed form. The powerplant is a direct drive Anzani. The aircraft was later rebuilt to include a pivoting rear wing and a raised undercarriage. (G.M. Cowie/Ken Ellis Collection).

An unidentified Carden Ford-powered Flea takes to the air in a pastoral setting.
(Ken Ellis Collection).

A simple aircraft, a simple philosophy of flight.

Mignet had brought about a powerful package that was going to capture many enthusiasts and stir them to do something that they had never considered before – to build and fly their own aircraft.

Mignet's thoughts on construction time
Throughout the constructional chapters of *The Flying Flea*, Mignet made constant references to the time needed to achieve each section or sub-assembly. At no stage does he define how many construction hours are within his 'day'. Despite this lack of specifics, herewith Mignet's breakdown of workload: Fuselage without accessories – four days Main landing gear – one day Control stick and accessories – one day Wing support – one day Main spars, front and rear wings – one day All ribs – 1½ days Both wings assembled, tanks fitted, covered and doped – eight days Rudder, construction, assembly, covering, doping – five hours.

Chapter 4

THE INVASION OF BRITAIN

TUESDAY EVENING, 13 AUGUST 1935. A LITTLE aeroplane approached the English coast, fighting a strong headwind. It was, of course, Henri Mignet in his HM.14, powered by the little 17 hp Aubier et Dunne. As he touched down at Lympne aerodrome, having taken off from St. Inglevort some 52 minutes earlier, he was clearly most satisfied. He had been escorted on his flight by a General Aircraft Monospar twin of Air Commerce Limited.

Just what Mignet expected beyond this achievement is unrecorded, but he was to swiftly find himself enveloped within the pages of the *Daily Express*, who had the man himself writing in their 15 August issue, when they also announced their sponsorship of a tour of coastal towns so that people could get a closer look at the machine that 'can be made by anyone with a slight knowledge of carpentry and mechanics'.

Mignet was an attractive proposition as a

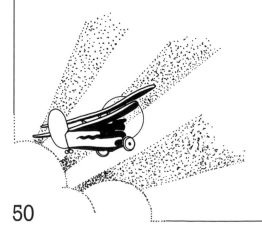

publicity device for the newspaper. He was ideal to take the public's mind (both in France and Britain) off the growing Abyssinian crisis as Mussolini flexed his muscles – this topic was the lead item in the *Daily Express* that day, but Mignet had secured the No. 2 slot. 'Holiday-makers will like this little Frenchman,' said the *Express*, continuing with a description of his arrival. 'He flew to England – his first visit – in an ordinary City suit. He wore a stiff starched collar. He stepped out of his machine and dived into the bottom of it for a small attaché case. And, in case the Flying Flea should drop into the Channel, he wore around his waist the inner tube of a bicycle tyre.'

One must applaud the foresight of the *Daily Express* which helped to propel the little man and the little aircraft into the public's imagination. One wonders, when the decision was taken for sponsorship, if any of the staff had in mind a historic parallel. Over a quarter of a century before, the rival *Daily Mail* had brought another Frenchman to the country by air. That was Louis Blériot who, aided by his Type XI monoplane on the power of a 25 hp Anzani, became the first man to fly the English Channel, on 25 July 1909. He was tempted across by the offer of £1,000 from the *Daily Mail* for the first person of any nationality to fly the Channel, from either direction.

In his own way, Mignet was as much a pioneer as Blériot, and certainly his arrival on British soil was to have a far more personal effect on the population than did the earlier aeronaut. Thousands were to be involved, in one way or another, in building his little invention.

Amateur Aviation before Mignet

Britain was not unused to individuals building aeroplanes to their own design before Mignet flew in. What was unusual was the notion that people could build their own example of an existing aircraft supported by ready-made plans, suggestions and, even, a supporting philosophy. All machines built by amateurs in the United Kingdom prior to Mignet had been 'one-offs'.

Following the Armistice that brought to an inconclusive end 'The War to End all Wars' in November 1918, there was seemingly no end to the supply of aircraft that could be bought quite cheaply and used privately by those that wanted to fly for pleasure. Many types, typified by the Avro 504 in all its variants, kept suppliers of ex-military aircraft richly stocked. In fact the availability of machines far exceeded demand.

While such types and post-war developments satisfied the needs of most of those who had learned to fly during the hostilities and those who had become caught up by the new spirit of aviation, there were those who were decidedly unfulfilled by this activity and wished to go aloft on wings that they had designed and built themselves.

Rules, regulations, paperwork and procedure, all designed to make sure that civil aviation was as safe as it possibly could be, tended to militate against the amateur builder in the pre-Mignet days. The mechanism that might allow for home construction, inspection and certification had yet to surface. It was far easier to join a club and fly in their aircraft, or buy one's own war-surplus type, if one had the money. If it was still impossible to suppress the desire to build one's own, then it was often a far easier option to build a machine and fly from a friendly farmer's field and never go much further than the adjoining fields, thus keeping the paperwork to a minimum.

Given that there may have been backyard aviators who have not become known to British aviation historians, it is generally accepted that the first homebuilt aircraft of the inter-war era was Harold Lowe's Marlburian, which first flew in the Spring of 1921. Mignet would have been captivated by Harold Lowe, and doubtless *vice versa*. Lowe had followed the same path as Mignet, without, it seems, the desire to tell the masses.

During 1917, with a war on and such things decidedly frowned upon, Harold built one of a series of aircraft (which, if the designation of the Marlburian – HL(M)9 – is anything to go by, was nearly into double figures) and succeeded in teaching himself to fly it. The Marlburian was a very orthodox design and was much influenced by some of the classic fighter types

Harold Lowe's Marlburian two-seater, arguably the earliest British 'homebuilt' aircraft. This aircraft was the final product of four years of experimentation.
(via Phil Jarrett).

of the First World War, amongst other characteristics having more than a passing streak of Morane-Saulnier in it.

Created at Heaton, outside Newcastle-upon-Tyne, the Marlburian used a war surplus Gnome rotary of 60 hp with other components, such as the undercarriage, the propeller, and instrumentation, coming from cheap disposal stock. A side-by-side two-seater of 28 ft 6 in wingspan, it apparently flew well. It was registered as G-EBEX in October 1922, but did not aspire to any form of certification, and was destroyed in a crash on 25 November 1922.

In the same year that Harold Lowe was successful in flying his two-seater, the Granger brothers, lace makers from Nottingham, built a glider for the expenditure of a few shillings. It and a subsequent design, called the Pink Emu, were not successes, but a biplane glider design was modified to take a 400 cc ABC engine and became the Granger Linnet of 1924. The Linnet was not a sparkling success but, clearly, the fires of enthusiasm were burning.

Next came the ambitious Archaeopteryx tailless design. By now the Grangers had teamed with B. Howard to form the Experimental Light Plane Club and had Captain C.H. Latimer-Needham as design consultant. Latimer-Needham was the designer of the Halton Mayfly G-EBOO for the Halton Aircraft Club. He was later to be the designer for Luton Aircraft and create their 'Flea' – but that story must await Chapter Six.

The brothers Granger had followed the work of Professor G.T.R. Hill and his Pterodactyl design, but Latimer-Needham provided for a conventional fuselage with fin and rudder with a large, swept-back, parasol wing with ailerons and elevators that comprised the entire outer sections of the wing. This device was to become known as the elevon.

Powered by a Bristol Cherub I of 32 hp, the Archaeopteryx made its first flight from Hucknall in October 1930. It flew well and made a series of cross-country excursions. At this stage it was blissfully without paperwork, but

The unusual Bircham Bettle, a combination of Fokker D VII wings and a fuselage based upon the rear section of a Bristol F2b Fighter.
(G.S. Leslie/J.M. Bruce Collection via P.H.T. Green).

the authorities could hardly fail to notice it, flying out of a popular airfield and making journeys further afield. Registered as G-ABXL in June 1932, it was retired in 1936 and survived to become part of the Shuttleworth Trust, who reflew the little aircraft following a restoration in June 1971.

The Grangers had used the wing of an Avro 504 trainer in the construction of their Pink Emu glider and two other 'pioneer' homebuilt types also mixed and matched production airframe components. At RAF Bircham Newton in the summer of 1924, a group of RAF officers combined a Bristol F.2b rear fuselage with a bespoke forward fuselage, the lower wing of a Fokker D VII, an Avro 504 rudder and a Douglas engine to create the Bircham Beetle. Its flying qualities were not recorded, though it must have been overweight. Carrying a 'G' on the tail and the somewhat truncated 'G-E' on the fuselage sides, it evaded the authorities and quickly dropped into obscurity.

In Devon, the brothers W.H.C. and R.C. Blake also used available airframe components in an effort to keep within the realms of their pockets their desires to achieve self-initiated flight. Using parts from Simmonds Spartan two-seater G-AAGN, Simmonds Spartan three-seater G-AAJB and Avro 504 components, they created a parasol monoplane two-seater powered by an ABC Gnat. The Blake Bluetit made its first flight on 19 October 1930. It flew, unhindered by officialdom, until an accident put it into store in 1932. Major components from this aircraft are held by the Shuttleworth Trust.

Examples of pre-Mignet homebuilt types within the UK could take up several chapters in this work so we will have to be satisfied with a tabular presentation. The description of another example will be useful, if only because it was the other end of the scale. A.L. Angus of Chippenham built himself a single-seater, the Aquila, in 1930, designed as a relatively high performance sports aircraft. Angus was not part of the 'market' that the Mignet philosophy was aiming at, being quite well-to-do.

Using a mixed construction of square-section steel tube and wood, covered in the main with aluminium skinning, the Aquila, G-ABIK, was completed by late 1930. Power came from a 40 hp Salmson AD9 radial and it first flew in February 1931 from Hanworth with its designer and builder at the controls, then with only about fifty hours' flying experience. On 21 March 1931 G-ABIK spun into the ground at Hanworth, killing Angus.

Other than the work of Harold Lowe, and to some extent the Granger brothers, the bulk of the pre-Mignet homebuilt types in the United Kingdom were trial-and-error 'one-offs' with little in the way of experimental flying with a series of types or developments to precede them. None of them were intended for construction by fellow amateurs – at least, not in a formalised manner.

Spreading the gospel

Mignet's ideas and the notion of building a little aeroplane of one's own were spread across Great Britain and into Eire through the printed word and through deeds. The words came from the pioneering support of the *Daily Express*, through the publication of his book in English by the Air League and in serialised form in *Newnes' Practical Mechanics*.

The Air League of the British Empire supported the Flea and Mignet in several ways, the principal manifestation being the translation of *Le Sport de l'Air* with introduction and other comments by Air Commodore John A Chamier. As *The Flying Flea* it appeared a month after Mignet's flight to Britain, published by Sampson Low, Marston & Co. Ltd with a first impression of 6,000 copies. Air League involvement went

The Blake Bluetit, assembled from several other airframes. Another example of the British pre-Flea 'one offs'.
(via Phil Jarrett)

much deeper than the publication of the book and is dealt with in greater depth in due course. The monthly magazine *Newnes' Practical Mechanics* started a three-part serialisation of Mignet's work in their October 1935 issue.

From these seeds the Flea 'craze' in the United Kingdom and Eire was to start. In terms of time, the craze was not to be long-lived, although it certainly involved a large number of people. Perhaps the height of the craze was the amazing Flea Rally held at Ramsgate in August 1936. That very month the Royal Aircraft Establishment at Farnborough had an example of the little aeroplane in their wind tunnel and a full scale investigation into its aerodynamics was under way. Before long the indulgence of the authorities was to be replaced by a less benevolent approach, which would manifest itself in an interdiction controlling the circumstances in which a Flying Flea might operate. This was to become famous, quite inaccurately, as a total ban.

Mignet's *Daily Express*-sponsored tour, starting at Shoreham on Saturday 17 August and hosted by the Southern Aero Club, was not

A beaming Henri Mignet flies past the press at Shoreham on 17 August 1935. This was the first of an extensive series of venues for the *Daily Express*-sponsored tour of Britain. Mignet's machine carried the banner *L'Autre Aviation* (Alternative Aviation) on the rudder.
(Ken Ellis Collection).

the first public appearance of the type in the British Isles. Stephen Appleby, of which more anon, gained the very first Authorisation (or Permit) to Fly in the United Kingdom for his Carden Ford-powered G-ADMH on 24 July 1935. On the 29th, while demonstrating it at Heston, it was damaged in a crash landing. Realising the potential of the first British-built Flea, the *Daily Express* gave Appleby £100 and with this L.E. Baynes rebuilt and redesigned the aircraft, to make perhaps the most promising of all of the HM.14s. Also in July, at West Malling airfield, W.G. Laidlaw of West Malling Aviation, showed off his, engineless, Flea, to interested audiences at the airfield's 'at home' day.

While Mignet was touring before his departure home and a triumphal return to Le Bourget (see Chapter Two) the Air League exhibited their own example G-ADME in the basement of Selfridges in London. With its modest dimensions the Flea lent itself admirably to being displayed within buildings and, as the craze gained momentum, so did their 'guest appearances', including being used on floats in town fêtes and parades. Appleby's machine was used for an extensive tour of major Ford dealers (having a Carden-converted Ford engine) going on exhibition in the showroom and making a public display from a local airfield at weekends.

Clearly the Flea had a good deal of public appeal so National Air Days Limited, the touring flying circus operation of Sir Alan Cobham, imported two Mignet-built aircraft in November

1935. Scott's Flying Displays Ltd, operated by C.W.A. Scott, built their own, the famous *Bertie Bassett* G-AEFK, which gained its Permit on 3 April 1936. These touring displays not only helped to give thousands of people a chance to make a joyflight, but also managed to show many Flea builders that the type really could fly.

On 13 April 1936 the Aero-8 Club at Ashington staged their Flying Flea Rally, with at least six attending (but more of this in Chapter Five). This was a sampler for the Ramsgate Rally of 3 August when a race for the little aircraft really caught the imagination. Mignet was there, this time showing off his enclosed cockpit HM.18. This was the heyday for the little aircraft in Britain; but the clamp down was not far away.

Bank Holiday Monday, 3 August 1936, was the day chosen by Ramsgate Municipal Airport to stage its First International Flying Flea Trophy Race and Flying Display. The large crowd was drawn to the newly-established airfield by the promise of a Flying Flea race and eagerly awaited the start. A seven mile course from the airfield to St Peters to RAF Manston and return would be lapped four times.

By the date of the race no fewer than 66 Fleas had aspired to a Permit to Fly in Britain.

The dapper-looking Mignet poses for the cameras in front of his HM.18 at Heston, August 1936. (Ken Ellis Collection).

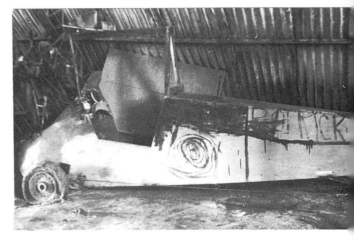

Prize money was generous and even the third prize would have gone a long way to building yet another Flea. The Challenge Trophy itself, destined to become a very short-lived annual award, would go to the winner along with £100. Second place would receive £60 and third £40. The organisers did well to conceal their dismay when the Flea count for the event came to ten, including Mignet's bullet-like HM.18.

Going by the competition numbers applied to the race aircraft there should have been at least another three. With Tom Procter's *Blue Atom* refusing to start, Arthur Clouston retiring from the race with a burst oil line and four Frenchmen flying there was plenty of interest for the large crowd.

The race was hotly contested. Edouard Bret came in first with a speed of 56.75 mph with the very popular Stephen Appleby second at a sizzling 59.5 mph in the Carden-Baynes modified G-ADMH. Coming in third at 50 mph and the first to take off was the 17 hp Aubier et Dunne-powered French machine piloted by Monsieur Robineau.

Irish interlude

Paddy went on flying
when all around were dying
in crashes when they flew.
Now Paddy has wings
plus harp and sings
and all that remains
is Patrick the Pou!

Anonymous ditty on the survival of Flea *Patrick* at Coonagh, County Limerick. (Via Bernard Martin.)

Construction of Flying Fleas in the Irish Free State (Republic of Eire from 1937) is not well documented. Press reports quote twelve machines under construction in February 1936 and record that the authorities were in the process of drawing up regulations for their administration and operation. By early summer two Fleas had flown in the skies over Ireland, this being the pair operated by Cobham's Circus when Phoenix Park, Dublin was used as a venue in 1936.

Only one Flying Flea got as far as the Irish

civil register, EI-ABH registered to the builder W.H. Benson of Dublin on 9 June 1936 which was fitted with a unknown belt-driven Vee-twin and had push-rod wing controls. It is not known if it flew. The registration was cancelled by the authorities at an unrecorded date but with the qualification that it had been cancelled after 'warnings to the owner'. The Flea was stored and next turned up in a loft in a plumber's yard. It was acquired by Dublin plumber Otto Reilly and moved to his house, by June 1952 at the latest. In 1954 Mr Reilly moved to the United States and set fire to his Flea.

J.C. Malone is known to have built an example in Malahide, although it did not fly. Two survive, by far the best being the engineless example held by Dick Robinson at Carbury, County Kildare. It was built by himself and his father and never aspired to a powerplant. This example is still kept at the owner's house.

The other survivor is *Patrick the Pou* referred to in the poem above. This battered fuselage was once a well-known landmark in the back of a hangar at Coonagh airfield, not far from the River Shannon. It is believed that wings were never fitted (in spite of what the poem implies), but it is known to have made engine runs. The engine survived for some time, attached to the fuselage, but eventually was sold for use on a motorboat. In August 1978 the Aviation Society of Ireland rescued *Patrick* and the aircraft is now kept in Dublin.

The disciple

Henri Mignet was working hard in a small workshop in the rafters of a friend's lorry garage in southern Paris and was busy pondering the construction of his wind tunnel. (Providing the power for this device would be the last use to which he would put his faithful Anzani engine that had been employed in several of his early designs.)

A young man, nineteen years old as it turned out, arrived, explained that he was a devoted reader of Mignet's work *Le Sport de l'Air* and announced that he and a mechanic were going to build and fly an HM.8 from the village of Beaulieu, near Nice. He said his name was Appleby – Stephen Villiers Appleby.

Mignet was polite, informative and very encouraging. This was his nature when faced with an enquiry, especially from someone who saw things his way. They became absorbed in discussion. As the two talked in front of Mignet's own HM.8, the conversation ranged from who were the best component stockists, to which people could give advice, to the technicalities of engines and propellers. Neither man could have realised just what an effect the other would have on his own immediate future. Mignet was to lead Appleby into a career in aviation and to bring him to prominence as a personality in Britain. Francophile Appleby was to be the instrument more than any other which would help Mignet spread the word within Britain about the Flying Flea.

Born in 1912, Stephen Appleby moved to Beaulieu from Britain in 1921 because his mother had been told to move to a better climate to help an illness. He was always fascinated by the thought of flight. Apart from throwing himself off a cliff on a pair of homemade wings as a child – which ended without serious repercussions – he did not get the opportunity to fly until he formed a friendship with Louis Delrue, a garage mechanic.

Appleby was convinced his Harley-Davidson motorcycle engine would power an aircraft. Researching this notion further, he became a reader of the French magazine *Les Ailes* where he read Mignet's advert for *Le Sport de l'Air* with instructions for building the HM.8. It was this that made him seek out Mignet to ask him personally about the little aircraft.

Appleby built the HM.8 largely alone, although Louis and his wife also gave assistance. Construction took exactly six months, being completed on 30 November 1931. On 3 December it made its first flight from Nice aerodrome piloted by a member of the local *Compagnie Aérienne Francaise*. On the power of the 34 hp Harley-Davidson it did not fly well. Stephen decided that now that he had built an aircraft he had better learn to fly it. It is interesting that he was not following Mignet's self-taught methods.

Stephen was employed by the American Mrs Barton-French at that time, and she was a friend of Sir Henry Newman, who had connections with the up-and-coming Heston Airport. In exchange for a write-up in *Les Ailes* Appleby got cut-rate flying lessons at Heston. While taking tuition, Appleby bought an ABC Scorpion which he described as being of 34 hp (most likely a Scorpion II, actually rated at 40 hp) and a propeller. These would be fitted to the HM.8 upon his return.

By now the HM.8 was banned from flying at licensed French fields, probably to allow the authorities to avoid the problems associated with the operation of an 'illegal' aircraft at a legal establishment. Having gained his flying licence Stephen returned home to Beaulieu and, early one morning, made a test flight of the re-engined HM.8 at Nice aerodrome. Upon return he was greeted by an enraged Airfield Manager. Robbed of a place to fly from, Stephen bought a set of floats from glider designer Roger Vuillemenot with a view to flying the HM.8 from Nice harbour. The floats had been designed for a sailplane and when the HM.8 was mounted on them it nearly went to the bottom. With the wings removed Stephen found that he had a phenomenally fast hydrofoil and used the former aircraft in this manner for some time. After this he bought a two-seater Caudron C109.

Aviation was now firmly in his blood and he made a return to Britain and to Heston. Here Stephen got himself a job with Airwork and worked in their traffic office, seeing off and greeting de Havilland Dragons, planning timetables, fuel uplift and other tasks. Airwork operated a daily newspaper flight from Heston to Orly and often Stephen could use a seat on flights to gain himself a weekend in France. During this time he looked up Henri Mignet and heard of the forthcoming HM.14 – he was getting hooked again.

A copy of the second version of *Le Sport de l'Air* giving full details of how to build the Flea was soon bought and a word with his employees allowed him space in a repair hangar to build his own HM.14. On his wages Stephen could afford to build the airframe, but he had no idea how he could acquire an engine for the little aircraft.

Heston had been central in Stephen's

Appleby at work on his Flea G-ADMH in one of the Airwork hangars at Heston. In the background is DH.84 Dragon G-ACHV of the Anglo Persian Oil Company.
(Ken Ellis Collection).

aeronautical career to this point, and it was to continue to foster him. Flying from Heston in his Pobjoy-engined Klemm L25 G-ABZO was engine pioneer Sir John Carden. He was formulating the conversion of the Ford 10 to become a reliable powerplant for light aircraft. He was in need of a suitable aircraft on which to try out his ideas and was well aware of the growing Flea craze in France and its early days in Britain. It was stretching co-incidence to an incredible degree that what looked set to be the first Flea to fly in the UK was at his local airfield and was without a powerplant.

With Sir John's backing and with Airwork providing more facilities, work progressed at a greater pace. G-ADMH, the first Mignet HM.14 to be completed in the United Kingdom, made its first flight, powered by the Carden Ford engine, on 14 July 1935, with SVA (as he was known to many) at the controls. It flew well and arrangements moved speedily through to the granting of Authorisation to Fly No. 1 on the 24th.

By now Sir John Carden had realised that his

Stephen Appleby taxying G-ADMH at Heston, almost certainly on 29 July 1935 – the day of the accident.
(MAP).

idea had great potential and that it was in his interest to popularise the Flea as much as possible, as the little aircraft represented the largest market at that moment for the engine. Encouraged by the successful first flight of G-ADMH a public demonstration was arranged to be staged at Heston on 29 July.

On Mignet's advice Appleby's Flea had the short-span wings. The day for the demonstration was very hot and right from the moment the little aircraft hopped into the air Stephen Knew all was not well. The

A proud Stephen Appleby with G-ADMH at Heston. Layout of the Carden-Ford engine can be seen to advantage.
(A.J. Jackson Collection).

combination of the heat, the short-span wings and the heavy Carden-Ford powerplant conspired with gravity to bring the aircraft down into the next field.

This was not the best of public début flights, but mixed fortunes were at work. While the Flea had crashed it was not so badly damaged that Stephen was not capable of effecting repairs. At the same time the guardian angel *Daily Express* was keen to make sure that there was a British Flea to show off while it wrestled with plans to bring Mignet to the country, by one form or other, for a publicity tour. A cheque for £100 from the newspaper and Sir John allowed the aircraft's rebuild and redesign to be entrusted to Jeffrey E.L. Baynes, designer for Abbott-Baynes Sailplanes of Farnham, Surrey. Baynes was responsible for the series of Scud sailplanes and had been approached by Sir John in 1934 with the notion of a self-launching sailplane. This eventuated as the revolutionary Carden-Baynes Scud III Auxiliary, featuring a retractable 9 hp Villiers single-cylinder engine, which first flew, from Woodley, in August 1935.

Jeffrey Baynes listened intently to Stephen Appleby and to Sir John Carden as both conveyed their knowledge of the airframe, of flying the Flea and of the engine. From this and his own observations came the new G-ADMH which featured the 22 ft (6 m) wing with a thickened and improved wing spar. More significantly, the pivot point of the wing (about which the wing moved to give Mignet's unique control system) was moved forward relative to the chord of the wing, giving a much better control response. This was married to the use of push-rods to connect the wing to the control column. Baynes had G-ADMH ready again on 12 September 1935.

September was to see Appleby leave Airwork and join Sir John in his engine business, Carden Aero Engines Ltd of Camberley and Heston, essentially as chief pilot for the Flea and to help in promotional work. Almost immediately the Ford connection was seized upon, and G-ADMH was to be found hoisted into the capacious roof of the Albert Hall at the Ford Motor Show which started on 17 October 1935. Plans were also laid to have the Flea moved around the country in a large van, equipped with a public address system, which could be used as a mobile hotel, engineering base and hangar as Appleby

toured the country, centred upon mainline Ford dealers. An extensive tour was made during the first half of 1936.

There was a greater plot afoot, for Sir John was convinced that if an Aubier et Dunne could prove reliable enough to bring a little Frenchman plus Flea across the Channel, there was no reason at all why the compliment should not be returned and a Carden Ford propel Appleby into France. The publicity potential of such a flight was enormous. And so it was that 5 December 1935 found Appleby and G-ADMH at Lympne aerodrome in Kent and 35 minutes later the Flea touched down at St.-Inglevert aerodrome, near Calais. Appleby plus 31 hp Carden-Ford had shaved fifteen minutes off the Mignet plus 17 hp Aubier et Dunne flight time.

Appleby's conquering of the Channel in his Flea on 5 December 1935 caught the public imagination, to the extent that this bogus photograph was circulated showing the achievement. Sadly the faker chose to use G-ADMH in its pre-Jeffrey Baynes guise! (Ken Ellis Collection).

Right: During the extensive sales tour, Appleby signed many of these postcards of the L.E. Baynes-modified G-ADMH.
(Ken Ellis Collection).

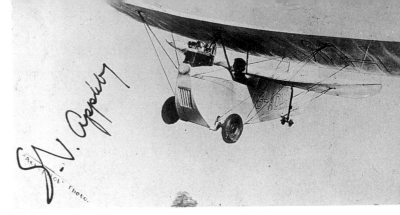

Below: Appleby flying the L.E. Baynes-modified rebuild of G-ADMH on one of its early test flights.
(*The Aeroplane*, via Richard Riding).

Five days later, the triumph was forgotten. Flying from Brussels to Croydon in a Sabena Savoia-Marchetti S.73 trimotor on 10 December 1935, Sir John Carden was among the fatalities when the flight ended in disaster at Tatsfield, near Biggin Hill. This was to be first of two deaths close to Appleby, and the first of more distant fatalities of those killed in British Flea accidents that were to make Appleby drop the Flea and its developments in 1936 and return to France. Appleby took with him the HM.18,

Below: A detailed view of G-ADMH in its second incarnation. The Carden-Ford installation is very neat for such a large powerplant. Note also the cockpit access door.
(*The Aeroplane*, via Richard Riding).

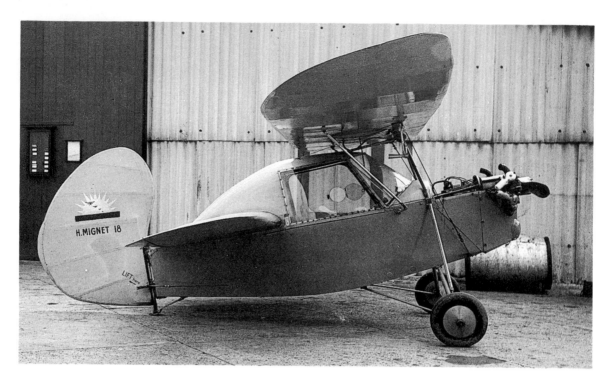

now registered G-AENV, which he had acquired from Mignet after the Ramsgate Race.

The interests of Carden Aero Engines Ltd were incorporated by Abbott-Baynes into Carden Baynes Aircraft of Farnham and eventually passed on to Chilton Aircraft at Hungerford. With the help of Martin Payne, an associate of Sir John, Appleby helped to establish, and then worked as Carden-Ford installation consultant for, Puttnam Aircraft of the Hornsey Road, London N19.

Puttnams offered a factory-made Carden Ford-powered Flea with the full Jeffrey Baynes modifications and a cut-out in the main wing to give the pilot some degree of upward visibility for £175 complete, but the Company completed only one aircraft, despite a heavy investment in premises and facilities. Martin Payne did not recover from a major operation and the fatalities in amateur-built Fleas took Appleby back to France in late 1936. For Stephen the aviation bug was incurable and in 1938 he joined de Havillands, working in the industry until 1947. Britain's first Authorisation to Fly holder died in 1984, proud of his achievements and the varied life they had given him.

Air League patronage

The Air League of the British Empire, then based at Berkeley Street, London existed then

After the Ramsgate Race, Appleby bought the HM.18 from Mignet and registered it as G-AENV. It went back to France with Appleby in late 1936. (A.J. Jackson Collection).

as it does today to promote all aspects of aviation and what could be generally termed 'air-mindedness'. Mignet's ideas and aircraft were bound to appeal to the League, for they comprised a method of getting more people to enjoy flying and so give impetus to a movement that needed support. As early as March 1935 *Flight* was recording the Air League's interest in the design, and in April a circular to members sounded-out the potential following of the notion of building one's own aircraft.

In May 1935 the Air League commissioned the construction of their own Flea. Registered in the name of Air Commodore John A. Chamier CB, CMG, DSO, OBE, the General Secretary of the League, the construction of G-ADME was undertaken in a cabinet-makers on the Fulham Road, London, under the supervision of Stephen Appleby. Strictly to the book, it was the only British-built Flea, as far as the authors can ascertain, to have an Aubier et Dunne of 17 hp engine –as per 'the master'. With Chamier at the helm it made its first flight at Heston in August 1935, gaining its Authorisation on 6 September after being shown off in Selfridge's Department Store basement. Such were the fortunes of the Flea as a type that 'ME was quietly put up for sale in October 1936 and was lost into obscurity.

The Flying Flea, the Air League translation of Mignet's *Le Sport de l'Air* appeared in September 1935 and was an instant success. By now the League has been engaged in talks with the Air Ministry to see how this new phenomenon would be legislated. In his summary in *The Flying Flea* Chamier referred to this and launched the system through which they planned to assist builders along a smooth path to legitimate flight. 'Here in England we fear no obstruction; we can confidently count on sympathy and assistance from the authorities. But we must organise ourselves as they have done in France because governments cannot deal with individuals each asking something different from his neighbour. It is for this reason that the Air League of the British Empire has formed a 'Pou Club' (keeping the French name in honour of the inventor) to help and encourage amateur constructors and all forms of cheap flying – it may grow into something far bigger.'

His conclusion was certainly correct, for today's Popular Flying Association, formed post-war to look after the interest of homebuilders, is a large and flourishing organisation overseeing the certification of hundreds of varied homebuild types from conventional wooden and fabric machines to all metal machines and to the new foam core and glass-fibre devices. In similar manner to today's PFA, the Air League sponsored local groupings where people could exchange ideas, hear guest speakers and have the construction of their pride and joy monitored.

A copy of *Flight* in early August 1935 said that the 'Air Ministry has implied the greatest possible freedom' in terms of legislation. In due course the legislation materialized in the form of an Authorisation to Fly. This piece of paper was a permit allowing operation of an aircraft without the need for full compliance with all articles needed for a Certificate of Airworthiness, as outlined in the Air Navigation (Consolidation) Order of 1923. The Air Ministry wished to establish that no third parties were to be put at risk by the operation of a Flea and that in order to achieve this, the aircraft would be flown within certain constraints and be adequately insured. It was an amazing

concession to individual flyers, considering that the Air League was asking the authorities to take a leap into the dark.

Essentially, the Authorisation or Permit holder could only fly his Flea within Great Britain and Northern Ireland (the Appleby migration to Calais requiring special permission) at the same time avoiding urban areas. The aircraft was not allowed to undertake aerial work for hire and reward, including the carriage of passengers, difficult though it would have been to achieve this in the first place. Leaving much to the common sense of the owner/operator the Flea could only be flown in 'sound working

The document that pioneered the adoption of homebuilt aircraft in Britain, the Authorisation to Fly. This is No.21, granted to Brian Park's G-ADYO. (Ken Ellis Collection).

AIR MINISTRY.

Authorisation No.21.

In exercise of the authority conferred upon me by the President of the Air Council (being one of His Majesty's Principal Secretaries of State) in pursuance of proviso (a) to Article 3 (1) and proviso (b) to Article 4 (1) of the Air Navigation (Consolidation) Order, 1923, I, John Gibson Gibson, Deputy Director of Civil Aviation, Air Ministry, hereby grant special permission for the following aircraft, viz.,

"Pou du Ciel" G-ADYO

registered in the name of Brian Henry Park of 22, Park Avenue, Southport, Lancs., to be flown without having been certified as airworthy as required by the said Order and without carrying a certificate of airworthiness as required thereby.

This permission is subject to the following conditions and limitations:-

1. This permit is valid only for the purpose of flights within Great Britain and Northern Ireland.

2. The aircraft shall not be flown over any populous area or concourse of people.

3. The aircraft shall not carry passengers, goods or mails for hire or reward.

4. The aircraft shall not be used for acrobatic flying.

5. The aircraft shall not be flown unless it is in a state of adequate repair, and in sound working order.

6. The aircraft shall not be flown on any occasion unless there is in force in relation to its flying on that occasion a policy of insurance approved by the Air Ministry for the purpose of the present permit against legal liability which may be incurred in respect of third party damage to persons and property on the ground.

7. The aircraft shall not be flown in any manner whereby the said policy of insurance would be invalidated.

8. This permission may be withdrawn at any time, and unless previously withdrawn, will continue in force until 14th November, 1936.

Deputy Director of Civil Aviation.

DATED 24th December, 1935.

order' and 'in a state of adequate repair', and acrobatic flying was forbidden – although not rigidly defined. Third party insurance was compulsory, to protect anyone who might suffer a Flea falling on them or their property.

The Permit would be current for a year and

Brian Park's Flea G-ADYO causes some interest during a lull in test flying from Southport Beach, 1936.
(Ken Ellis Collection).

Life after the 'ban'. T.H. Fouldes' G-AFUL, complete with pivoting rear wing, achieved its Authorisation to Fly on 1 May 1939, nearly three years after the imposition of the so-called 'ban'.
(Ken Ellis Collection).

was renewable only by the Air Ministry, and permission could be withdrawn at any time. When the Fleas' troubles came to a head, permission was withdrawn initially as a blanket move, but a ban, a term often used to describe the Ministry's action, did, in fact, not occur. Indeed Fleas were given certification beyond this time. The first Authorisation was granted to Stephen Appleby on 24 July 1935 and the last went to T.H. Fouldes on 1 May 1939. Fouldes' aircraft featured push-rod controls and a moving rear wing, the 'fix' needed to keep the Flea in favour with officialdom.

The Ramsgate Race, 3 August 1936

No	Pilot	Regist'n	Engine	Place	Speed	Comment
1	Stephen Appleby	G-ADMH	Carden Ford 31 hp	2nd	59.50 mph	L.E. Baynes modifications
2	Edouard Bret(Fr)	–	unknown	1st	56.75 mph	–
3	Robineau (French)	–	Aubier et Dunne 17 hp	3rd	50 mph	–
4	Colli (French)	G-AEJC	Carden Ford 31 hp	5th	56.25 mph	Owned by E.D. Abbott Ltd. Cantilever variant.
5	Tom Procter	G-ADDW	Anzani 32 hp	–	–	Would not start. Much modified airframe.
6	Claude Oscroft	G-AEJD	Carden Ford 31 hp	4th	57.5 mph	Owned by E.D. Abbott Ltd. Cantilever variant.
9	Lane (French)	–	–	6th	43 mph	–
11	F/L Arthur Clouston	G-ADPY	'Bristol 60 hp'	–	–	Did not finish, oil line broke – see notes.
–	C.L. Berrington	G-AEKH	Anzani 35 hp	–	–	Withdrawn before race.

Note: In his book *The Dangerous Skies* (Cassell, 1954) Arthur Clouston describes the fitting of a 60 hp Bristol engine to the Flea that he flew in the Ramsgate race, giving him 'the fastest Flea in England'. G-ADPY was loaned to Clouston by the builders, E.G. Perman and Company, at which stage it was fitted with a Scott A2S Flying Squirrel of 16 hp. The largest of the 'small' Bristols was the Cherub III, rated at 36 hp – a 60 hp 'Bristol' engine is not a possibility. Just what Clouston had on the front of his aircraft cannot be confirmed. The handicappers made him take off last, so it was clear that they, too, considered he had the 'hottest' aircraft of the race.

British homebuilt aircraft before Mignet

Type	Regist'n (if any)	Designer/ Builder	First Flown	Powerplant	Configuration, etc
Angus Aquila	G-ABIK	A.L. Angus Chippenham	–/2/31	Salmson AD9	low-wing, single-seat
Baldwin Aeroplane	–	T.S. Baldwin, Totnes	–/–/30	Anzani	parasol monoplane, single-seat
Bircham Beetle	–	RAF Officers	–/8/24	Douglas	low-wing, single-seat, built from parts of other aircraft
Blake Bluetit	–	W.H.C. & R.C. Blake, Winchester	19/10/30	ABC Gnat	parasol monoplane, single-seat built from parts of other aircraft
Buckle Parasol	–	S.L. Buckle	–/–/29	Anzani	parasol monoplane, single-seat Sopwith Snipe mainwing and centre section
Clarke Cheetah	G-AAJK	J. Clarke, Brough	–/–/29		Blackburne Thrush biplane, using lower wing of Halton Mayfly G-EBOO. Convertible to parasol monoplane.
Dudley Watt DW. 2	G-AAWK	K.N. Pearson, Brooklands	–/–/30	ADC Cirrus III	biplane, two-seat
Gibb Biplane	–	John & James Gibb, Hamilton	–/–/30	Rover 8?	biplane, single-seat
Granger Linnet	–	R.F.T. & R.J.T. Granger, Nottingham	–/7/26	ABC 400 cc	biplane, single-seat
Granger Archaeopteryx	G-ABXL	as above	–/10/30	Bristol Cherub I	tailless parasol monoplane, single-seat
Hill Pterodactyl	J8067	G T R Hill and wife	3/12/25	Bristol Cherub pusher	tailless parasol monoplane, adopted for Air Ministry evaluation
Hinkler Ibis	G-AAIS	H.J. Hinkler & R.H. Bound, Hamble	–/5/30	Two Salmson AD9s, one tractor, one pusher	two-seat monoplane, wing professionally built
Lowe Marlburian	G-EBEX	F.H. Lowe, Newcastle	–/–/21	Gnome	two-seat monoplane
Noel Wee Mite	G-ACRL	C. Noel, Guernsey	10/4/33	ABC Scorpion	parasol monoplane, single-seat
Pearson-Pickering KP.2	G-ACMR	K.N. Pearson & G L Pickering, Hanworth	–/–/33	Aeronca E, 117 pusher	single-seat monoplane
Worsell Parasol	–	E Worsell, Sevenoaks	–/–/30	Singer, water-cooled	parasol monoplane, single-seat possibly using parts from other aircraft

Note: All the above designed and constructed essentially by individuals, and all achieved flight, either with or without Air Ministry knowledge. Other light aircraft built under the aegis of aero clubs and similar bodies have not been included.

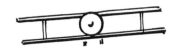

Chapter 5
THE CRAZE TAKES HOLD

A Motorcycle of the Air?

'I've got an itch to fly,'
Said he.
'Let's see if we can make
a Flea!'
The thing complete,
he tries to rise.
To view the landscape
from the skies.
The engine snorts,
it coughs in vain.
It makes no difference
to the plane.
To get her home,
he has to lug her.
It's not a Flea –
the thing's a bugxxx!

Above: **Douglas Henry Shrimpton's sketches.**
(via David Shrimpton).

(Poem and sketches from a collection of Flea memorabilia from the late Mr Douglas Henry Shrimpton; written in 1935.)

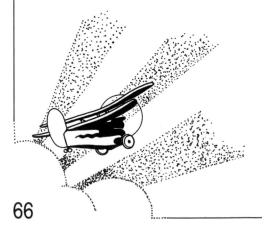

THE FRUSTRATION SO NEATLY EXPRESSED IN the poem was to be the chief sensation that many would be flyers of the HM.14 were to experience. Few would deny that, while being robbed of the opportunity to see air under the tyres in a sustained and controlled manner, the excitement of building, the trials and tribulations of adapting and making do, of cadging skills from friends, made it all worthwhile. Many builders, be they working alone or in an informal group or a well stratified club, built nothing more than a noisy, ineffectual, lawn mower.

No sooner had the craze started – Stephen Appleby's G-ADMH took to the air for the first time at Heston in July 1935 – than it was over. Anderson died in Paterson's G-ADVL in Scotland in April 1936 – G-AEFV went into the wind tunnel at Farnborough in August and the report came out in October. Modifications were easily made, but the bubble had burst and only four more machines were to receive Authorisations to Fly after Farnborough's analysis.

Even today, in an age when an essentially amateur-built aircraft (the Rutan Voyager) has managed to fly non-stop around the world without refuelling using a form of construction that was unheard of in the mid-1930s, to leaf through Henri Mignet's book *The Flying Flea* is to flirt with an invite to a gentle, but highly effective, seduction. As translated for the Air League of the British Empire and published by Sampson Low, Marston & Company it is still a powerful document – the enthusiasm of the man and the passion of his feelings come over graphically. (A handwritten note on the flyleaf of one copy of *The Flying Flea* sums this up nicely: 'WARNING! READING THIS BOOK IS DANGEROUS! You will be compelled to clear the mother-in-law's bedroom and chop up her bed to build a 'Flea'!')

In his Preface, Air Commodore (Retired) John A. Chamier CB, CMG, DSO, OBE, describes Mignet's writing as 'vivid and arresting' and hoped that 'very many young men . . . will be encouraged to follow . . .'.

Chamier could not have envisaged the explosion of interest effected by the publication of Mignet's words, both in the 270 page hardback, and through the inserts in *Newnes' Practical Mechanics*. Through the books, the magazines, the personal appearances, the sponsorship of the Air League, the publicity of a willing and air-minded popular press and the pioneering work of Appleby the word was to permeate across the whole country. The desired effect was to get people who had not flown before, or who thought aviation was beyond them, into the air. This was achieved.

Beyond those immediate aims came something that rose out of the Flea and all that it stood for – a movement that is still going. The advent of Mignet's little aircraft brought about changes in aeronautical legislation within Britain that are, in essence, still with us.

Although the HM.14 faded away under a shroud of fatal accidents and the so-called 'ban', many of the thousands who had taken part in the Flea craze, having experienced the possibility of building an aircraft for themselves, continued to design and to build, using the Authorisation to Fly system that had been brought about to cope with Mignet's creation. The Second World War was to put all of this on ice, but after the conflict the Ultra Light Aircraft Association was born and was to gel into the Popular Flying Association, now boasting thousands of members with hundreds of aircraft of many types, configurations and materials built, under construction or under development.

To return to pre-war days, while wood, ply, fabric, dope, nuts and bolts could all be found in equivalents to the French ingredients Mignet had used, French motorcycle engines were a rarity in Britain. Builders used Chamier's conversion tables in the Appendix of *The Flying Flea* or just guessed at English equivalents. (And in many cases, for the want of a more methodical approach to mathematics, built very heavy aircraft, destined never to take off.)

A whole host of possibilities presented themselves and the ripples of the Mignet invasion were to extend into a search for air- and water-cooled engines adaptable to the needs of light aviation. Britain's motorcycle industry was the envy of the world and adaptations abounded.

Building Fleas, and in some cases rebuilding them, gave individuals experience of aircraft construction and a practical ability to experiment, alter and refine. The little HM.14 also gave more than a jolt to the established light aircraft industry in that there was a clear market below the level of the DH.60 Moths and the Avro Avians.

Perhaps one of the current homebuilt types most closely following the design philosophy of Mignet – the single-seat, easily-built 'fun' aeroplane – is Eric Clutton's FRED (Flying Runabout Experimental Design). The prototype G-ASZY has another link with the HM.14 it flew with a Scott A2S in the early 1960s.
(Ken Ellis).

In reaction to, and from experience of the breed, a flock of ultralight aircraft was to come about, factory-produced or available to amateurs through the purchasing of plans or partial kits. The Brawney, Perman Parasol, the Gurney-Grice Mosquito were all Flea-inspired. (The professionally built Flea and design reactions to the Flea concept are discussed in Chapter 6.)

Through his book and through magazine serialisation Mignet provided a boost to the British light aviation movement almost without parallel. The table at the end of this chapter gives the bare bones of factual information on the hundreds of Fleas started in Britain during the 'craze'. Here we will examine in a more detailed manner some of the individuals, clubs, groups and professionals who were inspired by the 'vivid and arresting language' of that enthusiastic Frenchman.

Flea search

Putting a total to the number of Fleas built in Great Britain during the Flea craze is a very difficult exercise. All Fleas in the UK *should* have attracted *some* paperwork, and if this were, in fact, the case a very precise

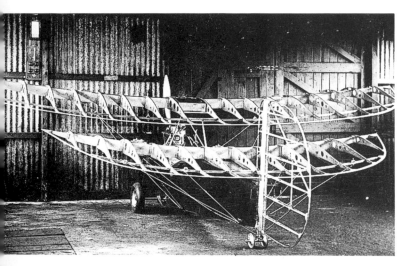

Left: Skeletal view of G-ADZV built by H. Dodson, a joiner, and R.C. Caunce, a motor engineer, on the Wirral. It flew from Hooton Park but was given up at the request of their wives.
(Ken Ellis Collection).

Below: Proud group in front of Brian Park's Scott-powered G-ADYO. Brian's trade was in the making of axles and shovels.
(via Brian Park).

Left: A Douglas-powered example of the HM.14 built by F. Jowett and E. Jackson at the Blackpool Flying Club. It was finished by April 1936 and was never registered.
(Ken Ellis Collection).

'Cumberland's First Flying Flea' built by W. Myers of coachbuilders Myers & Bowman. Douglas-powered, nothing else is known of it. (J.M. Bruce/G.S. Leslie Collection).

assessment could be made. As it is the authors feel safe by merely saying that the Flea constituted the biggest outbreak of building a

James Hill and Glyn John of Swansea pose with their Douglas-powered version. It was reputed to have had a variable pitch propeller. It made hops only in 1937.
(Ken Ellis Collection).

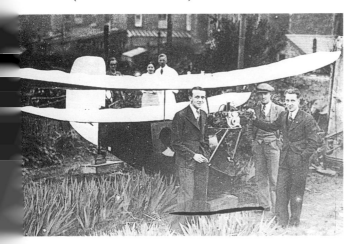

single type of aircraft ever undertaken outside of the major aircraft industry in Britain – and possibly in Europe.

To tie the statistics down further, 119 were registered, but not all of these flew, or were completed and some only existed in the form of paperwork. Of these 76 received Authorisations, although not all of these flew.

The authors have managed to track down many more that do not fit either of the two categories given above. As these, essentially, do not exist in officialdom, it is interesting to establish just how they have managed to be catalogued at all.

At this point mention must be made of Peter Schofield, Manchester-based pioneer of studying the British Flying Flea as a breed. A former Flea-owner himself, Peter deserves a place in the history of the HM.14 through his tireless seeking out of unknown Fleas and their builders during the 1960s. At that time there were many more Flea builders alive to interview and to quiz.

This task is still continuing and through many different sources, the picture of the past can be still further enlarged. One of the principal weapons used by Peter and his disciples, and by the authors, has been the study of local newspapers. The comparative brevity of the craze helps in the number of editions that need to be surveyed.

Newspapers were fascinated by individuals and groups building such devices. Flea builders could be reported upon first with incredulity and then with some pride if they succeeded in their aims. The national publicity afforded Mignet and Appleby, then the crashes and the deaths, all helped to make the Flea 'good copy'.

From the newspapers came names, and into the newspapers went appeals for anyone who had built, helped to build, or knew of, or thought they knew of a Flea builder. This led to the most interesting and yet difficult part of the search. Knocking on doors and asking apparently daft questions like 'Did anyone build an aeroplane here?'

More often than not negative answers, total astonishment or even abuse would follow. Once in a while material *did* come forth. Once every blue moon Flea parts of even whole Fleas were discovered.

This was certainly the pattern in past research and, although odds are dwindling, it

is likely that more research will fill in more holes. Many of the illustrations in this book, much of the background notes and quotations, and knowledge of some of the Fleas still extant arose out of such research.

From 'house-to-house' enquiries come further hints, suggestions and leads. Builders would know of other builders. Names and locations come forth all needing to be checked out. If such a method of research strikes the reader as haphazard, this cannot be denied. Research into any aspect of social or folk history almost invariably is of this nature. Documenting the entire history of the Flea in Great Britain is an open-ended task.

Having bestowed a little of the 'science' required to dip into this fascinating subject there remains an open invitation to dip into local libraries and faded back-issues of long-defunct newspapers, or strain eyes under the fluorescence of a microfilm reader to see if our view of the Flea craze can be expanded upon.

A task for the man-in-the-street

Inevitably choices must be made to illustrate the experiences of those who built, or flew Fleas. A selection of individuals have been singled out for this purpose here. One source that has survived through to print is a vivid blow-by-blow account of the construction, operation and frustration of a Flea: Joseph Wood's diary of G-AEBT. This appears later in edited form and is a tribute to a determined builder who also had an eye to the recording of history.

'There are three main features about the machine which account for its appeal to the public. Its simplicity of construction, its simplicity of flying and its safety of flying. Nobody can possibly question the first two, and its history so far seems to confirm its safety'. So wrote Philip Priest in *The Aeroplane* for 9 October 1935. The article was published just two days before his example, G-ADPZ, gained its Authorisation. Priest's machine was only the third Flea to achieve such a document and was the first 'non-Appleby' example. Before him had been Appleby's own, G-ADMH, on 24 July, and Chamier's, G-ADME, built with Appleby's supervision.

G-ADPZ was built in a stable loft at Crosland Moor, near Huddersfield, from May 1935. Choice of engine lay with the 500cc Douglas conversion and it was in this form that it first

An example of the fruits of a 'Flea-search'. Co-author Geoff Jones 'discovered' the remains of 'The Guernsey Pou' during the research for this book. The Flea was built in St Martin's in 1936 by Edward W. Laker and John E. Beasley. (Geoffrey P. Jones).

flew from Sherburn-in-Elmet, going on to gain a modicum of fame on exhibition in Lewis's store, Leeds, during the latter part of September.

While the article in *The Aeroplane* also gave warning of one of the problems of Mignet's style, 'times given in the book of words for constructing each section are far shorter than will be found in practice', it dwelt on the powerplant possibilities at length. Priest considered they 'would be the subject of considerable debate'. His own experience would bear out his comments on the choice available at that time: '. . . the Scott and the Douglas are the only special jobs, and the former is nearest to Monsieur Mignet's ideas on the subject. To see whether this engine with its 650cc is going to cure the apparent lack of power in reserve of the present 500cc twin two-stroke engines will be interesting'.

G-ADPZ was to suffer damage at Sherburn in an accident, date unrecorded. The Douglas was consigned to a speedboat owned by one of Priest's sons and a Scott A.2S was installed; what results were achieved with this are unknown. Priest also planned to fit a Harlequin, but this was not carried out. The Flea was sold off in 1936 and later burnt.

Owner of West Malling airfield, W.G. Laidlaw, also wrote of his experiences, but this time in *Popular Flying* for November 1935. Laidlaw contracted the Flea 'bug' in advance of many British builders through reading the French magazine *Les Ailes* in February 1935 and then purchasing the book *Le Sport de l'Air* from Hachettes. Mignet certainly got to Laidlaw, as he talks of the Frenchman's writing being a 'blend of unmalicious sarcasm with sound advice'. Laidlaw started construction around March 1935 and is reported to have finished by September, although only photographs of it uncompleted were shown in the October *Popular Flying*. There is no evidence of this Anzani-fitted example having flown. Laidlaw had to pioneer conversions of metric into inches and millimetres to standard wire gauge or to BSF measures. He tracked down a handy conversion ready-reckoner, called '*Instantus*', at 6d which would have proved a wise investment for many frustrated builders.

Possession of a 750 cc OHV Douglas was a major reason for motor engineer Syd Butler to build his Flea, at the Studley Green Garage, High Wycombe. Construction started in November 1935 with flying taking place in June 1936. The green and silver machine was named *Doroli* in honour of his fiancée, Dorothy, who became his wife a fortnight before the Flea's test flights. Dorothy was to have a great influence on this machine. Syd wrote (in 1968) of his experiences:

'At the time of the trial the Flea was as per book with the undercarriage according to Mignet with the exception that the cables controlling the front wing incidence were replaced by tubes, or rather steel tubular rods.

'The Douglas engine was not the type supplied for the light aircraft, it was an engine which had been built for the (Isle of Man) TT Races in the sidecar event and I made up a 2-1 reduction gear which was chain driven, the engine bearer and airscrew shaft was in one unit and was a very difficult thing to make. I remember it had a total of 48 welds; however, it was very rigid and the chain tension remained good throughout. The propeller was made by my brother and it was an excellent piece of work.

'Unfortunately after flying or hopping in this field a number of times I yanked on the stick a bit too much with the result that the aircraft ballooned up and I was a bit scared, shut the throttle and she dropped her nose and we finished up on the ground in an upside down position. The damage was a broken prop and damage to the top of the rudder. A new prop was made and the other damage repaired but at this time we had contacted Mignet who was over here from France and he gave us details of how to modify the rear wing and use elevators [this is believed to be a reference to the small 'tabs' placed on some Fleas in an effort to overcome its aerodynamic problems]. This I did and made up a new undercarriage on my own oleo leg principle; this was much more business-like. The accident happened two weeks after being married and my newly-wed witnessed it also. It so upset her that I decided to part with the aeroplane. I enjoyed making it.'

A story not unfamiliar to other builders!

Another man with engineering skills was Henry Killick of Hale, Cheshire. He, too, used a 750 cc Douglas, but elected for direct drive with an unusually high engine mounting. Henry was the proprietor of H.D.K. Trailers and he built his example in his garage at Ashley Heath.

Syd Butler at the helm of his 750 cc Douglas-powered Flea, showing off the gearing and pushrods.
(Mrs D. Butler via Mike Vaisey).

In front of his wife of just two weeks Syd Butler suffered a flying accident in his Douglas-powered Flea. The traumas of this led to it being sold off.
(Mrs D. Butler via Mike Vaisey).

In an interview with the local press Henry talked of making the first crossing of the Irish Sea in a Flea and this may have been the reasoning behind the motto *I Conquer* that was painted on the silver rudder. Killick, also a scoutmaster, had previously built racing cars

Henry Killick tries out the fuselage of his Flea G-AEII for size in the yard of his trailer-making business. Killick had plans to cross the Irish Sea in this machine, but it had a problematical flying career.
(Ken Ellis Collection).

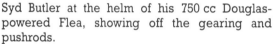

to his own design. Construction began in September 1935 and was completed in April 1936. The Flea was moved to Barton aerodrome for testing, gaining its Permit to Fly on 11 May and registered as G-AEII two days later. The aircraft suffered several mishaps during its brief flying career at Barton.

At one time a Praga B engine was mooted for G-AEII, but there is no evidence that this was fitted. Killick gave the aircraft away while it was at Barton, but returned to aviation in 1963 when he built a man-powered gyroplane, which is still extant in Leeds.

Another example of a Flea builder who later returned to building a flying machine was Sid Miles who built the red and white G-ADZT in Bedford. Constructor's number SSM.1, this Flea succeeded only in making hops before it was sold off. Powered by a 35 hp Henderson, Miles acquired the wheels and wood for 'ZT from Permans. SSM.2 had much greater success, being an American-designed Stolp SA.500 Starlet parasol monoplane. Registered G-AZTV, it first flew on 4 July 1973, powered by a 90 hp Continental C90-8F flat-four. At the time of writing 'TV could be found at Old Warden.

Beyond the 'ban' Fleas did fly, including a quartet that aspired to Authorisations, once they had been suitably modified. Just as examples flew quite happily without paperwork and oblivious to the fact that paperwork was even needed while the craze was on, so beyond the 'ban' HM.14s are known to have flown – some quite recently.

Most recent UK Flea builder is Mick Ward of North Scarle, Lincolnshire. Mick has reversed the trend taken by most builders of evolving from the Flea to other types. He has built three aircraft to date, *ending-up* with an HM.14! Mick's first design was the P45 Gnome, at the time Britain's smallest aircraft with a wing span of 15 ft 9 in and a length of 11 ft 6 in. Of all-wooden construction it was a simple single-seat low wing monoplane powered by a Douglas conversion. Registered as G-AXEI, it made its first flight on 4 August 1967 and subsequently found its way into the Lincolnshire Aviation Museum, where it is still held.

Next came the E47 Elf, a small biplane started in November 1980 and completed in June 1984 and registered in the microlight category as G-MMUL in October 1984. With a span of 15 ft 10 in and a length of 11 ft 10 in it was not far removed from the dimensions of the Gnome. Unladen weight was 250lb and power came from a 600cc Citroen Ami engine conversion. Mick sold the Elf airframe, but hung

Latecomer to the building of Fleas, Mick Ward of Lincolnshire started-off by building Britain's smallest aircraft, the Gnome, in 1966. (Lincolnshire Aviation Museum).

on to the Ami – he had plans for it.

At the age of 67, Mick embarked upon the construction of a very orthodox HM.14 in November 1988. It was completed in June 1989 and was awaiting suitable weather to 'hop' as we closed for press. Designated by Mick as the F50 Flea, it used the Ami conversion from the Elf biplane.

Writing in August 1966 Mr J. Ogle of Ribbleton, Lancashire, recalled a series of flights in a Flea of unknown pedigree made in late 1939. All the more remarkable was the fact that these flights were made with some degree of legitimacy! The Flea in question was bought by John Lockley for about £15 and was said to have been made in Manchester and was thought not to have flown properly, if at all.

Private flying was strictly sanctioned and petrol was rationed.

Mr Ogle takes up the story: 'My friend had cheek enough to write to the Air Ministry, or somewhere like that, saying we were experimenting with something of military potential . . . To our surprise, (they) sent us some petrol coupons and instructed the Chief Constable of Lancashire that we were to have every assistance. So all our performances were watched by an amused police constable. Our Flea was quite normal, with the Scott A.2S twin two-stroke engine, one of the nicest little engines I have known. Being inverted, its plugs filled with oil while standing.

'Our field was very bumpy, and when the lower fuselage caught the mole hills, the Flea sometimes rolled onto its nose, breaking the propeller, if we were unlucky.' Tom Procter, a woodworker from Blackburn and a well known supplier of Flea parts, kept Lockley and Ogle in props throughout these flights. (He also

loaned them a Flea fuselage with an Anzani attached for grounding running: this is most likely to have been his own G-ADDW.)

At one stage this wartime Flea was fitted with a higher undercarriage, with a compression strut to take the shock, this being attached to the forward cockpit bulkhead at the base of the windscreen. This came from Alec Latus, whose own much-modified Flea is described in Chapter 6. The twin-vee units were fitted to the base of the fuselage. It did not fly in this configuration, doubtless because of the considerable nose-up attitude.

Sociable Fleas

Henri Mignet built his Fleas largely unaided – that was, after all, the whole idea. Many individuals in Great Britain followed his example and built their aircraft with the minimum of help from others. Others – ideally a woodworker and a mechanic – paired up to tackle the work. Building a Flea lent itself admirably to a club or a group project, and in Britain such clubs were to be found liberally scattered about the realm. Through such groupings the skills of a variety of volunteers could be tapped but, more importantly, the cost of owning and operating an aircraft could be brought down still further.

In his article 'Pou-Planes' in *The Aeroplane* of 9 October 1935, Philip Priest had a clear idea of from where and when many future Flea builders would come, 'There is the intense enthusiasm of the motor-cycling and small-car groups, suppressed by the crowded condition of the roads and the recent restrictions. They are likely to build these machines in very large numbers this winter.'

Priest also latched on to one of the major pitfalls of group building and operation: workload definition. Many a group, then and now, has suffered from the difficult problem of a member not pulling his weight. '. . . it would be a mistake to start off without a very clear understanding at the beginning of what they are going to do about the flying when some members with equal money at stake seldom turn up, and others work nearly every night'.

Other problems envisaged were that such groups or clubs would probably have to find their own flying field as the established airfields and flying clubs might not take too well to 'beginners hopping about their aerodromes on these simple little machines'. Mignet had

developed an aircraft that was accessible to the working classes, and Priest was aware that this too would cause disharmony on the plush carpets of many clubhouses by bringing 'a new social class to their clubs which they may resent'.

One club that had no problems in mixing Fleas with more conventional flying machines was the Aero-8 Flying Club, based at their own Canute Air Park, near Ashingdon, Essex. The club came about through a demand locally for an organised way of building a Flea. At its height Aero-8 boasted some 700 members, but soon settled down to the more standard operation of a flying training school, under the guidance of instructor V. N. Dickinson. During mid-1936, as well as their Flea, the Aero-8 Club and the associated Canute Air Park Company operated two de Havilland DH.60 Moths, an Avro Avian, a BAC Super Drone (most likely G-AEDC, of which more later) and Avro 504N G-ADBD. Additionally a General Aircraft Monospar was reported to be on order.

Aero-8's contribution to the history of the Flea in Great Britain was two-fold: their own much-modified and refined example, G-AEFW,

Close up of the Douglas installation on the Aero-8 Club's very unorthodox G-AEFW. (Ken Ellis Collection).

Aero-8 Flying Club's heavily modified G-AEFW. Almost a completely new type, it owed only the design concept to Mignet. (A.J. Jackson Collection).

and the organising and staging of a Flea Rally at Ashingdon on 13 April 1936.

Prior to their 'Super Flea', the Club had built a very orthodox HM.14 which did fly, but had its performance limited when a heavy landing cracked the longerons. After this it was labelled 'Taxying Machine' and used for initial training of the Mignet 'hops' variety. G-AEFW on the other hand, was heavily streamlined and at first glance only owed the concept to Mignet. With a very sleek nose, conventionally sprung undercarriage, cleaned up flying wires and struts it looked more akin to the much later HM.360 than the HM.14. It was powered by a very standard Douglas Sprite, rated at 23 hp.

By the time of the Ashingdon Rally, G-AEFW was unflown, or at least remained static throughout the day. It was eventually flown by Claude Oscroft and received its Authorisation on 16 May 1936. Flushed with the success of possessing this piece of paper, the following day, the little Flea set off on a cross-Channel attempt. This was to end somewhat prematurely in a forced-landing near Lympne in Kent. It is thought that the damage incurred put the aircraft into store. It was certainly to be found gathering dust at Canute Air Park during 1939.

The Flea Rally held at Ashingdon on 13 April 1936 was attended by, in all, eight Fleas (including their own G-AEFW and almost certainly the flightless 'Taxying Machine'). This figure is quoted in local press, in *The Aeroplane* for 15 April 1936 and by Joseph Wood in his diary. As well as G-AEFW, only five have been identified: Pearce's G-AEDN; Appleby in G-AEEC all the way from Heston via a top-up at Hatfield; Broughton in G-ADMH; Mercer in G-AEFV; and Cooper's G-AEEI. Additionally, Joseph Wood records a Flea flying overhead at about 500 feet, but not landing, and a Flea ending up in the hedge.

Other notable happenings at the rally included the 'partial burning' of Drone G-AEDC (the words being from a typical caustic report from the pen of C.G. Grey in *The Aeroplane* and a 'ground crash' (Wood's terminology) of an autogiro.

Birkenhead Flying Club managed to squeeze

Members of the Birkenhead Flying Club hard at work on the rear wing of their Flea in Oxton Church Hall.
(Ken Ellis Collection).

twelve men and a lone woman into the workshop end of the Church Hall in Newburns Lane, Oxton, Wirral, for a publicity shot during early 1936. Their aircraft, G-AEIZ, was started in November 1935 and was tested in a field near Irby in July 1936. It is reported to have flown only poorly and was abandoned after a crash. It never achieved a Permit. Power came from a Scott A.2S.

The Flea element of the Glasgow Corporation Transport Flying Club clearly suffered from the syndrome about which Philip Priest had written. While the main flying club could use the facilities of Renfrew Aerodrome, the Flea-builders were confined to a field at Gartsherrie. Built in the Corporation's Coplawhill Works, Airdrie, G-AEFP was fitted with a Ford 10 conversion. It flew, although how well is not recorded. In any event it acquired a Permit on 16 April 1936. It was abandoned when the investigation results were announced.

Ipswich and District Pou Club had more than their share of troubles, although they did manage to lodge on Ipswich Aerodrome. Secretary of the club was E.L. Maule, who was later killed in a gliding accident. The club ordered a Carden-Ford for their G-AEEJ, but delivery was so protracted that they elected to

purchase a water-cooled Ford 10 and convert it to their own specification. Most unusually, G-AEEJ featured a ply covered rudder. It was also fitted with large disc-type wheels that had previously been on Robinson Redwing II G-ABRM which had been damaged beyond repair at Ipswich in 1935.

Flight trials at Ipswich were not very successful, although G-AEEJ did get its Authorisation on 9 April 1936. Writing in June 1966 Charles Coote described its flying ability: 'During tests it went on to its back and the maximum height achieved in its hops was no more than four feet'. The final straw came in November 1936. During a frost the water jacket cracked on the Ford 10 and G-AEEJ was scrapped before the month was out.

The final word must go to the Flea built by the Leek Amateur Flying Group. Formed in September 1935, their anonymous aircraft was built in the Premier Garage (proprietor Mr H. Trafford) in Leek and featured a geared 600 cc Douglas. It was completed in July 1936 and hopped in a nearby field. The little group gave up the Flea when the adverse publicity then abroad gave them cause for concern, and it was put into store.

In 1938 the Flea was sold to farmer Mr S. Hobson of New Mills. He also got it to hop, this time from his farm. During a flight it was damaged. Perhaps he tried to effect repairs, which might offer an explanation for the aircraft's next appearing in the main street of the lovely Peak District town of Chapel-en-le-Frith. Whatever the Flea was doing in town only adds background to the final chapter in its career. It ran amok in the little town and wrote itself off in collision with the Town Hall! Mr Hobson was in due course sent a bill for £28 by way of repairs to the building. The Flea, having disgraced itself, was broken up, although Mr Hobson hung on to the engine.

1935

Jun 14   Received letter from the Air League concerning the Pou Club.

Jun 19   Called at the Air League [19 Berkeley Street, London W1] and went and saw a Pou being made at a cabinet maker's in Fulham.

Jul 29   Called on Charlie Vaughan about plywood and found that he was keen on building a Pou with me.

Jul 30   Charlie came round and we discussed building the Pou.

Jul 31   Drew out a rib section.

Aug 4   Started making a few metal bits for the Flea [22 days to become Anglicized!]

Aug 10   Went on fourteen day holiday at uncle's – took the Flea book and the Scott engine mounting blueprint with me.

Aug 31   Charlie starts work on our trestle table.

Sep 2   Our first night working on the Flea – gluing up longerons.

Sep 3   Had tailwheel parts welded. Stuck two sides of the fuselage together.

Sep 5   Charlie and I went to Shenstone to inspect a Flying Flea that Cobham had with him [G-ADSC]. The Flea did not fly. Met [Frank] Chapman, another Flea builder.

Sep 6   Two sides of the fuselage ready for assembly with seat back.

Sep 10   Got a Dunlop wheelbarrow tyre and tube. Showed it to Charlie and we adapted it for the Flea. Saving of £2/14/0 on wheels.

Sep 19   Called in at Perman & Co. [Brownlow Mews, London WC1] to see a Flea being built.

Sep 20   Called at Dunstable about a Bristol Cherub – it had been sold.

Oct 7   Charlie and I busy in the evening. Fuselage nearly finished.

Oct 8   Landing wheels and axle fitted.

Oct 11   Fitting rudder controls and rear landing gear.

Oct 21   Worked until 1 am on ribs.

Oct 23   Called at Ford [Motor] Show in the Albert Hall to inspect the Carden Flea hung up in the centre of the Hall. [Appleby's G-ADMH.]

Oct 25   Rang up Hanger Motors about a new Ford 10 engine. Charlie and Don Burgoyne [of Knowle, built G-AECN] and I went along to town for a meeting to form a Pou Club. Lots of arguments.

Oct 28   Worked hard to finish twelve ribs. Knocked off at 1 am.

Nov 1   Letter from the Air Ministry.

Nov 6   A new Ford 10 engine arrives for us to convert.

Nov 7   Dad worked all day stripping the engine. Charlie and I went over to see Linklater and McLeod's Flea at Handsworth. [Not registered.]

Nov 8   Carden modification sketch arrives from Appleby.

Nov 11   Charlie came over and wanted to give it up. Argued with him for a couple of hours.

Nov 13   Charlie and I busy on little wing main spar.

Nov 20   Ackers [Local builder - see later] called for ply and glue –10/- .

Nov 29   Charlie and I covered and doped the little wing – did not tighten up much.

Dec 2   Moved little wing into lounge for sewing on fabric.

Dec 4   First coat of dope on little wing – still in lounge. Finished rudder and painted it aluminium.

Dec 10   Charlie and I go to see Ackers building his Flea, then take him to see Burgoyne's Flea.

Dec 11   Rigging wire arrives from John Cleveley – AID Engineer.

Dec 12   Painted a few squares on fuselage.

Dec 16   Builders knock down my dividing wall in garage.

Dec 19   Towed fuselage to father's garage.

Dec 22   Finished boxing mainspar.

Dec 24   Charlie and I busy on the main wing. Ackers and his father call.

Dec 28   Fitted all ribs and leading edge to main wing.

Dec 31   Fitting trailing edge to main wing.

1936

Jan	1	2.4 pitch prop arrived from Appleby.
Jan	4	Made rear petrol tank in copper sheet.
Jan	13	Sew fabric on main wing.
Jan	16	No Charlie this evening.
Jan	24	Dad and I busy mounting engine for test running.
Jan	25	I silvered main wing. Engine ready to run.
Jan	26	We went to see Burgoyne taxi his machine at Bushwood. [His had a Scott A.2S.] I had a few runs up the field in it.
Jan	27	Ran Ford engine for four hours on test – running it in.
Feb	2	We go to see Don's Flea. Very wet conditions, but I had a run up and down the field. Chapman there, also Mottram [L.E. Mottram, G-AEFI, Anzani] at Court Laundry (Northfield).
Feb	5	Went over to Ackers, he has to go to Penang on the Malay Straits.
Feb	6	Took main wing to garage on top of Austin 7.
Feb	9	We went to Don's field and do a few runs. Don flies it a few feet up.
Feb	14	Charlie not well, Don came and gave me a hand. Gaumont Graphic took movie shots of Don and I working on the Flea in the garage.
Feb	18	Don and I mount the engine on the fuselage.
Feb	19	We all went over to Coventry Technical College to hear Air Commodore Chamier give a talk on the Flea. [Aircraft registered as G-AEBT to J.H.V. Wood and C.S. Vaughan on 20 February]
Feb	21	Charlie and I bolt up the engine.
Feb	25	Don and I visited Appleby at Heston and he flew his Flea for us. Took delivery of new prop.
Mar	5	Appleby rang and asked me to send prop to Permans.
Mar	15	Mottram takes his flea to Tallis's field. Don flies his upside down into a tree.
Mar	17	John Lidstone [first visit March 12]

		came along and got on well with painting the squares.
Mar	24	Ackers brought round his rev counter and I paid him £7 for his Flea parts.
Apr	7	Charlie and I went over to Don's to work on our prop.
Apr	13	Arthur Felton and I go to Don's at 7 am and we set off for the Flying Flea Rally at Ashingdon, near Southend. [Aero-8 Club.] Eight Fleas there [six traced - G-ADMH, G-AEDN, G-AEEC, G-AEEI, G-AEFV and G-AEFW], Appleby started his up and flew around [flew G-AEEC from Heston via Hatfield]. One Flea flew over at about 500 feet, but did not land. [No other reports of this.] One taxied into a hedge. A BAC Drone caught fire and an Autogyro 'ground crashed'.
Apr	15	Mottram crashed at Leamington Aero Club-smashed front fuselage, prop and main front wing spar.
Apr	17	Don and I took his Flea to Leamington Aero Club and we joined up.
Apr	29	Testing engine with radiator filled all day. Don and I fetched the parts from Ackers' Flea.
Apr	30	Don towed our Flea to his place.
May	2	Had eight runs up and down at Leamington in the evening. Short hops, wheels seized.
May	5	Cowell, the Air League test pilot for Fleas was killed while testing Doig's aircraft [G-AEEW].
May	10	I took Don's machine out and found that it was still flying right wing low. Tried adjustments and tried again. I had to pull it up over some sheep and then it cartwheeled into the ground. Lucky the prop was not broken.
May	11	Finished off my Flea at Don's. All ready to go to Leamington.
May	12	Charlie and I went over to Don's, loaded the Flea onto Don's trailer.
May	13	Don and I took my Flea to Leamington, assembled it and taxied it around a bit. Loaded Don's crash onto his trailer.

May 15	Don, Charlie and I go to Leamington and had the machine out. I did one run up the 'drome, turned round and the machine did a complete somersault, breaking the prop and the rudder. We worked until 1.30 am at Don's repairing the damage.		Jun 6	Fitted prop, but the wind was in the wrong direction.
			Jun 9	Two hops. Tailwheel collapsed. Lots of little problems.
May 16	Don and I over at Leamington to refit rudder and tail unit after repair.		Jun 16	Mottram's machine crashed – a total write-off. He was not flying it. Charlie had a few runs on ours.
May 17	Charlie taxies the Flea about, using the homemade prop. Engine revs 100 down. Running time one hour fifty minutes.		Jun 18	I finished up in the hedge. [G-AEBT's last flight.]
			Jun 28	Flea will not take off. Grass cuts into prop. Fed up.
May 26	Don, Charlie and I taxied it up and down half a dozen times.		Jul 22	Don and I bring my Flea away. I left it outside Don's workshop.
May 28	More taxying, and a few hops.		Jul 28	Went with Don to take his Flea to Leamington.
May 31	Taxied the Flea all day. Managed to get it to fly short, straight, hops. Running time three hours. Airfield owner took me up for some crazy flying in his DH.60 Moth.			

1937

May 14 — Fetched main wing of the Flea from Don's and placed it in the garage.

Jun 11 — Rigged up the fuselage and wing to a girder in the garage roof.

Jun 1 — Don flies our Flea well. We both had six short flights. All very pleased.

1938

[Registration G-AEBT cancelled on 30 April.]

Jun 2 — We had some good flights. I crashed it into a hedge near a hayrick after a good flight across the 'drome. This broke the end off our homemade propeller. Take prop off for repair.

1946

May 6 — Sold the Flea to Forte [J.A. Forte, who had plans to fit a 600 cc Blackburn] for £10.

And so the diary ends. In June 1961 Forte sold the Flea to A.J. Walker of the Birmingham Branch of Air-Britain, and it was kept at Kings Norton. After this it was acquired by Mr Vincent, who used G-AEBT as an attraction outside his antique shop, the *'Treasure Trove'* in Birmingham. Mr Vincent died in February 1963. In 1964 G-AEBT went the way of several Fleas that survived the war – it 'disappeared'.

Joseph Wood inside his Flea following its retirement in mid-1937 to a position of permanent 'flying' in the garage.
(Joseph Wood).

The main wing of Joseph Wood's G-AEBT prior to covering. Mignet's book encouraged builders to take a photo of the completed wing and to send it to him as a token of friendship.
(Joseph Wood).

Chequerboard G-AEBT in completed state. As with many Fleas, it carried the motif of the Air League on the rudder. (Joseph Wood).

UK Fleas – Authorisation to Fly dates

The following HM.14s received Authorisations to Fly in the months given. Initial powerplant is also listed.

1935

July (1) G-ADMH (Carden Ford)

Sep (5) G-ADME (Aubier et Dunne); G-ADPP (Scott); G-ADPZ (Douglas); G-ADSC (Mignet-built, Mengin); G-ADSD (Mignet-built, Mengin)

Oct (6) G-ADOU (Scott); G-ADOV (Scott); G-ADPW (Anzani); G-ADSE (Cherub); G-ADUB (Scott); G-ADVM (Scott)

Nov (2) G-ADWR (Scott); G-ADXF (Scott)

Dec (4) G-ADVI (Scott); G-ADXS (Scott); G-ADXY (Scott); G-ADYO (Scott)

1936

Jan (4) G-ADPV (Scott); G-ADZP (JAP); G-ADZV (Scott); G-AEBS (Scott)

Feb (6) G-ADPX (Perman Ford); G-ADPY (Scott); G-AEAD (Scott); G-AECE (Scott); G-AECV (Carden Ford); G-AEDP (unknown)

Mar (9) G-ADDW (Anzani); G-ADVS (unknown); G-AEBB (Henderson); G-AEDF (Anzani); G-AEDM (Scott); G-AEDN (Scorpion); G-AEEC (Carden Ford); G-AEEF (unknown); G-AEFV (Scott)

April (13) G-AECM (Perman Ford); G-AEEI (Austin 7); G-AEEJ (Ford 10); G-AEEW (Anzani); G-AEEY (Anzani); G-AEFD (unknown); G-AEFE (Scott); G-AEFG (Scott); G-AEFK (Carden Ford); G-AEFP (Ford 10); G-AEGD (Carden Ford); G-AEIA (Scott); G-AEIP (Carden Ford)

May (10) G-AEEH (Scott); G-AEFW (Douglas); G-AEGU (unknown flat twin, 9 hp); G-AEGV (Douglas); G-AEHG (unknown); G-AEII (Douglas); G-AEIO (Scott); G-AEJO (unknown); G-AEJU (Scott); G-AEJZ (Scott)

June (3) G-AEHD (Austin or Ford); G-AEJX (unknown); G-AEKR (Anzani)

July (4) G-AEJC (Carden Ford); G-AEJD (Carden Ford); G-AEKH (Anzani); G-AELN (Coventry Victor)

Aug (2) G-AELM (unknown); G-AEME (unknown)

Sep (2) G-AEBR (Scorpion); G-AEND (Henderson)

Oct (1) G-AEOH (Scott)

Dec (1) G-AERJ (Austin 7)

1937

Feb (1) G-AEOJ (Anzani)

Aug (1) G-AFBU (unknown)

1939

May (1) G-AFUL (Scott)

(76) Total number of UK Fleas to receive Authorisation to Fly.

British-Registered Fleas

Builder/Location	Regist'n	Powerplant	Authorisation
E. D. Abbott Ltd, Farnham	G-AEGD	Carden-Ford	25 Apr 1936
E. D. Abbott Ltd, Farnham	G-AEJC	Carden-Ford	28 Jun 1936
E. D. Abbott Ltd, Farnham	G-AEJD	Carden-Ford	28 Jul 1936
E. D. Abbott Ltd, Farnham	G-AEIE	Carden-Ford	-
E. D. Abbott Ltd, Farnham	G-AEJE	-	-
E. D. Abbott Ltd, Farnham	G-AEJF	-	-
E. D. Abbott Ltd, Farnham	G-AEJG	-	-
Aero-8 Flying Club, Ashingdon, Essex	G-AEFW	Sprite 23hp	16 May 1936
Aircraft Constructions Ltd, Croydon (R. G. Doig)	G-AEEW	Anzani	1 Apr 1936
Stephen Appleby, Heston	G-ADMH	Carden-Ford	24 Jul 1935
Stephen Appleby (HM.18)	G-AENV	Mengin 38hp	18 Sep 1936
Dr. M. D. S. Armour, Fife	G-AEOJ	Anzani 30hp	7 Jul 1937
A. S. Bacon, Canterbury	G-AEBR	Scorpion	22 Sep 1936
C. E. Baker & ptnrs, Wimborne	G-AEJU	Scott A2S	27 May 1936
R. L. Baker, Forest Hill	G-ADVW	-	-
L. V. G. Barrow, Colchester	G-AEFE	Scott A2S	3 Apr 1936
C. L. Barrington, Burnham	G-AEKH	Anzani 35hp	18 Jul 1936
N. M. Bird, Stowmarket	G-AEMY	-	-
Birkenhead Flying Club, Birkenhead	G-AEIZ	Scott A2S	-
H. F. Bouskill, Leeds	G-AEIA	Scott A2S	24 April 1936
G. F. Briggs, Preston	G-AEFD	-	7 Apr 1937
Cyril Brooke & ptnrs, Huddersfield	G-ADPP	Scott A2S	25 Sep 1935
Don Burgoyne, Knowle	G-AECN	Scott A2S	-
R. Butler, Hastings	G-AEEY	Anzani	1 Apr 1936
Fred Brown, Peterborough	G-AENI	Austin 7 (?)	-
E. H. Chambers, Princes Risborough	G-ADXF	Scott (?)	20 Nov 1935
John A. Chamier, Heston	G-ADME	Aubier & Dunne	6 Sep 1935
Cheltenham Light Aircraft Club	G-AELN	Coventry Victor (?)	30 Jul 1936
E. Claybourn Co.,	G-AEKR	Anzani	23 Jun 1937*
Clyde Battery Co, Glasgow	G-AECV	Carden-Ford	25 Feb 1936
C. H. Cooper, Derby	G-AEHH	Harley	-
Cooper's Garage, Surbiton	G-AEEI	Austin 7	1 Apr 1936
Leslie Crosland, Hull	G-AEJZ	Scott A2S	29 May 1936*
E. Crossley, Banbury	G-AEFF	Scott (?)	-
M. L. Curtis, Enfield	G-AEFJ	-	-
Dart Aircraft, Dunstable	G-ADSE	Cherub III	19 Oct 1935
C. R. Davidson, Digby	G-AEBS	Scott A2S	29 Jan 1936
E. G. Davies, Bath	G-AEEH	Scott A2S	16 May 1936*
H. Dodson & R. C. Caunce, Wirral	G-ADZV	Scott A2S	1 Jan 1936
H. J. Dolman, Bristol	G-AEHM	Douglas II	-*
L. R. Dover-Beck, Hansworth	G-ADZY	-	-
H. J. Dunning & G. E. Ferguson, Shoreham	G-AEEF	-	1 Mar 1936
E. Dutton, York	G-AEDR	Anzani	-
East Midlands Aviation Co. Sywell	G-AEGV	Douglas	27 May 1936*
G. A. Essex, Penrhyn	G-AEGU	'flat twin'	15 May 1936
T. H. Fouldes, Derby	G-AFUL	Scott A2S	1 May 1939

Fraser Bros, Dingwall	G-ADWX	Scott A2S	-
Glasgow Corporation Transport Flying Club	G-AEFP	Ford 10	16 April 1936
J. Goodall, Keith, Scotland	G-ADXY	Scott A2S	24 Dec 1935
E. H. Gray, Swindon	G-AEKA	-	-
J. C. C. Green, Stroud	G-AEIX	-	-
C. C. L. Gregory, Broxbourne	G-ADVS	-	9 Mar 1936
W. B. Haddow, Glasgow	G-ADVI	Scott A2S	3 Dec 1935
R. P. Hartley, Windermere	G-AEGT	Anzani (?)	-
F. Hills & Sons, Manchester	G-ADOU	Scott A2S	9 Oct 1935
C. Howitt, Oxford	G-AEEX	Douglas	-
Ipswich & District Pou Club	G-AEEJ	Ford 10	9 Apr 1936
E. W. Kendrew, Middlesbrough	G-AEAD	Scott A2S	2 Apr 1936
Harry Killick, Hale, Cheshire	G-AEII	Douglas	11 May 1936
M. G. Lazars & A. L. Bieber, Liverpool	G-ADUB	Scott (?)	23 Oct 1935
Leicestershire Flying Pou Club	G-AEHG	-	1 May 1936
G. A. Litchfield & ptnrs	G-AEHD	-	30 Jun 1936
R. R. Little, Canterbury	G-ADZS	Scorpion	-
C. E. Mercer, Lewisham	G-AEFV	Scott A2S	26 Mar 1936
National Aviation Day Displays Ltd, Ford	G-ADSC	Poinsard	11 Sep 1935
N.A.D Displays Ltd, Ford	G-ADSD	Poinsard	11 Sep 1935
Sidney Miles, Bedford	G-ADZT	FN	-
B. W. Millichamp, Belton	G-AERJ	Austin 7	1 Dec 1936
L. E. Mottram, Birmingham	G-AEFI	Anzani	-
John Nolan, Accrington	G-AEFG	Scott A2S	1 Apr 1936
North Liverpool Light Plane Club	G-AELM	-	1 Aug 1936
Oldham Welding & Central Motor Co.	G-AEJA	Anzani	-
A. Oliver, St Teath, Cornwall	G-AEBA	Anzani	-
K. W. Owen, Southampton	G-AEBB	Henderson	2 Mar 1936*
Brian Park, Wigan	G-ADYO	Scott A2S	14 Dec 1935
R. H. Paterson, Glasgow	G-ADVL	Anzani	-
J. Patston, Peterborough	G-AENJ	Austin 7	-
W. A. Pearce & ptnrs, Southend	G-AEDN	Scorpion	10 Mar 1936
E. G. Perman Co., London	G-ADOV	Scott	2 Oct 1935
E. G. Perman Co., London	G-ADPU	-	-
E. G. Perman Co., London	G-ADPV	Scott A2S	24 Jan 1936
E. G. Perman Co., London	G-ADPW	Anzani	18 Oct 1935
E. G. Perman Co., London	G-ADPX	Perman Ford	2 Feb 1936
E. G. Perman Co., London	G-ADPY	Scott A2S	14 Sep 1936
E. G. Perman Co., London	G-ADZG	-	-
E. G. Perman Co., London	G-ADZW	-	-
E. G. Perman Co., London	G-AECK	-	-
E. G. Perman Co., London	G-AECL	-	-
E. G. Perman Co., London	G-AECM	Perman Ford	8 Apr 1936
Phoenix Aircraft Construction Co., London	G-AEIP	Carden-Ford	9 Apr 1936
Planes Ltd, Chelmsford	G-ADVM	Scott A2S	25 Oct 1935

J. B. Plant, Manchester	G-ADZP	JAP	7 Jan 1936
Philip Priest, Huddersfield	G-ADPZ	Douglas	11 Sep 1935
Tom Procter, Blackburn	G-ADDW	Anzani	31 Mar 1936
Puttnam Aircraft Co., London	G-AEEC	Carden-Ford	21 Mar 1936
Puttnam Aircraft Co., London	G-AEED	-	-
Puttnam Aircraft Co., London	G-AEEE	-	-
A. Roe, London	G-AEDF	Anzani	11 Mar 1936
Scott's Flying Display Ltd, Hanworth	G-AEFK	Carden-Ford	3 Apr 1936
N. H. Shaw, Stafford	G-AFBU	-	23 Aug 1937
C. R. Shoults, Nazeing	G-AEFL	Douglas	-
E. Small & A. D. Hardie, Brechin	G-AEJX	-	12 Jun 1936
W. V. Smedley & C. Bell, Wisbech	G-AECD	Scott A2S	21 Feb 1936
Snelling's Light A'craft Service, Darwen	G-AEDM	Scott	11 Mar 1936
J. S. Squires, Barrow-on-Soar	G-AEIO	-	11 May 1936
C. L. Story, Southend	G-ADXS	Scott A2S	9 Dec 1935*
R. C. Streather, Sutton	G-AEOH	Scott A2S	5 Oct 1936*
John Stubbs, York	G-AECE	Scott A2S	27 Feb 1936
R. L. Thorne, Hull	G-AEFC	-	-
A. U. Tomkins, Brooklands	G-ADWR	Scott A2S	13 Nov 1935
H. R. Toy & D. P. Riley, Ormskirk	G-AEND	Henderson	17 Sep 1936
H. J. Tuckett, Chelmsford	G-AEJO	-	20 May 1936
W. Turner, Helensburgh	G-AEFO	-	-
W. H. Wandby, York	G-AEDP	-	24 Feb 1936
C. Watson, Portsmouth	G-AEDO	-	-
R & D. Weaver, Wolverhampton	G-AEME	-	26 Aug 1936
Whyteleafe Motors, Surry	G-ADWS	-	-
Joseph Wood, Solihull	G-AEBT	Ford 10	-
F. G. Wright, Louth	G-AEDS	-	-

Additionally, the registrations G-ADVU and G-ADYV were reserved for Fleas, but not taken up.

Notes: Engine given is the first application. Where an engine is queried (?), type cannot be confirmed. Where no engine is given the type is unknown. If no Authorisation date is quoted, none was granted. Aircraft marked * are currently extant.

Chapter 6

THE MIGNET EFFECT

HENRI MIGNET'S LITTLE AEROPLANE ALLOWED the term 'amateur' (or *Autre Aviation* – Alternative Aviation – as the man proudly proclaimed on the rudder of his HM.14) to become a respectable and workable element of the aviation world. This was not all, however, for the ripples from his arrival in the established and tranquil pond of flying are still moving outwards.

In Britain and France the pattern of reaction to the endearing little man was much the same. Because the Flea was an aircraft for individuals, there were endless variations on the basic design, no two Fleas being the same. Beyond this there was more major surgery to the basic HM.14, the Jeffrey Baynes modification to Appleby's machine having already been discussed in Chapter Four, the Aero-8 Club's version in Chapter Five and the quite radical rethink of Francis Kohler and André Baumann in Chapter Two.

Apart from a few die-hards Britain was to drop the Flea like a hot brick after the 'ban' and to date only two of the later Mignet designs have been attempted by homebuilders. Only one, Bill Cole's HM.293 has flown. Anyone attending the *Réseau de Sport de l'Air*'s superb international rally at Brienne-le-Château, near Troyes, (and, more recently, at Moulins,) will know that in France Mignet designs have not just been avidly taken up as he developed further ideas, but a whole series of other designers have taken the whole philosophy into

the 1980s, as witnessed in Chapter Fifteen.

Particularly in Britain, the advent of the Flea gave birth to many cottage industries across the country feeding the amateur builder, some even offering the Flea on a professionally manufactured basis. Some of these companies were as short-lived as the British Flea craze itself, but others went on to establish themselves and produce other aircraft. Britain also went on to develop rivals, or alternatives, to the Flea, offering the concept without the wing layout and control systems that were to come into question very quickly. In France the work of Léon Lacroix was to give birth to a series of aircraft that were to continue post-war.

A little variety

In Britain most of the major surgery undertaken on Fleas was carried out by those concerns offering professionally built examples, and these will be dealt with a little later. A scan of every photograph of a British Flea will reveal differences of detail, and certainly of powerplant; this variety is one of the delights of studying the little aircraft.

The most radical alterations to a basic Flea in the United Kingdom were to be found in aircraft built and operated by Alec Latus, the owner of a radio shop in Preston, Lancashire. He built a conventional aircraft, powered by an ABC, although it is not known if it flew in this guise. For one reason or another, perhaps an attempt to gain more lift without the need for more power, Latus then fitted the wing of a Dagling glider – presumably with its conventional ailerons, although these would have needed major changes to the other flying surfaces and the control system to have been utilised. Its flying career is thought to have been brief. Its last flight was brought to an abrupt end, the ABC dropped a valve, smashed a piston, bent a conrod and gravity took over. Latus was not hurt, but the wing was. The undercarriage was donated to John Lockley's Flea that managed to fly during the Second World War, as related in Chapter Five.

The Dagling was a primary glider, based upon the German Kassal Zogling and manufactured in 1930 by R.F. Dagnall's RFD Ltd (Dagnall and Zogling being combined to produce the type name). The name did become more or less generic for all British built pre-war primary gliders of this configuration so it is possible that the wing could have come from an imported Zogling, an Abbott-Baynes Sailplanes-built version, a Zander and Weyl-built version, the later Slingsby T.3 Primary, or even from the plans released by the British Gliding Association (for £3) in 1933.

Designs from Lacroix and Bourdin

Very much in the mould of Mignet, another Frenchman, Léon Lacroix had experimented with his own aircraft designs in the Agen region of France both before and after the 1914-1918 war. It was Mignet in 1934 who was responsible for Lacroix getting back into homebuilding and, like hundreds of others, it was through the HM.14 Pou du Ciel.

Dr Barret de Nazaris was a close neighbour of Lacroix and started independently to build a HM.14. Lacroix's Flea, called *Toto* and de Nazaris's example both made tentative hops into the air, but neither flew to their satisfaction. Comparing notes, they soon came to the conclusion that one of the major problems was airframe weight and poor engine power. It was 1936 and Flea fatalities were hitting the headlines, so the pair decided to use the basic Mignet concept but to fit a larger engine and more conventional controls. Through a process of experimentation the first two-seat Lacroix et de Nazaris Autoplan was created in 1937. Powered by a Salmson radial, it featured ailerons on the forward wing and elevators on the rear. The main wing did not pivot either, but it was still a true tandem giving excellent

slow speed handling. Lacroix built several versions of the Autoplan, the LN.2 and LN.4, at Villeneuve-sur-Lot, but also dabbled with other designs including his 1942 flying wing.

Showing its Flea-like configuration, but being a much more 'conventional' aircraft, the first Lacroix/de Nazaris Autoplan of 1937. (Geoffrey P. Jones Collection)

In 1943 Lacroix designed a single-seat version of the Autoplan, the LL.7. This was built by Raymond Bourdin and completed in 1946, designated as the LB.7 Autoplan. In the following years several variants of the Lacroix-Bourdin Autoplan were built, all with tandem wings. None were given registrations nor acquired the then-new *Certificat de Navigabilité Restreinte pour Avions* (CNRA), broadly similar to the British pre-war Authorisation to Fly and the post war Permit to Fly. Under the CNRA system aircraft were instantly recognisable as having a restricted category certificate by being registered in the F-Pxxx batch. Bourdin wrote of these aircraft: ' . . . from the very first flights these aeroplanes were a success, and I admit to having very fond memories of the thirty or so hours spent flying the LB.7 and LB.9.'

One of the next aircraft designed and built in Agen incorporated the work of all three up until then involved with the Autoplan family. This was the LNB.11 Autoplan, taking the 'L' from designer Lacroix, the 'N' from de Nazaris who supplied the finance and the 'B' from Bourdin, who built it. It featured staggered side-by-side seating (to lessen its cross-section) and great attention was paid to weight saving in its construction. Power came from a Continental engine (probably an A65) taken from a Piper Cub and it could cruise at just over 100 mph (165 kph). Production plans for the LNB.11 included a batch of twelve aircraft powered by

a Bausier engine, derived from the 2CV Citroen car engine. A single seat version of the LNB.11, the LNB.12 and the true side-by-side LNB.13 were on the drawing board, but were overtaken by the tragic events of 1952.

It was in the LNB.11 in 1952 that de Nazaris attempted to take the world record for the longest flight in a straight line for an aircraft of less than 1,102 lb (500 kg) loaded weight. The attempt ended tragically and fatally in Spain. There were numerous explanations, but the cause of the accident is thought to have been a combination of problems. The canopy had been opened in flight causing the aircraft to turn over and enter a spiral dive. The probable reason for de Nazaris doing this was a design fault that allowed fuel vapour to leak into the cockpit from the pipe feeding the carburettor. Pilot fatigue due to the length of the flight was also a likely contributory factor. 'I've destroyed everything,' said Lacroix afterwards, 'and I don't want to touch it again.'

Death had again thwarted attempts to put a tandem-wing aeroplane into production. Although several subsequent designs were worked on, the last being the L.16 single-seat Autoplan, of 1969 – none have so far been built. A complete dossier of plans for the L.16 had been lodged with Raymond Bourdin for safe keeping with the proviso that they were not used for the construction of the aircraft until thirty years after the death of de Nazaris. In June 1985, having complied with this wish, Bourdin handed the dossier to the President of the RSA, who in turn passed it to the RSA Regional Group at Villeneuve-sur-Lot.

Reappearance of an Autoplan was not long coming and at the RSA International Rally at Brienne-le-Château in 1986, a single-seat L.12 Autoplan was displayed, built by Roland Cuvelier at Villers en Argonne. His aircraft had taken 1,500 hours of work over eighteen months and was close to its first flight. Power came from a 40 hp converted Citroen engine. Although it has a fixed front wing with ailerons, the Autoplan is a classic example of the

The LN.7 built by M. Valadeau. The LN.7 was a single-seat version of the Autoplan, stemming from 1943. The illfated LN.11 in which de Nazaris lost his life in 1957 is shown above the LN.7. (Geoffrey P. Jones Collection)

tandem wing formula and can trace its history directly back to the HM.14.

Mauboussin Hemiptère

In 1935 Pierre Mauboussin established Avions Mauboussin at Puteaux to develop several aerodynamic innovations, in association with Louis Peyret. From these were to come the M.40 Hemiptère tandem wing single-seater which presented yet another interpretation of the Mignet principle. One of the company's other experiments was in the development of the 'vee' tail (also known as the 'butterfly') championed by such aircraft as the Beech Bonanza cabin monoplane and the Fouga CM-170 Magister jet trainer. In the case of the latter, the pretty jet can trace its tail directly back to the work of the mid-1930s. Société Fouga came to a marketing arrangement with Avions Mauboussin for the promotion of any production possibilities from the research at Puteaux.

The Hemiptère was a conventionally designed single-seat light aircraft in every respect apart from its tail surfaces. A dramatically enlarged tailplane carried twin fins and rudders on its tips. There were pedals for rudder control, but the 'ailerons' on the forward wing acted as flaps, while the 'elevators' on the rear plane acted as either elevators or ailerons. The forward wing was low set on the fuselage, much in the manner of low-wing single-seat light aircraft and carried the well-spaced main undercarriage. The rear wing was mounted on top of the fuselage at the rear. Power came from a 40 hp Train 4T in-line engine.

Professional options

Britain was only just showing the signs of pulling out of the depression – a depression that would only be truly relieved by the massive rearmament programme initiated to counter the threat of Fascist expansionism within Europe – thus 1935 and 1936 were not ideal times for the population to take to an expensive hobby, still less for other individuals to group together and form companies based around the idea of building, supplying and supporting the Flea boom.

Yet, as the table shows, from June 1935 onwards a whole barrage of company names were established in which the magic words 'Flying Flea', 'Flea', *'Pou du Ciel'* or 'Mignet' appear in their Articles of Association. That many of these cannot be connected with Flea

activity, no matter how small, is perhaps a measure of what living there was to be made out of the craze.

As well as those professing a wish to adopt production of the Flea as their chief means of making their livelihood, there were plenty of other concerns who could lend their skills, predominantly occupied in other things, to the production of Fleas to order, from people who wished to avoid the construction phase, or to building the more complex components. The Fazakerley Cycle and Baby Carriage Company was quoted in the *Liverpool Daily Express* as 'building' Fleas. Because their name did not crop up elsewhere, it is safe to assume that the reference overstated the case. Such a firm would certainly have skills in tubular work, wood working and the all-too-complex problem of wheels, so it is not unnatural to assume that Liverpool- and Lancashire-based builders may well have turned to such a firm. There are many other examples that could be so cited.

A handful of companies became well established in the production of Fleas, or in the support of others. F. Hills and Son moved swiftly from 'sampling' the Flea to becoming a major builder of aircraft. Hills and the major professional builders are given in more detail below. Other concerns, such as the Phoenix Aircraft Construction Company of Ashingdon and Planes Limited of Chelmsford built but one aircraft each. Snelling's Light Aircraft Service of Darwen, Lancashire, also merit a mention, they too built their own Flea, G-AEDM, but were prolific suppliers of kits and components.

Abbott-Baynes Aircraft

Abbott-Baynes Aircraft was part of a marriage of talents, linking E.D. Abbott Ltd, coachbuilders of Farnham, Surrey, with the design skills of L.E. Jeffrey Baynes. Through Abbott-Baynes Sailplanes they built the Scud series of sailplanes and had linked up with Sir John Carden with the self-launching Carden-Baynes Scud III Auxiliary which had its début in August 1935 (see Chapter Four).

Following the accident to Stephen Appleby's pioneering Flea G-ADMH at its first public demonstration on 29 July 1935 at Heston, Baynes was asked to effect a rebuild and redesign through Sir John Carden, whose Ford conversion had been fitted to the unfortunate Flea. As described in Chapter Four, Baynes modified the aircraft and it made its first public appearance in its new guise at Heston on 2 October 1935. By that time Appleby had joined Carden Aero Engine Ltd, who were offering the Ford conversion and was to act as test pilot for Abbott-Baynes and their ventures.

G-ADMH represented the mid-point in Baynes' thinking on the Flea. He was to go on to produce possibly the most workable and reliable example of the type, the so-called Cantilever Pou. This was of Mignet philosophy and starting point, but the design took in much more and really should be regarded as a separate type. Baynes employed struts to support the wing, arising from near the main undercarriage fitment and also from the engine bearers, thus the wing was cantilever and had two pivot points, sharing the wing loading in a more tolerable manner. The wing section was to Baynes' own design and he claimed it had a stationary centre of pressure. Among other improvements a set of counterbalance weights were added to the control horns (which worked a pushrod in similar manner to G-ADMH) so that when the wing was not in lift the weight was not transferred to the pilot's wrist.

'The aft plane, instead of looking like a garden seat, now seems to be a kind of orthodox tail-plane. The hay-wire bracing has given place to bicycle-tubing, and the gap between the wings has grown so that there seems little chance of the slot taking charge of the aft plane. A few more steps in evolution and it will not be unlike a real aeroplane of 1911 or thereabouts'. The caustic words were by C.G. Grey, the editor of *The Aeroplane,* written about what he called the *'Cantilouse'* in the 13 May 1936 issue. No matter how hurtful he may have been about a very genuine design improvement, he was precise about the slot effect and that aft tailplane, on standard HM.14s at any rate.

Abbotts' advertising offered the whole aircraft, including engine, for £150; an extra £15 would pay for its assembly and test flight. For £90 a customer could have a complete airframe packed and ready for assembly. The first *'Cantilouse',* G-AEGD, was tested by Appleby in April 1936 and gained its Authorisation on the 25th. Despite much pushing, the market was not large for professionally built machines and only four were completed, the last one not gaining its Authorisation document. Abbotts did claim to have done well out of selling components and knock down kits, as many as 100 kits being reported, although this seems high in the light of these airframes needing the comparatively expensive Carden-Ford to power them, being very different at the nose from the standard HM.14.

As with Appleby and Puttnam Aircraft, the fortunes of Abbott-Baynes Aircraft were linked with those of Sir John Carden. His death in an air crash on 10 December 1935 was a severe blow. Appleby had turned his attentions to the Puttnam Aircraft Company. Both Baynes and Carden had been hard at work on the Carden-Baynes Bee, a side-by-side two-seat tourer with two of the projected 40 hp Carden Ford SP.1 supercharged four-cylinder developments of the basic engine mounted in pusher configuration on the wing. Development of this aircraft, G-AEWC, continued and it first flew at Heston on 3 April 1937. Bugged with developmental problems, including the engines, the Bee was scrapped in 1939.

G-AEGD, the prototype Abbott-Baynes Cantilever Pou, or 'Cantilouse' with Appleby at the controls. The substantial strut structure was part of the Jeffrey Baynes rethink. Abbotts advertised aircraft to this specification as being ready to fly for £150. (via Richard Riding)

Proud Abbotts workers pose next to their product, the Abbott-Baynes Cantilever Pou with Imperial Airways Short S.17L G-ACJK 'Syrinx' to give scale. (Ken Ellis Collection)

Dart aircraft

German-born Alfred R. Weyl and Eric P. Zander formed Zander and Weyl and Company at Dunstable, building several gliders. Their first powered aircraft was Flying Flea G-ADSE, built to the order of C.F. Rae Griffin, who also assisted in its construction. Powered by a Bristol Cherub III that had been previously fitted into Avro Avis G-EBKP and found at Wilstead, *Winnie the Pou* as the craft was called, gained Authorisation No.12 on 19 October 1935. The company went on to build other Flea parts for owners and on 11 May 1936 became Dart Aircraft Ltd.

In the light of the Flea boom, Weyl was convinced that ultralight aircraft had a future. First off was the Dart Pup with a 27 hp Ava 4a-100 French-made pusher engine, designed to compete with the Kronfeld/BA Drones that were gaining in popularity. Known initially as the Dunstable Dart until the company changed its name, the sole example, G-AELR, made its first flight in July 1936. A commission from Dr H.N.Bradbrooke resulted in the Dart Flittermouse G-AELZ. Using the wing of a previous Zander and Weyl glider, the Totternhoe, the Flittermouse had a single-seat nacelle fuselage with a pusher 25 hp Scott A2S engine with a framework-mounted tail and high wing. It first flew shortly after the Pup, but also remained the only one of its kind.

Dart's main claim to fame was the delightful Kitten single-seat monoplane, also initially powered by the 27 hp Ava. The first example, G-AERP, made its first flight on 15 January 1937. A second aircraft, G-AEXT, was termed Kitten II and fitted with an Aeronca JAP J-99 and was ready by April 1937. A Kitten in kit form was also sold to a customer in the Midlands, but was not completed. Post war another Kitten, a Mk III, G-AMJP was completed. A two-seat version, the Weasel, was planned, but Weyl was interned as an alien when the war began and these, and other, plans came to nought.

Dart Aircraft's most famous product was the shapely Kitten single-seater. Illustrated is Kitten II G-AEXT powered by a JAP J-99 and lovingly restored by the late Clive Stubbings. (Duncan Cubitt/*FlyPast* Magazine)

F. Hills and Son

In 1935 three employees of the Trafford Park, Manchester-based woodworking concern F. Hills and Sons set to building a very standard Flea, powered by a Scott A2S. These men were to have a great influence on the next ten years of the company's history. The Flea was registered as G-ADOU on 23 September 1935, and it made its test flights from the nearby Barton Aerodrome – then Manchester's airport – gaining its Authorisation on 9 October. A second aircraft was started, about August 1935, but was never completed; it was reported that it was planned to power it with a Praga engine.

This Flea building exercise ran in parallel with the acquisition of the licence-building rights to the Czech CKD-Praga Air Baby side-by-side two-seat trainer/tourer, powered by a Jowett Cars-built Praga B engine of 36 hp. Hills were to complete 28 as the Hillson Praga between 1936 and 1938. It was not an astounding success, but was certainly cheap at £385 for a two-seater (the Ava-powered Dart Kitten single-seater being offered at £345 at the same time).

Underpowered with its 36 hp Praga B engine, the Hillson-built Praga found some popularity in Britain in the immediate pre-war years. G-AEON illustrated was exported off the Manchester production line in December 1936.
(MAP)

Relative success in this area brought in a designer, Norman Sykes, and the totally in-house, but in configuration very similar to the Praga, Hillson Pennine, G-AFBX, appeared. Praga-powered, it made only one flight, on 4 February 1937. Sykes went on to design the Helvellyn military trainer for Hills in 1939, but only the prototype, G-AFKT, was completed. By this stage Hills were a major sub-contractor for Avros on Anson production and a major producer of wooden propellers. During the war, Hills built 812 Percival Proctors under sub-contract and also built the amazing slip-wing Hillson Bi-Mono, a research aircraft for their FH.40 Hawker Hurricane which took off as a biplane to extend its operational range, jettisoning the upper wing in flight.

Luton Aircraft Ltd

The Dunstable Sailplane Company was founded, at Dunstable Downs, in January 1935 by C.H. Latimer-Needham and William L. Manuel, both of whom were well versed in the art of designing gliders. Latimer-Needham had several light aircraft designs under his belt, including the Mayfly and Minus for the Halton Aero Club, had had a hand in the Martin monoplane G-AEYY and was consultant to the Granger brothers on their Archaeopteryx (see Chapter Four). Manuel had just completed at Dunstable design of the abortive, Flea-like Gurney Grice Mosquito (see below). On 4 November 1935 the company was renamed as the Luton Aircraft Company as a result of its changing base to Luton Aerodrome, Barton-in-the-Clay, and the wish to expand into powered flight. The trade name Dunstable Sailplane Company was retained. A major fire at the Barton plant in 1936 was the occasion of another move, this time to the Phoenix Works, Gerrard's Cross.

Luton Aircraft became a major supplier of components and kits for the Flying Flea, offering a comprehensive brochure on the subject. A complete set of manufactured parts and covering materials for the Flea, including spars, ribs, leading and trailing edges, longerons, plywood panels, struts, tanks, fittings, wheels, 36 yards of fabric, five gallons of dope, the control assembly, bolts, turnbuckles and cables could be had for £62 10s 0d and, of course, all parts could be bought separately. A complete Flying Flea, fitted with a Scott A2S or a 34 hp Anzani, finished in any colour and ready to fly was £165, or a straight £100 less engine and airscrew. Dr M.D.S.Armour's G-AEOJ (see Chapter Three) used many Luton-manufactured components and doubtless many other Fleas took advantage of this service. Luton themselves had a Flea half built when it perished in the Barton fire.

Luton Aircraft's Buzzard relied very much on the the firm's previous glider experience and first flew in the summer of 1936 powered by a pusher Anzani.
(MAP)

Under Latimer-Needham, Luton were to try their hand at other ultra-lights and were unique in being the only British firm to try again the tandem-wing concept. First product was, however, a throw-back to the designer's gliding days, this being the sailplane-like LA.1 Buzzard powered by a pusher 35 hp Anzani engine, although it was designed to use a Scott A2S. The one and only Buzzard (G-ADYX) made its first flight in the summer of 1936.

To have been called the Minor, the next design, the LA.2 featured that tandem wing, although it had ailerons and a conventional tail unit – a compromise of aerodynamics. The wing was supported from a central cabane and had two flying struts as well as wire bracing. Constructional technique on the fuselage was very different from that of Mignet, but it certainly had the 'Flea-look', especially around the undercarriage. Powered by the faithful

Anzani, the LA.2 made its first flights in late 1936, but was not deemed a success.

The fuselage was incorporated in the LA.3 Minor, G-AEPD, which featured an entirely new wing. Starting in January 1937, the new aircraft was ready for flight test the following month at Gerrard's Cross, powered by a Luton-Anzani. With detail refinements the LA.4 Minor prototype, G-AFBP, flew in 1937 powered by an ABC Scorpion II of 40 hp. Luton Aircraft intended the LA.4 Minor only for sale as plans and components, learning from their days of being a prominent Flea stockist.

Luton built one LA.4 for a South African customer and this was despatched, unflown, before the war broke out and Luton Aircraft wound down. Two Minors were homebuilt before the war, both by former Flea builders. Jack Carine of the Isle of Man bought his Flea as a kit (possibly from Luton Aircraft) and announced that he intended to fly to Liverpool in it upon its completion. The flight ended in his turning back and it was damaged on landing. Carine sold it to a local, Reggie Bimson, but he did not fly it. By now Carine had received his LA.4 kit from Lutons which, powered by 35 hp Luton-Anzani as G-AFRC, gained its paperwork on 8 March 1939, flying from Hall Caine airfield. It was damaged beyond repair at Jurby airfield on 2 September

Poor quality, but historic, shot of the Luton LA.2 tandem wing aircraft under construction. It was not a success, but via the more conventional LA.3 gave rise to the well known Luton LA.4 Minor.
(via Phil Jarrett)

1939. J.S. Squires of Barrow-on-Soar, Leicestershire, completed his Flea, JSS.1, G-AEIO, in the Spring of 1936, gaining its Authorisation on 11 May and flying from Rearsby airfield, powered by a Scott A2S. JSS.2 was LA.4 G-AFIR, powered by a Luton-Anzani and gaining its vital piece of paper, on 14 August 1938. Stored through the war and later given a JAP J-99, G-AFIR is still with us, undergoing a rebuild to flying condition in Buckinghamshire.

G-AFIR was one of two amateur-built Luton LA.4 Minors flown before the outbreak of the Second World War. It was completed by August 1938 by J. S. Squires of Leicestershire, who had previously built Flea G-AEIO.
(Charles Boxer)

E.G. Perman and Company

From their factory, located in Brownlow Mews off the Grays Inn Road in London WC.1, E.G. Perman and Co. were to complete the largest number of professionally built Fleas, although of the total only six gained an Authorisation. They were largely to the Mignet design and used a variety of engines, including their own Ford conversion, the Perman-Ford of 32 hp. In the middle of their small production run, a constructor's number (and very little else) was taken and applied to another design, the Broughton Midget, which was to become the alliterative Perman Parasol and then, towards the end of its brief career, the Perman Grasshopper.

Perman's first Flea, G-ADOV, was to the order of J.E.W. Wheatley of Walton-on-Thames and was a very orthodox machine, featuring a Scott A2S engine. It was tested at Lympne and gained its Authorisation on 2 October 1935. As part of their lively advertising campaign, Permans promoted the '£10 Club', an arrangement whereby would-be Flea buyers could order an aircraft on a subscription basis to spread the financial load. Second off was G-ADPW, with a 35 hp Anzani previously fitted to a Hawker Cygnet for R.G. Doig for use in Scott's Flying Circus. It received Authorisation No.5 on 18 October 1935 and moved down to Lympne. Here it was damaged on 10 November 1935 when it was blown over. Doig had it on the Kent coast for a cross-Channel attempt, but the accident was to put paid to his chances and Stephen Appleby took this accolade in G-ADMH on 5 December. Doig formed Aircraft Constructions Limited in December 1935, but only G-AEEW resulted.

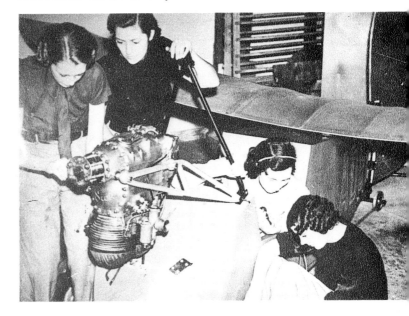

E. G. Perman and Company built the largest production run of Fleas in Britain, here the first, G-ADOV, receives adjustments from a female workforce.
(Ken Ellis Collection)

Third off, also with a Scott engine, but with pushrods and a 21 ft 4 in (6.5 m) wing was G-ADPV. It received its Authorisation on 24 January 1936 and was transferred that day to E.W.H. Cavendish and based at Heston. G-ADPX was the first to be fitted with the Perman Ford and also featured pushrods. The Permit was issued on 2 February 1936 and the aircraft became F.W. Broughton's on 7 March 1936 and

F. W. Broughton's Flea replacement, the Perman Parasol G-ADZX. The project started as the Perman Midget and ended up being called the Grasshopper. It made its first flight in May 1936, but did not go into production. (A. J. Jackson Collection)

was flown from Gravesend. Broughton was already working on the Flea replacement, the Midget.

Fifth was another Scott machine, G-ADPY, and the subject of Arthur Clouston's (who was Perman's test pilot) 'Bristol' claim at the Ramsgate race (see Chapter Four). It gained its Permit on 14 February 1936. Last of the line was G-AECM, Perman-powered, receiving its Permit on 8 April 1936. Permans had several other registrations reserved for them, but they were not taken up.

While sampling Perman-built Flea G-ADPX, F.W. Broughton was scheming a single-seater of reasonable performance available for less than £200 professionally built. This was the Broughton Midget, powered by a 32 hp Perman-Ford. It used the same wing section as Mignet's Flea, but otherwise was a very different aircraft, being a nice-looking single-seat strut-braced parasol monoplane with completely conventional controls and flying surfaces. Broughton and Permans got together to build the type and Perman Flea constructor's number EGP/SS/56 (in an already complicated constructor's number sequence), allocated G-ADZG, became the basis of the renamed Perman Parasol, G-ADZX. With Clouston at the controls the Parasol made its first flight, from Gravesend, on 23 May 1936 and was offered to the buying public at £175 ex-works.

The Flea was shortly to take on a bad name, and it would seem that the very distantly related Parasol was tarred with the same brush. With no more orders for Fleas

coming in, Broughton left to form Broughton-Blayney Aircraft to build the Brawney (of which more later); Permans were not doing well. The Parasol was renamed the Grasshopper, but it did not change its fortunes. G-ADZX was sold off in October 1936 and was the centre of attention in a fire fighting display at Gravesend in July 1937.

Puttnam Aircraft Company

With the death of Sir John Carden, Stephen Appleby moved his interests from Abbotts-Baynes to the Puttnam Aircraft Company of the Victory Works, Hornsey Road, London N.19, to build and market another version of the L.E.J. Baynes-modified, Carden Ford-engined HM.14. Established with the help of a friend of Sir John, Martin Payne, PAC built only G-AEEC, although it had the intriguing constructor's number PAC.5, possibly acknowledging the four under way at Abbott's. Appleby tested G-AEEC at Heston and it gained its Authorisation on 21 March 1936 and attended the Aero-8 Rally at Ashingdon on 13 April. Payne did not recover from an abdominal operation and Puttnams

The only Baynes-style Flea to be completed by Puttnam Aircraft Company, G-AEEC. Others were in the process of construction when the project fizzled out.
(A. J. Jackson Collection)

folded, although at least two other aircraft were close to completion.

More spin-offs

Mignet's creation inspired not only professional concerns to build the type for the general flying market and then to develop other ideas from it; the Flea had still further effects. From the E.G. Perman Company came F.W. Broughton, who proceeded to take his ideas for a 'super-Flea' further with the fateful Brawney. Several Flea builders graduated to designing and building their own aircraft beyond their dabblings with the HM.14. Mr Gurney Grice built a somewhat massive-looking tandem winged aircraft, clearly influenced by Mignet, the Mosquito. While, perhaps, representing somewhat obscure aircraft, predominantly 'one-offs' (there were three Brawneys), they show the extent of the effect of the craze, not just people queuing to build Fleas, but also a stimulus to thought and development.

Broughton-Blayney Brawney

As related earlier, E.G. Perman and Co. took up F.W. Broughton's idea of a follow-on to the Flea, initially termed the Midget, marketed as the Parasol and later renamed the Grasshopper. Only one example was built and Permans lost interest by late 1936. Meanwhile Broughton left and teamed up with A. J. Blayney, supplying the finance, to produce a more developed and refined version under the aegis of Broughton-Blayney Aircraft Limited of Hanworth. Their product was the Brawney, the name presumably coming from an amalgam of the proprietors' surnames.

Broughton commissioned three Brawnies from T.H. Gill and Son of Kilburn Lane, London W10. The Brawney followed much the same idea as the Midget/Parasol/Grasshopper, including using the same Carden-Ford powerplant. The wing was generally similar, but mounted lower in relation to the fuselage and supported by seemingly enormous struts, of 'N' configuration on the prototype (G-AENM). On the two 'production' aircraft the diagonal component of the 'N' was a bracing wire.

Carrying no visible registration marks, G-AENM made its first flight at Hanworth on 19 September 1936 in front of the assembled junketers for the annual Hanworth Garden Party. After H.J. Wilson returned from the successful maiden flight, the price tag of £195

Convivial atmosphere surrounding the prototype Broughton-Blayney Brawney following its first flight at Hanworth on 19 September 1936, the occasion of the annual Hanworth Garden Party. Three Brawnies were built, two were bound for tragedy.
(via Phil Jarrett)

was painted on the Brawney's cowling – Broughton was just inside his less-than-£200 target. Orders were slow in coming and the three aircraft achieved their Authorisations (G-AENM on 8 October, G-AERF and G-AERG both on 23 December 1936) and were kept looking busy at Hanworth.

What followed was to deal a mortal blow to the Brawney, and deliver a hefty swipe at the whole ultralight aircraft concept at the same moment. Yorkshireman Alexander Scaife acquired G-AENM and came down to Hanworth to ferry it home himself. On his first flight in the Brawney it crashed at Feltham, killing Scaife.

Alfred Stanley Bacon ran a tobacconist's shop in Canterbury and had earned himself quite a name as an amateur motorcycle racer and stunt rider. He had served in the Royal Naval Air Service and later with the RAF. He and shopkeeper Mr H. Sower-Butts built Flea G-AEBR in the back of Bacon's shop. The 30 hp ABC Scorpion fitted featured 2:1 reduction gearing and an impulse starter. It was tested from a nearby piece of land called The Old Park and gained its Permit on 22 September 1936. Bacon considered it to be underpowered and in early 1937 it was damaged and abandoned. The wings were sold to a young Flea builder locally. The fuselage was passed on post-war to a man in Ramsgate who intended to turn it into an aquaplane.

Both Bacon and Sower-Butts put their money into buying the second Brawney, G-AERF, and both journeyed to Hanworth to pick it up on 6 June, 1937. Sower-Butts flew it around Hanworth and Bacon elected to fly it to Ramsgate aerodrome. Bacon is thought to have encountered engine trouble near Bromley Hill. An eyewitness recorded that he only just made the hill, tried to climb and the engine seemed to cut out. G-AERF crashed almost vertically into the local cemetery, killing Bacon instantly.

Although the remaining Brawney continued to be demonstrated in the capable hands of Jenny Broad, the aircraft clearly could not overcome such a terrible reputation as that of killing its owners on first acquaintance. G-AERG languished at Hanworth after its Authorisation had expired and quietly slipped into oblivion. An amateur-built Brawney is reported to have been some three-quarters complete by mid-1937, but was not completed.

Brown Monoplane

Frederick W. Brown worked for the Aeronautical Corporation of Great Britain at their factory in Sages Lane, Walton, near Peterborough, building Aeronca 100s and their derivatives under licence from the Aeronautical Corporation of America, Cincinnati, Ohio. Of an evening he would return home to his house in South View Road and, after tea, conduct his small engineering business. Included in this work was the conversion of the Austin 7 powerplant for John Patston's Flea G-AENJ, being built at nearby Eye.

Frederick was keen on the idea of building a Flea, but with an engine costing £50 or thereabouts – about six months wages – he felt it was prudent to form a local Pou Club and see if he could attract help. So Flea G-AENI was born and Mr W. Ward and Frank Serjeant added their assistance. G-AENI was also Austin 7-powered, and Brown hopped it with limited success from Patston's field in Eye.

After the Flea, Frederick Brown turned to his place of work to help him with his next project.

Using Aeronca 100 components, including the wings, he created the Brown Monoplane, believed to have been powered by the same powerplant as its production cousins, a 40 hp Aeronca JAP J-99. Its flying career is thought to have been brief, and Frederick Brown (who died in 1980) was convinced of its existence in a barn in the Peterborough area well into the mid-1970s.

Burgoyne-Stirling Dicer

Don Burgoyne and his Flying Flea G-AECN have already been mentioned in Joseph Wood's diary (see Chapter Five). His Flea was built at Heronfield Farm, Knowle, Worcestershire and was completed in January 1936. It featured pushrod controls and a Scott A2S and made its first definite flight on 9 February. G-AECN never achieved an Authorisation and its flying days were finished at Leamington aerodrome when it cartwheeled with Wood at the controls on 5 May 1936. A second machine was started, but not finished. Pulled by ponies, children used the fuselage as a cart and it was still at Knowle Hall when the Air Ministry carried out an inspection on 31 August 1939.

Along with Mr H. Stirling, Don Burgoyne built a large single-engine low-wing monoplane in 1939, called the Burgoyne-Stirling Dicer, and may well have employed the fuselage of a BAC Drone in its construction. Powered by an Aeronca-JAP J-99 of 37 hp, it did not fly before the war. During the war Burgoyne repaired training gliders. In 1948 the Dicer took to the air, wearing the markings G-AECN, previously worn on his Flea. This was a totally unofficial

Flea-builder Don Burgoyne went on to produce the single-seat Dicer monoplane with H. Stirling. Started in 1939, it was not flown until 1948 when it used the registration of Don's Flea, G-AECN, for an identity.
(A. J. Jackson Collection)

move. The Dicer was scrapped in the late 1950s.

Crossley Tom Thumb

Another Midlands Flea builder who went on to build his own aircraft was Mr E. Crossley from Banbury, Oxfordshire, although the aircraft was not completed. Crossley's Flea was G-AEFF, registered to him in March 1936. It was powered by a Scott A2S, but it is not known if it flew at all. The registration was cancelled in December of that year. The Flea was followed in 1937 with the Tom Thumb, a high wing cabin monoplane of his own design. This aircraft was not completed and the fuselage and wings are now kept by the Midland Air Museum at Coventry.

Another product of a Flea-builder. E. Crossley of Banbury went on from Flea G-AEFF to build the Tom Thumb, a high wing cabin monoplane, but it was not completed.
(Ken Ellis Collection)

Gibb Biplane

John and James Gibb of Hamilton, Scotland, built a Flea in late 1935. Jack Gray worked on the engine for this example, being two 500 cc Dunelt motorcycle engines joined together to create a new engine of just under 1,000 cc. The Flea is thought not to have flown and was stored in a hangar the brothers built at Limekiln Burn, above Hamilton. The Gibbs and Gray then turned their attention to the construction of a small single-seat biplane, possibly of original design, although some sources believe it was built to plans acquired from the United States. Gray again supervised the engine

conversion, this time using a 1924 aircooled side-valve horizontally-opposed Rover motorcycle engine of 1,000 cc and about 8 hp. Bits of the aircraft came from a scrapyard in Paisley, the control column being from a Bristol Fighter cut down to size. In 1937 the hangar and the aircraft within them were dismantled. Parts of the biplane survive in the local museum.

Gurney Grice Mosquito

William R. Manuel teamed up with Gurney Grice to design and build a most unusual looking machine, the Mosquito, along the same tandem wing lines as the Flea, but in a much more substantial aircraft. Grice, an engineer who had developed, among other things, an expanding axle wheel brake (fitted on the main gear of the Dart Pup G-AELR) was responsible for the powerplant on the Mosquito. This consisted of two JAP motorcycle engines of 250 cc and 15 hp each being joined together, driving the propeller through a chain drive. The Mosquito pre-dated the Flea in the United Kingdom, as it was ground run at Dunstable in November 1934, the month in which *Le Sport de l'Air* was published in France. While the forward wing pivoted in exactly a similar manner to the control system in the Flea, the rear wing was mobile and could rock up and down by moving the control wheel; there was no rudder. On the ground the tailwheel on the almost racing car-like 'fuselage' could be coupled to the control wheel. The Mosquito did not fly, but achieved some very high speed taxying without the wings!

Howitt Monoplane

Built in a barn at Garsington, near Oxford, was Flea G-AEEX, with the constructor's number H.32C. What logic there is in this number has not been explained, although the builder's next project, a small single-seat parasol monoplane registered G-AEXS, was constructor's number H.32D.

The 'H' doubtless stood for their creator, Mr R.C. Howitt. The Flea featured a 600 cc ohv Douglas motorcycle engine of 18 hp driving a 4 ft 3 in propeller carved from solid beech and 12 inch 'doughnut' wheels to quote the builder. It was flown for the first time by Flight Lieutenant H.R.A.Edwards from nearby RAF Abingdon. Mr Howitt, who emigrated to Australia post-war, last saw the Flea at the town

The amazing Gurney Grice Mosquito with designer William Manuel in the cockpit and Gurney Grice, who devised the linked JAP engines that powered it, at the propeller. Predating the Flea in Britain, it used a more unconventional flying control system than even the HM.14. It did not fly.
(via Phil Jarrett)

to his own design. Registered as G-AEXS, it featured the same Douglas engine and used the same test pilot from the same airfield, making its maiden flight in 1937. It was later fitted with a 1,000 cc Brough Superior motorcycle engine. With the advent of war it was stored at Abingdon and 'lost' prior to 1945.

headquarters of Oxford University Air Squadron, St Cross Road, Oxford.

The Oxford UAS connection was maintained for his follow-up aircraft, the Howitt Monoplane,

Starting the 600 cc Douglas on the Howitt Monoplane G-AEXS. Howitt had previously built Flea G-AEEX.
(A. J. Jackson Collection)

'FLEA' Companies

Companies registered after June 1935 in which the Articles of Associated specifically mentioned construction, support or similar of the Flying Flea. Aircraft known to have been produced or associated with the company are given, if no aircraft are mentioned, research has failed to identify any products, if indeed there were any.

Name	Date	Location	Starting Capital	Official(s) etc
Aircraft Components Ltd	26/3/36	–	–	
Aircraft Constructions Ltd	6/12/35	Sidcup	£2,000	R.G. Doig, G-AEEW only built.
Aircraft Improvements Ltd	35/3/36	–	–	P.P.Nazin, E.G.Smith
Amalgamated Aircraft Builders Limited	20/4/36	London EC4	–	
Carden Aero Engines Ltd	11/3/36	Camberley	–	Lady D.M.Carden, H.H.S.Wright. Registered after the death of Sir John Carden. Carden-Ford conversion and the rights to the Scud III Auxiliary retractable engine mounting.
Carden-Baynes Aircraft Ltd	3/4/36	Heston	£5,000	L.E.Baynes, H.Pemberton, Registered as above, E.D.Abbott Ltd produced the aircraft.
Clyde Aircraft Construction Company Ltd	25/3/36	London EC2*	£100	
Coventry Aero Engines and Components Ltd	25/5/36	London EC2*	£100	
Dart Aircraft Limited	11/5/36	Dunstable	£5,000	A.J.Lucas, E.P.Zander, A.R.D.Weyl, Formerly Zander and Weyl, made parts to order, built G-ADSE and other designs.
East Midlands Aviation Company	4/11/35	Northampton	–	C.G.Brown, S.P.Seddon, A.Chappel, F.M.Rouse, J.I.Bazely, A.Woodhouse Gardner. Only G-AEGV built.
Flea-Type Plane Construction Ltd	11/9/35	London W1	£100	Cmdr S.D.H.Grey RN, DSO.
Flying Flea Ltd	29/8/35	London EC2	£100	
Light Aircraft Ltd	8/35	London WC1*	£100	
London Aircraft Development Corporation	31/8/35	London EC2	£100	
Luton Aircraft Ltd	4/11/35	Barton, Beds	£100	E.F.Needham, build to order, kits and supplies.
Oxford Flying Services Ltd	29/6/35	Wheatley, Oxon	£2,500	H.V.Kimberley Atkinson, G.W. Woodhouse, Also traded as Oxford Aircraft
Walker Aircraft Ltd	11/9/35	Durrington, Wilts	–	W.E.Read, F.W.A.Williams, G.E.Walker

* Solicitor's address

Chapter 7

WHICH ENGINE ?

CHAPTER X OF *THE FLYING FLEA* BRINGS TO a conclusion Mignet's philosophy on flying and the step-by-step construction of the airframe. It finishes on the following words: 'It remains to adapt it to the motor-airscrew group, without which it is a face without an eye, a body without a soul, and is not any good to anybody.'

Chapter XI considers the powerplant, in a mere eight pages. There is a chapter on engine management later on. Mignet's scant attention to the engine has often been criticised as a cop-out. Mignet knew full well that the choice of powerplant would depend totally on the financial state of the builder and, accordingly, he understood that a set of guidelines would be more important, and more practical, than a detailed appraisal of individual engines.

Engine choice had clearly been a painful experience for Mignet, who had become somewhat disillusioned that no French engine manufacturer had decided to make an aircraft adaptation of one of their production two-strokes. Using public transport, he visited at least five (unnamed) motorcycle engine manufacturers. He summed up the response as follows: 'I talked on these lines in three factories. In another my explanations were continually interrupted by the telephone. In yet another they were hardly polite to me.'

With the craze yet to blossom, their reaction is understandable. The investment required to convert a production run of ground-based engines to flying status would only be practical if a market clearly existed. Experience of the HM.8 was not sufficient to convince managing directors to take the risk. Most builders would buy either second-hand or from the factory and convert them to their own satisfaction.

Just as Chapter X closed on flowery rhetoric, so the chapter dealing with the powerplant, among other topics, launched off in fine style: 'Without an engine no flying is possible. That is a basic principle which no man with a conscience can deny, even in so far as it concerns the sport of the amateur. A bad engine . . . bad flying. A good engine . . . good flying.'

Mignet's own engine performance figures in *The Flying Flea* are based upon the 540 cc Aubier et Dunne, rated at 20 hp at 4,000 rpm. Mignet also used Mengins in his HM.14s and exhibited great experience of the powerplants

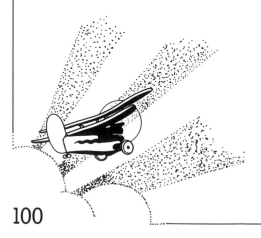

available within France and showed more than a passing knowledge of British engines and their accessories.

In his assessment of the powerplant needs of the HM.14, Mignet was at pains not to mention a specific engine type, although he came down firmly on the two-stroke as the best breed for the Flea. While he could be quite specific about how the wing should be built, he could not constrain the choice of device that would be bolted on the nose.

Strength, Sweetness, Flexibility and Fire Risk were the four characteristics Mignet cited for his choice of the two-stroke engine. It was strong because, in his opinion, the two-stroke had 'nothing to break nor to come to a stop'. 'Sweetness' was a delightful concept used to emphasize the 'less brutal' operation of the two-stroke, in which chains and gears in the reduction system, and the mounting frame, would not suffer as much. This alluded to strengthening and perhaps rethinking the nose section and the load lines if anything other than a two-stroke was opted for.

In Mignet's opinion a two-stroke gave a more suitable power delivery than the four-stroke because the power curve was flatter and a good power output could be had over a much greater range. He claimed his own engine to give 18/20 hp at 3,500 to 4,000 rpm, making it more tolerant to the choice of airscrew. With the fuel tank up in the wing and isolated from the, albeit, uncowled engine by a region of strong airflow fire risk would be low anyway, but the two-stroke cycle meant that a carburettor fire was a remote chance.

Quoting a reconditioned Harley-Davidson at 1,000 Francs and a similar Indian at 600 Francs, Mignet conceded that many builders would want to go for a 'bargain' engine, even if it were only to be used for ground trials and initial test flights. He preferred the purchase of a new engine, hoping that friends would pitch in for the asking price of 4,000 Francs. Besides, a reconditioned or second hand engine would be good experience for the Pou pilot: 'The worse it flies, the better pilot you will become.'

British engine choice

With an indigenous, and high quality, motorcycle industry, British Flea builders were bound to have leanings towards home-spun powerplant answers. The choice that faced builders in the years 1935 and 1936 widened as the craze developed and manufacturers could see the potential market opening up.

Builders could opt for reconditioned or home-modified motorcycle two-strokes, similarly adapted motorcar engines, imported or licence-built French engines or the professionally produced and purpose-designed or adapted Cardens and Scotts. Additionally, there was a growing stock of British light aero engines, designed from scratch.

The variety of powerplants on British Fleas was compounded by the choice of cooling (air-cooled or water-cooled) and by the method of prop drive (direct, geared or otherwise). In many cases the powerplant of particular examples has eluded the writers and other researchers, let alone particulars such as drive and cooling system. Where such variations are known, these details are given with the examples listed on Page 109.

The remainder of this chapter will look in brief detail at this array of powerplants, and the use that they were put to on Fleas. Adaptations and modifications dictate that data quoted can only be regarded as a guide, and installations can only be regarded as the 'standard' engine before going into the hands of the builder/tinkerer!

ABC Scorpions

The All-British Engine Company of Walton-on-Thames, Surrey, had a chequered association with aero-engines. Established in 1912, ABC produced a series of problematical engines during the First World War.

From the end of the war to 1923 the company turned to motorcar and motorcycle production. Then came three adapted two-cylinder engines aimed at the light aircraft market; an unnamed 400 cc, motorcycle-based engine, followed by the car-based 30 hp Scorpion I and the 40 hp Scorpion II.

Despite finding some success with the Scorpions and the later 'double Scorpion' (described by Herschel Smith as 'the world's first flat-four' in his book *A History of Aircraft Piston Engines* Sunflower University Press, 1986) ABC departed from the manufacture of aero-engines in 1929 even though they had designed and built their own single-seat cabin monoplane, the ABC Robin, in that year. This timing dictated that all Fleas using the Scorpion did so with reconditioned powerplants.

Examples of usage: A.S. Bacon's G-AEBR

with 30 hp (assumed to be a Scorpion I) with a 2:1 reduction gearing and impulse starting; J.N. Gladish's had a direct-drive 600 cc ABC; F. Salmon and L. Jones with their own conversion of a 1198 cc ABC car engine.

Anzani

French motorcycle builder Alessandro Anzani started building aero-engines in 1909 as *Anzani Moteurs d'Aviation*. The British Anzani Engine Company of London built a 1,100 cc V-twin which found a considerable following with Flea builders. Luton Aircraft acquired the rights to this engine in 1938. Examples of usage: Dr M.D.S. Armour's G-AEOJ, direct drive, rated at 30 hp; E. Claybourne & Co's G-AEKR rated at 25 hp; Tom Procter's G-ADDW.

Aubier et Dunne

Mignet's first-choice engine for the HM.14, the 17 hp Aubier et Dunne two-stroke was rated at 4,000 rpm, geared down to 1,600 rpm at the propeller. A motorcycle engine, it found favour in France as a Flea powerplant, being of very simple layout. Only J.A. Chamier's G-ADME is known to have used this engine in Great Britain.

A schoolboy watches as Cooper's Garage G-AEEI runs up its Austin Seven conversion without the apparent aid of the pilot! Proprietor Charles Cooper was father of the famous racing car builder and Mini-tweaker John Cooper.
(A. J. Jackson Collection, via John Bateman)

Austin Seven conversion

Converting the reliable and readily available 747 cc Austin 7 motorcar engine occurred to at least eight Flea builders. Rated at 13.5 hp, two of these are known to have been converted to air-cooling. Examples of usage: J. Boulton's air-cooled, but not flown as such; Coopers Garage's G-AEEI with chain-drive (first engine); B.W. Millichamp's G-AERJ with cowling.

Bristol Cherub

Conceived for the Light Aircraft Trials of 1924, the Cherub was the brainchild of Bristol's Roy Fedden. The Cherub became a well-regarded aero-engine and found many applications, including a successful migration to the USA. Development of the 34 hp direct-drive Cherub I led to the geared Cherub II and the more developed 36 hp Cherub III.

Only three British Fleas are known to have been fitted with Cherubs. The high price of the Cherub must have been a contributing factor. The Cherub also had a motorcar potential, but Fedden's best offer to the Morgan Motor Company for supply of each engine for use in their three-wheelers was higher for the engine than for the complete car when fitted with a JAP! Only with the Dart Aircraft example, G-ADSE, is the series of engine known, a Mk III. The other two known applications were on A.C. Dale's and Fernley & Shatwell's aircraft.

Bristol Cherub I installed in the Granger Archaeopteryx G-ABXL on show at the Shuttleworth Trust, Old Warden.
(Alan Curry)

Douglas/Aero Engines Sprites

Douglas was another motorcycle engine manufacturer of high regard that found great favour with British Flea builders. Adaptation to aeronautical usage of the various available engines was relatively straightforward, as they had longitudinal finning stemming from the fore and aft motorcycle application. The Douglas engine, built in Bristol, grew from the original 17 hp /500 cc two-cylinder horizontally-opposed engine of the 1923 Light Aircraft Trials. There were 600 cc and 750 cc factory originated versions, but there were enlargements, the East Midlands Aviation Company's G-AEGV having a 850 cc version. In 1935 Aero Engines Limited, still at the Kingswood plant, took over the 750 cc version

Shots of Fleas with air under their wheels are not easy to come by, so the often poorer quality can be forgiven. The Burns Garage, Congleton, 750 cc direct-drive Douglas-powered example in flight with Harold Burns at the helm. Note the cowled area under the engine.
(via H. Burns)

and after some refinement it continued in production. Factory-fresh engines and former motorcycle versions found their way on to British Fleas.

T. Steele claimed to have a 1,000 cc Douglas on his Flea, but it is doubtful if the original cylinders of the 500 cc engine could stand such reboring. In about 1914 Douglas did make several cyclecar prototypes that used a flat-twin engine that was then available either air-cooled or water-cooled with a capacity of 1,070 cc. It is thought, but cannot be confirmed, that Steele's engine was one of these. Examples of usage (in addition to the two mentioned above): Aero 8 Club's G-AEFW, defined as 23 hp; Burns Garage's 500 cc then 750 cc, initially chain, then direct; James Hill with a former motorcycle 500 cc unit; C. Howitt's G-AEEX rated at 18 hp and 600 cc; Leek Amateur Flying Group, 600 cc geared drive; E.G. Perman & Co's G-ADPW direct-drive (second powerplant).

R. G. Doig's Permans-built G-ADPW inside a Blackpool garage awaiting repairs to its exhaust while touring with Scott's Flying Circus. The small size of the direct drive Douglas (though to be 500 cc) is evident.
(Ken Ellis Collection)

Ford 10 conversions; the Carden- and Perman-Fords

In 1936 £51 10s 0d bought a ready-to-install 30 hp Carden-Ford four-cylinder four-stroke, complete with airscrew hub. For another £8 10s 0d (£8.50) dual ignition came as standard. The first conversion of a Ford engine for use in an aircraft had been by B.H. Pietenpol in 1927 for his famous parasol-winged Aircamper. Only two Fleas are thought to have had Fords fitted that were not Carden- or Perman-converted. Conversion was not as straightforward as other engines and even second-hand prices put them beyond the means of many would-be builders. The two aircraft were Glasgow Corporation Transport Flying Club's G-AEFP and the Ipswich & District Pou Club's G-AEEJ.

In the year before Pietenpol dabbled in Ford conversions, Sir John Carden built a 750 cc two-stroke to his own design and became fascinated by the notion of cheap and reliable powerplants for light aircraft. He came up with a variation of the Ford 10 in 1935, reducing weight through using light alloy instead of cast iron. Reliability and the ready supply of Ford spares were strong points in its marketing campaign. Another sales point that was of incalculable value was the success of the Carden-Ford in the nose of Stephen Appleby's G-ADMH – the first British Flea to fly. Carden Aero Engines of Heston was formed to market this powerplant, with a particular view to the Flea, although it was to power other types as well, notably the Chilton DW.1.

Sir John was tragically killed in an air crash on 10 December 1935 and Carden

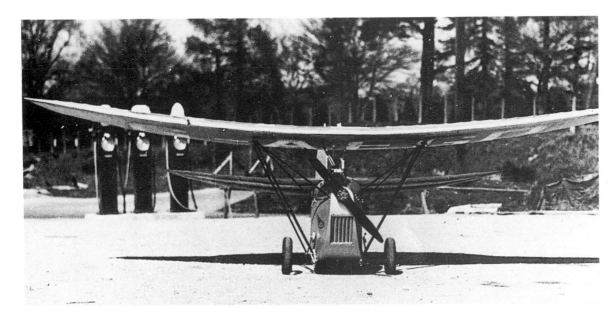

Nose-on view of the neat engine and radiator installation on the Abbott-Baynes Cantilever Pou prototype G-AEGD.
(Ken Ellis Collection)

Aero Engines was absorbed into Carden-Baynes Aircraft of Farnham. In 1937 the rights went to the Chilton Aircraft Company of Hungerford. Examples of usage: E.D. Abbott's

Almost certainly the most well known Flea apart from those of Mignet and Appleby was the 'Bertie Bassett' painted example G-AEFK. Built by Scott's Flying Display Limited, it was powered by a Carden-Ford. It is seen here during a lull at Whitchurch, Cheshire in mid 1936; Airspeed Ferry behind.
(Ken Ellis Collection)

G-AEGD, G-AEJC, G-AEJD, G-AEIE; Clyde Battery's G-AECV; Puttnam's G-AEEC; Scott's G-AEFK; Wood & Vaughan's G-AEBT.

Puttnam Aircraft Company of Hornsey, established by Stephen Appleby, also had a conversion of the Ford 10, along with very similar lines to the Carden variety. This was intended for use in PAC's production line of L.E. Baynes-modified Fleas, of which only G-AEEC flew.

JAPs

From 1928 in Cincinnati, Ohio, the Aeronautical Corporation of America – universally known as Aeronca – started to build a line of classic light aircraft leading to the famous C-3. Along with the airframe came a series of powerplants, also

and 1,100 cc, air cooled V-twins in the power range of 30-45 hp also found applications on Fleas. These could be found in Brough-Superiors, and in the Morgan three-wheelers. R. Machin's Flea is thought to have had a 500 cc single-cylinder JAP from a dirt-track racing motorcycle with a reduction chain to the propeller.

J-99s and other JAPs saw only limited usage on Fleas, but with the Aeronca 100 (C-3), Hillson Praga and other applications, found a fair market in Britain. Post-war it was much sought-after to power the early homebuild revival aircraft. Examples of usage: R. Machin's (see above); J.B. Plant's G-ADZP. Additionally J. Ashworth's and Mr Isaacs' Fleas are reported to have been JAP-powered, but could have had Anzanis fitted.

Mengin

While only one aircraft flew in Britain powered by a Mengin (Appleby's imported HM.18, G-AENV) the powerplant came about in response to Mignet's aircraft designs and was clearly favoured by the man himself. A range was established for this two-cylinder horizontally-opposed design, the Mengin B rated at 28 hp, the C at 38 hp (and therefore the assumed

Above: **The distinctive Y-shape of the exhaust pipe on the Aeronca/JAP J-99 makes it an easy to identify powerplant. A example is seen here on Ben Cooper's superbly restored Aeronca C-3 G-ADYS.**
(Ken Ellis)

built by Aeronca: the E-107 30 hp and E-113 40 hp both horizontally-opposed twin-cylinder engines.

The Aeronautical Corporation of Great Britain was established in 1936 to build the C-3 at Peterborough. At the same time a company called Light Aircraft Limited took on the E-113C licence but this soon moved to the well known motorcycle manufacturers J.A. Prestwich Limited who built the engine (with its easily recognisable Y-shaped exhaust system) as the JAP J-99. JAP motorcycle engines of 1,000 cc

Below: **Alan Troop's aircraft on show at the Lincolnshire Aviation Museum at Tattershall, giving an excellent view of the Scott A2S, its bearers and the rigging on a 'by the book' Flea. (Duncan Cubitt/*FlyPast* Magazine)**

power of G-AENV) and the 45 hp GHM. The type was also built under the Poinsard name after the designer.

Scott A2S Flying Squirrels

The Scott is the engine most associated with the Flea. Shipley-based Scott Motorcycles, manufacturers of an excellent series of motorcycles, including the Flying Squirrel, turned their skills to producing a light two-stroke air-cooled engine for use on the new breed of ultralight aircraft –particularly the Flea. Scott went as far as acquiring Mignet-built HM.14 No.6 G-ADSC for use as a testbed. The A2S was closely associated with its famous water-cooled motorcycle forebear. An inverted, air-cooled in-line twin, the A2S had power take off between cylinders to reduction gear built into the crankcase casting.

Through a lively marketing campaign, the little aero-engine became the most used of all the Flea powerplants for British builders. Sadly, other uses on light aircraft were restricted to one-offs, such as the Luton Buzzard. Scott

claimed that the Flying Squirrel had 'the ability to maintain the power output at low engine revolutions', and that 'with the comparatively wide revolution range afforded, provides an ample margin to meet all flight conditions'. Thus it supplied the tolerant power curve that Mignet wanted from an engine fit to motivate his creation. Examples of usage: L.V.G. Barrow's G-AEFE; D.C. Burgoyne's G-AECN; W. Miller's 'G-AEOF'; K.W. Owen's G-AEBB (second engine).

Other Options

As might be expected, builders experimented with other engine choices, predominantly other motorcycle powerplant conversions. Many of

Nostalgic pastoral scene with builder C. H. Cooper at the prop of the chain drive Harley-Davidson on his G-AEHH. The transparent doping of the wing well shows the increased tankage that Cooper built into the aircraft (shadows at the centre of the main wing) and the spar and rib layout.
(Ken Ellis Collection)

the aircraft in this section are far less documented and for several descriptions of powerplants we have to rely on eye witness accounts or builders' memories, a long time after the event.

Most numerous usage in this category is shared (four applications each) between two motorcycle engines, the V-twin Harley-Davidson and the four-cylinder in-line Henderson. Use of the Henderson engine as an aircraft powerplant came with Ed Heath's search for a suitable engine for his Heath Parasol, the result being the 1,300 cc Heath-Henderson B4 rated at 48 hp. The British Fleas that had Hendersons were Cooper's G-AEEI (second engine); J. Middlehurst's; K.W. Owen's G-AEBB (first engine); and M.R. Toy's G-AEND. The Harley-Davidson engine was a neat V-twin which lent itself well to aircraft usage and to gear reduction. The Flea applications known were in J.O. Bayliffe's, C.H. Cooper's G-AEHH; L.&.H. Geeson's using direct drive and H.R. Metcalfe's.

The FN four-cylinder in-line air-cooled engine, produced by the Belgian arms manufacturer, found favour with C.W. Blankley and S.S. Miles (G-ADZT). Two Rover powerplants were also harnessed to Fleas, Mr Woodward of Nantwich using an 8 hp air-cooled conversion and Tom Phillips using a 1,000 cc twin, claiming 34 hp. These are almost certain to have come from Rover 8 light cars, produced between 1919 and 1925. Originally flat-twin air-cooled side-valve 8 hp engines of 998 cc they were later enlarged to 1,100 cc. Two examples from the French Salmson range were employed. I.H. Cameron's Flea used a 10 hp four-cylinder Salmson from a motorcar, while the Busfield and Ingham machine is quoted as having a nine-cylinder 45 hp engine, almost certainly an AD9, and quite possibly from the British Salmson Aero Engine Company.

One-off choices recorded are: the AJS V-twin engine, circa 1930, fitted to E.G. Davis's G-AEEH; the intended use of a Coventry Victor on the Cheltenham Light Aircraft Club's G-AELN; Philip Priest used a 30 hp Harlequin, based on Harley-Davidson components and developed by Les Long in the USA for his Longster design. John Gibb's example had a coupled engine produced by Jack Gray, using two 500 cc Dunelt motorcycle conversions, but is though not to have flown (see Chapter Six under the Gibb Biplane reference). Finally the post-war Juggins and Heyden BAPC.77 was fitted with a Norton engine, but was not intended for flight.

Mignet's Performance Data for an Aubier et Dunne-powered HM.14
(As given in *The Flying Flea*)

Total Span: 6
Engine: Aubier et Dunne 540 cc standard model, 20 hp at 4,000 rpm
Propeller diameter: 1 m 60 cm
Pitch: 1 m 30 cm, 1,600 rpm at rest on the ground

Actual Certified Performances
Passes Over: 40 feet at 300 yards from the standing start
Slow Cruising Speed: 50 mph at 1,350 propeller rpm
Consumption: $1\frac{1}{2}$ gallons of petrol and oil per hour
Range: 3 hours
Fast Cruising Speed: 62 mph at 1,500 propeller rpm, throttle half open
Climb Fully Loaded: Propeller speed 1,500 rpm, 1,000 metres in 19 minutes, 1,700 metres in 38 minutes
Landing Speed: 19 mph

30 hours of flying comprising 70 trips – Soissons to Reims, Soissons-Meaux and back, etc. . .

Data on principal British Flea powerplants

Engine	Cyls	cc	hp	Bore/Stroke	Layout	Cooling	Wt (lb)	Applications
ABC '400'	2	400	8	2.7 x 2.2	HO	A	35	} 6
ABC Scorpion I	2	1100	24	3.6 x 3.6	HO	A	90	
ABC Scorpion II	2	1500	40	4.0 x 3.6	HO	A	109	
Anzani	2	1100	?	?	IvV	A	?	19
Austin 7	4	747	14	2.2 x 3.0	I	A or W	120	8
Bristol Cherub I	2	1095	34	3.4 x 3.8	HO	A	81	} 3
Bristol Cherub III	2	1228	36	3.5 x 3.8	HO	A	95	
Douglas Sprite	2	500	17	?	HO	A	58	} 24
Aero Engines Sprite	2	803	25	2.7 x 3.2	HO	A	82	
Carden-Ford	4	1172	31	2.5 x 3.7	I	W	131	15*
JAP J-99 (and E-113C)	2	1860	40	4.2 x 4.0	HO	A	121	4
Scott A2S	2	690	16	2.9 x 3.1	IvI	A	85	39

Notes: HO = Horizontally Opposed; Iv = Inverted; V = Vee; I = In Line; A = Air cooled;
W = Water cooled.
* Includes Ford conversions and the Perman-Ford.
Applications include all known uses of the engines fitted on British Fleas.
While installed, these aircraft may not have flown with that particular powerplant.

Chapter 8

THE BUBBLE BURSTS

MIGNET'S WHOLE PHILOSOPHY OF FLIGHT was intended to reach people who had never built anything as complicated as a flying machine before, let alone flown one. His book, *Le Sport de l'Air* included details of how a potential pilot could teach himself to fly, step by step, from the merest hops to the first circuit, and the writing was full of enthusiasm, directness and above all else, encouragement. What may have seemed to be an impossible dream became true for many builders: they had completed a working aeroplane. The logic of taking that machine into the air in the same learn-by-deed approach was compelling.

Accidents, and deaths, were inevitable from such ventures. There would be those who would circumvent the authorities and even common sense, and create death-traps. There would be those who would chance their flying luck, or who would find themselves in a situation where their lack of experience would

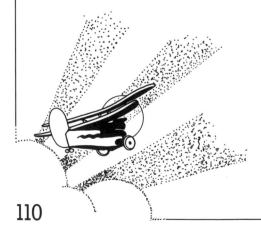

Accidents with Fleas were an inevitability, as with any sport. Many accidents were more hurtful to the ego of the flyer than to his person. Here is G-AEBA, built by A. Oliver, inverted in a corn field. The number of aircraft that ended up upside down, but not through flip-overs on the ground, is evidence that a little more height would have killed the occupant.
(Ken Ellis Collection)

prevent a recovery. As it turned out, the bulk of the crashes, certainly from the British experience at least, were due to the aircraft itself. Building quality, engine characteristics or hopelessly overweight powerplants, pilots' experience seemed not to be components in the disasters that were to overcome the little HM.14.

The first reported fatal accident to a Flea pilot

occurred on 19 August 1935 in Algiers (then a French colony) when Monsieur Marignan spun and crashed. This was one of about forty Fleas reported to be under construction in Algeria at that time. On 14 September at Marseilles Henri Chapalet, an instructor at the *Aéro Club Provençal*, was killed when the Flea he was piloting made a vertical dive while landing. Reports relating to both accidents talked of the pilots having problems keeping their mounts level followed by dives into the ground.

Just as the Flea craze was beginning to take hold, so the accidents were to apply a brake that was to have an effect almost as sharp as the meteoric rise of the little design. With no jurisdiction on the HM.14, the French Air Ministry could do little more than release a notice of caution to Flea builders and flyers, this being published on 24 September. Following the death of Marignan in Algeria *The Times* reported that the flying of Fleas in that country had been forbidden. This was September 1935, a month prior to Mignet's triumphant *Rassemblement* at Orly and before matters had really taken hold in Britain. On the Continent the pace of accidents and fatalities quickened as the numbers of Fleas multiplied. On 26 November 1935 at Caen in Normandy René Besnard was killed in a crash of the same character as the previous ones and by the turn of the year, another Frenchman's life had been claimed. At Sergnyin in Switzerland on 15 March 1936 a pilot called Kuffer was killed when his creation dived uncontrollably into the ground. Like their Algerian counterpart, the Swiss Aviation Bureau immediately forbade the operation of Fleas in their country.

Suggestions, theories and hypotheses as to the cause of the crashes and how they could be avoided or overcome became rife, not only in France, Switzerland and Algeria, but around the world. In Canada Professor Louden of the University of Toronto undertook an independent investigation. Louden concluded that it was most important for the centre of gravity and the position of the Flea's rear wing to be located correctly. In Holland the *Nederlandische Vereeniging ter Beoefening van de Kleine Luchtvaart* (homebuilding association, or Pou Club) started investigations in Amsterdam and commented on the aeroplane's flight characteristics following purely theoretical research. They concluded that overlap of the wings had an important

bearing on the fore and aft stability and the less the overlap, the greater the stability.

Pressure to carry out official tests on the Flea-formula resulted in a series of examinations at Villacoublay, near Paris, the home of the Air Force-run experimental and trials unit (the equivalent of today's *Centre d'Essais en Vol* at Bretigny or Britain's Royal Aircraft Establishment at Farnborough). In this initial report, the first major appraisal of the aerodynamics of the Flea, several items were highlighted, all possibly related just to the trials aircraft, or representative of the many variables to be experienced when builders work to different standards, skills and budgets. Fitted with a 25 hp Ava, the test aircraft had a limited range of engine speeds, often between only 2,100 and 2,310 rpm – although, as *The Aeroplane* of 15 April 1936 put it, 'The maximum possible speed of this motor is 2,800 rpm and so the probability seems to be that the airscrew was not quite right'. Other points highlighted were the long take-off run, that flying was best accomplished in calm conditions and certainly not in winds exceeding 20 mph (32 kph), and that if landed at 45 mph (72 kph) or above the aeroplane would land itself normally and without difficulty.

This report, which came out in March 1936, was somewhat academic in its tone and certainly was far from damning. As the Spring of 1936 progressed, concern for the safety of the innumerable Flea pilots mounted. By far the best method of testing the Flea was to pop an actual example in a wind tunnel – easily achievable because of the little craft's dimensions. This would provide an accurate, and above all else safe, method of examining the whole flight envelope. At Chalais Meudon, near Paris, the French Air Ministry's *Service Technique* possessed such a tunnel. At first they refused to undertake such full-scale tests. 'The Joke' was having another laugh for despite the fatalities no official body was under any obligation to concern itself with the Flea. By June they had changed their minds, the Minister for Air, Pierre Cot, stopped all Flea flights in France pending the results of full-scale wind tunnel tests at Chalais Meudon. In truth, the last days of 'legal' Flea flying in France had gone.

The machine chosen for the Chalais Meudon test was No. 10, built by the Lambert Brothers, and it became the first full-size aircraft ever to

Flea No.10 inside the tunnel chamber at Chalais Meudon, near Paris. Fitted with a dummy pilot, it 'flew' inside the tunnel from 2 July to 26 July 1936.
(Geoffrey P. Jones Collection)

be tested in a wind tunnel. This aircraft had been built 'to the book' and had been used for extensive testing by Mignet and Robineau as part of the designer's own investigations into what was going wrong. Through Mignet and Robineau's experiments and through the incredibly detailed report that *Service Technique* were about to publish, a Flea was modified to give the main wing a greater degree of travel so that a recovery could be made from the critical attitude. Sadly, in September 1936 while testing this device on a

Flea, Robineau himself was killed in similar circumstances to the other victims. The loss of Robineau was devastating to Mignet and must have helped in his decision to move to the United States the following year.

Chalais Meudon's report was a major document which outlined precisely what was wrong with the design and how such conclusions had been arrived at. The very 'slot effect' that Mignet felt made his design safer than any other type flying was working against the little aeroplane in certain attitudes. Basically, in a shallow nose-down attitude (it would be unfair to term this a 'dive') the 'slot' was lost and essentially the two wings became one large wing. The amount of travel on the pivot of the front wing could not correct this and the aircraft would continue in an ever-increasing dive; indeed, several aircraft crashed inverted. Pilots, realising the loss of control, would without thinking move the control column forward in an attempt to gain speed and come out of the descent, but this only made matters worse; recovery was impossible beyond fifteen degrees of pitching moment.

Mignet came up with several 'fixes' all of which cured the fault. The rear wing had to be made to move, so that it could act as a conventional elevator and help the aircraft to effect a recovery from such a dive. Differential cams working on both wings produced what Mignet termed the 'conjugated wing'. A different aerofoil section on the rear wing was also a possibility as this would produce a tail-down moment as speed increased should the aircraft start to enter a dramatic dive. Both modifications were effective but were taking the Flea away from its original concept, because they were both complex and costly to install.

By moving the centre of pivot of the main wing and by making rigging changes, the basic HM.14 could be altered quite quickly and rendered safe. Public faith in the design had gone, however, and almost overnight Mignet found himself developing remedies for retrospectively fitting to Fleas that nobody seemed to want to undertake. The bubble had burst on him. The findings of this investigation were published in late September 1936, a month after the British Royal Aircraft Establishment placed a Flea into their wind tunnel to carry out similar tests. In France, and then Britain, the HM.14 as a breed was never to recover.

Don Burgoyne's G-AECN inverted following an accident on 15 March 1936. G-AECN was destroyed when it cartwheeled on 10 May 1936, thankfully without injury to its pilot Joseph Wood. (Don Burgoyne)

Engine drivers in charge of lorries

'At the outset the amateur building and self-instruction of Pou enthusiasts were seen to contain the germs of plentiful crashery, which was freely prophesied verbally on aerodromes, but in this paper alone.

'The Pou has obliged with an excessive percentage of breakages to flying, and of fatal accidents, which now number seven.' Acid words in *The Aeroplane* for 13 May 1936 immediately after the death of Flight Lieutenant Ambrose Cowell at Penshurst on 4 May 1936, while air testing R.G. Doig's G-AEEW. With five fatalities in the land of its birth and the death of A.H. Anderson at Renfrew Aerodrome, Glasgow, on 20 April 1936 marking the first in Britain, the craze that was in full swing of building and operating HM.14s was beginning to lose momentum. Editor C.G. Grey was soon to have more to write about, for exactly eight days after the publication of that issue, Squadron Leader C.R. Davidson died in G-AEBS at Digby.

Anderson had received some flying instruction, but prior to the findings of the aerodynamic investigation being made available, his demise could have been put down to inexperience. Not so for Cowell who was the official Air League test pilot for the Flea. Likewise Davidson, who was the Chief Flying Instructor with No 2 Flying Training School at Digby equipped with Avro Tutors. To paraphrase words from *The Aeroplane* neither of these two pilots could be described as 'an engine-driver suddenly put in charge of a lorry'; here seasoned pilots had got themselves into the same terminal situation as the rank novices.

The short interval between these crashes and the obvious competence of the pilots involved in the second and third British fatalities convinced the Air League and others that the time had come for someone to accept the responsibility for looking into the aerodynamics of the aircraft. As a result of Davidson's death, the matter of the Flea was brought up in the House of Commons, by the Hon. Oliver Simmonds, Tory Member of Parliament for Duddleston, with the demand that the Air Ministry undertake an investigation. Under-Secretary of State for Air, Sir Philip Sassoon, did not rule out testing at Farnborough (the National Physical Laboratory was also a possibility) but wished to point out that, not being a production aircraft, no two Fleas were the same, and it would be very difficult to be conclusive on the type in general. This all formed the preamble to the famous 'ban'. One more death was to follow Davidson's, when J. Goodall died on 20 September 1936 in the cockpit of his machine: he broke his neck when he ran into a ditch at speed. It is as well to take a deeper look at each of the fatalities, before moving on to the findings that were to deal a mortal blow to the HM.14.

20 April 1936

In Flea G-ADVL *White Eagle* A.H. Anderson, a friend of the aircraft's builder, R.H. Paterson, entered the history books by becoming the first British fatality while flying the little aircraft. At Glasgow's Renfrew Airport the Anzani-powered aircraft went into an uncontrollable dive while preparing for a flying exhibition. Paterson, an employee of the Glasgow-based F.D. Cowison & Company, had built G-ADVL in what he claimed was just five weeks from August 1935 at his employer's premises. It made its first trials from St. Rollox in Glasgow, before moving on to Renfrew. G-ADVL did not get a chance to achieve a Permit. The accident was regarded as part of the inevitable cost of amateur construction and operation. Anderson was inexperienced; accidental death was a not surprising conclusion to the sad episode.

4 May 1936

'During a test flight the aircraft dived to the ground completely out of control.' So concluded Air Ministry Form 528, Number C339 relating to the fatal crash at Penshurst, Kent. Flight Lieutenant Ambrose M. Cowell was killed at the controls of G-AEEW, built by R.G. Doig, trading at Aircraft Constructions Limited. Cowell was the Air League's official test pilot for the Flea, and was available to undertake trials on any HM.14 built in Britain, should the builder so wish. This death, the second in the United Kingdom and the seventh in total, was the watershed in the Air League's attitude. Air Commodore John Chamier recommended that the Air Ministry request Fleas not to be flown again until an investigation could look into the design. Cowell's flying credentials were excellent and alongside Stephen Appleby, he must have been the most experienced Flea-aviator in the country.

As Air Ministry accident investigator Major J.P.C. Cooper went to work on the mangled remains of G-AEEW – it had made the by-now familiar headlong dive into the ground – a Coroner's inquest was undertaken. On 7 May the inquest gave Cowell's fate as accidental death, and made two recommenda-tions: that the Air League's request for an investigation be followed up and that test-flying of Fleas over in-habited areas be banned. (The Authorisation to Fly already specified that built-up areas be avoided, although it was not specific as to what constituted such an area.) Just as in France, the very nature of the Flea was beginning to work against the little design. The Air League could put pressure on the Air Ministry, but the latter was not obliged to act and indeed the Secretary of State for Air announced that he would not revoke Authorisations at that time. The Air League acted alone and advised builders not to fly from mid-May onwards. Despite approaches, neither the Royal Aircraft Establishment at Farnborough nor the National Physical Laboratory were willing to undertake an investigation of the design. If commissioned to do so, both bodies would investigate Mignet's design, but the cost they would have to levy would be beyond the means of the Air League, the only organisation showing any real concern at that stage.

R.G. Doig had taken on the Perman Flea G-ADPW *Robin Goodfellow* on 18 October 1935. Fitted with an Anzani from a Hawker Cygnet, it made its first flight at Lympne, Kent, seven days later. Doig planned to make a cross-Channel flight, but his plans were squashed when it was blown over at Lympne on 10 November. Later fitted with a Douglas, Doig flew it with C.W.A. Scott's travelling air circus. (A photograph of G-ADPW was appended to the accident card for G-AEEW in lieu of a shot of the actual aircraft.) Meanwhile Doig had founded Aircraft Constructions Limited at his Sidcup home with a share capital of £2,000. G-AEEW, powered by an Anzani, possibly from G-ADPW, was awarded its Authorisation to Fly on 1 April 1936. It is not clear if Cowell was conducting the craft's first flight when it plunged into a sheep field at Penshurst on 4 May – certainly it was an early flight.

Remains of Squadron Leader C. R. Davidson's G-AEBS following its fatal crash at Digby on 21 May 1936, just seventeen days after the death of the Air League's test pilot, Cowell.
(via Mike Hodgson)

21 May 1936

Britain's third Flea fatality also claimed the life of an experienced aviator, it also brought another powerplant, the Scott A2S, into the argument. Squadron Leader C.R. Davidson was killed in his stylish G-AEBS while undertaking the final rehearsal for RAF Digby's Empire Air Day on 21 May 1936 –the big day taking place four days later. G-AEBS had been built in the hangars of 2 Flying Training School at Digby under the supervision of Davidson, who was the Chief Flying Instructor for the unit. The Flea was given its Authorisation to fly on 22 January 1936 and had flown a fair bit, each time with its owner at the controls. Like the others before it, it entered a dive that the pilot clearly could not bring it out of.

20 September 1936

The death of garage proprietor James Goodall in his Flea G-ADXY was well separate from the previous three in time and also in circumstance. It is recorded here because it has entered history in several references as the last of four British Flea deaths due to the same aerodynamic causes as those accidents that befell Anderson, Cowell and Davidson. This is not so; Goodall was killed in and by a Flea, but it was not airborne at the time. Goodall completed G-ADXY, powered by a Scott A2S, and received the Authorisation to Fly on 24 December 1935. It flew regularly from Aberdeen's Dyce Airport. Goodall was taken with the Flea sufficiently to have started the construction of two others at his premises, but they were never completed. In what is best described as a forced landing at Dyce on 20 September 1936 Goodall brought his Flea down for a fast but controlled landing. The Flea was brought to an abrupt halt by a drainage ditch and it was this impact that killed Goodall, breaking his neck.

Into the tunnel

From 13 August 1936 C.E. Mercer loaned his Flea G-AEFV, powered by a Scott A2S to the Air League. It was moved to Farnborough and was installed into the Royal Aircraft Establishment's 24 ft wind tunnel under the guidance of A.S. Hartshorn BSc. Air League pressure had been decisive in getting the Air Ministry to foot the bill for the investigation, but the fact that the French authorities had also put a Flea into their tunnel at Chalais Meudon must have helped to convince the Secretary of State for Air that a full and swift account of the Flea's flying qualities was needed. G-AEFV was perhaps an unusual choice for the tests as it had been built under the auspices of Malling Aviation, the operators of West Malling airfield

in Kent, and therefore could be termed a 'professional' build. (Malling Aviation had previously been the aegis under which W. Laidlaw had built his Flea.) The Scott A2S put it in line with many others, but the pushrod wing controls and rear compression struts certainly made it non-standard, in terms of what 'the book' stipulated, at any rate.

As related earlier, in September 1936 the French *Service Technique* produced a very comprehensive report that centred upon the terminal problems relating to the tandem wing layout in a restricted flight regime. Hartshorn's document (the RAE called it BA 1333 with Reference BA/549.R/117, the Air Ministry gave it a 'parallel' reference 430302/35/DDSR), while much shorter, came down to the same conclusions. Briefed only to cover 'the requirements of the Air League' the report was not an attempt at a full investigation of the flying characteristics of the Flea, and the conclusions were restricted to its flight characteristics in relation to the diving phenomenon – hence the comment 'None' under the pro-forma heading 'Further Developments'. The report made no recommendations, did not look into any 'fixes' and as such its conclusion could only be seen in a damning light.

The test specimen was rigged in the massive tunnel to a rigid tower structure attached at the axle, giving the Flea movement about this axis. A wire control to the tail altered the incidence. The control column was locked in any position desired for the experiment, G-AEFV being 'flown' by a dummy pilot while in the tunnel. Following several trials in the tunnel, the RAE team had sufficient data to calculate the aircraft's pitching moment about any axis. From these figures, the RAE could extrapolate figures for all of the Flea's flight regimes. Flea G-AEFV (Tunnel Item Number 19B/8/36) was therefore measured mathematically to ascertain the longitudinal control available at incidences representing the conditions during a dive. Hartshorn concluded that this aircraft was unstable in normal flight when the centre of gravity was further back than 0.4 of the main wing chord. In the dive this instability became more marked.

A positive pitching moment (that is, one with enough control movement to correct the dive) could be achieved at angles of incidence down to -15 degrees. Negative angles greater than this brought about the diving condition experienced in Algeria, Britain, France and Switzerland (and probably elsewhere) where recovery was no longer possible. Hartshorn also noted that a movement of G-AEFV's centre of gravity backwards or forwards by $7\frac{1}{2}$ in (14 cm) made little difference to the amount of control available. As the French had found, the Flea as it stood was lethal in certain flight regimes: no amount of experience would bring it and its pilot out of a self-deepening dive. Mignet had the 'fix', but it was a complex job, his so-called 'conjugated wing'. Determined Flea builders could have employed such a device, and did, but in general the press publicity in the British Isles had moved from one of marked benevolence to the little French aeroplane and its little French creator, to one of doom and gloom. The public dropped the Flea like a hot brick and in Britain hundreds

Stephen Appleby conducting tests on the Abbott Flea G-AEJD. Tufting on the wing upper surfaces shows the port forward wing to be stalled. (via Richard Riding)

were quietly shelved, stored, thrown away, burnt or scrapped.

Air Ministry reaction was to stop the renewal of Authorisations to Fly; many owners stopped flying of their own accord. The last 'conventional' HM.14 to receive an Authorisation was R.C. Streather and partner's Scott-powered G-AEOH, being given Authorisation No. 109 on 5 October 1936. To talk of a 'ban' as such, as many sources happily and widely do, is not strictly accurate so far as Britain is concerned. After the publication of the RAE report in October 1936, the Air Ministry did not renew the documentation of non-modified Fleas, but others, either modified or built from scratch to the new standard, went on to receive Authorisations, ending with T.H. Fouldes' G-AFUL as late as May 1939. Of course, other aircraft continued to fly, in ignorance or in defiance of bureaucracy and a good number were totally unburdened by such pieces of paper.

After the 'Ban'

Adverse publicity and ignorance of what was possible despite the apparent lethality of the HM.14 meant that in Britain only four Flea builders were to take their projects beyond the so-called 'ban' and to gain Authorisations to Fly. Two of this quartet are known to have flown with a good degree of success. Many other British Flea builders and flyers either 'went underground', or did not bother to channel their creation through the authorities, thus avoiding the 'ban' anyway. It was B.W. Millichamp of Belton, Suffolk, who received the first post 'ban' Authorisation to Fly when he was given No. 114 for his Austin 7-powered G-AERJ on 1 December 1936. It boasted a sleek cowling to the engine and of course the pivoting rear wing modification as advocated by Mignet. The Millichamp Brothers had an interest in seeing the Flea come through this slump, as they had made and marketed a Flea hangar, costing £17 10s 0d including delivery and erection. *Madam Butterfly* as G-AERJ was called flew with some degree of success from Ely, until it was sold, minus engine, in July 1938.

Dr M.D.S. Armour of Anstruther, Fife, started construction of his HM.14, G-AEOJ, prior to June 1936, using many components available 'off the shelf' from Luton Aircraft of Gerrards Cross (see Chapter Six). Anzani-powered, the aircraft was completed by October 1936, just in time

Above: A legitimate Flea after the so-called 'ban'. Dr Armour's G-AEOJ in its fully modified state with pivoting rear as well as main wing and much-heightened undercarriage.
(Dr M. D. S. Armour/Ken Ellis Collection)

Left: Close-up of Dr Armour's G-AEOJ showing the 'fix' needed to give it an Authorisation to Fly. Complex faired push-rods control the pivot angle of the rear wing, in concert with the main wing.
(Dr M. D. S. Armour/Ken Ellis Collection)

for the Doctor to appreciate what officialdom would think of his Flea. He employed the bulk of Mignet's modifications, making the rear wing pivot using faired pushrods. At the same time *Marmath,* as it was called, was given a much-modified undercarriage to enhance ground-clearance – always problematical on 'standard' HM.14s. As such it received Authorisation to Fly No. 124 on 7 February 1937 and continued to fly until the advent of the war in 1939 when the Doctor considered it prudent to cease. N.H. Shaw of Stafford was also granted an Authorisation to Fly in 1937, his G-AFBU acquiring the necessary piece of paper on August 23. Its powerplant is unknown, but it is known only to have completed hops, from Oxford Gardens.

The final HM.14 Flea of the British era was T.H. Fouldes' G-AFUL, which was built in Porter Road, Derby and flown from Chaddesdon. It is thought that Fouldes built this Flea (or possibly another) to the 'book', when it was powered by an Anzani. Photographic evidence of the Anzani shows the mainwheel in view as only a 'classic'

Close up of the Anzani installation on the 'conventional' Fouldes's Flea. Note the position of the mainwheel as in 'classic' HM.14 format. (Ken Ellis Collection)

HM.14 would have from such an angle. Later the Flea was fitted with an Anzani engine (most likely the same one) in a complicated tubular frame engine mount and an equally complex

undercarriage of similar construction. In its final guise G-AFUL had a Scott A2S, a moving rear wing, pushrod controls for both wings, a complex split undercarriage with oleos, and was modified from a single tailwheel to a double one after initial flight trials. In this guise it gained its Authorisation to Fly on 1 May 1939. In this state, G-AFUL flew well from Chaddesdon until it had an argument with a tree. It (or possibly the 'normal' HM.14) was stored in Derby until being burnt mid 1965.

So, despite the mythology, the HM.14 did, in fact, live on beyond the Air Ministry's 'ban', although in tiny numbers compared to the heady days of the craze. Post-war, with the blossoming of the homebuilding movement in Britain again under the Popular Flying Association, only two individuals have chosen a Mignet-related design. A HM.380L Ladybug was started by a builder in Harrogate in the mid 1970s, but was later shelved. This left only Bill Coles and his HM.298 G-AXPG, which first flew in 1972 to be the only *legal* 'Flea' flyer in Britain post-war – although a couple of HM.14s are known to have put air under their wheels since 1945!

Britain's first (and so far only) post-war Flea with a Permit is this HM.293 built by Bill Coles and powered by a Volkswagen conversion. It took nearly 500 hours of writing, letters, discussions, paperwork and patience to get the Civil Aviation Authority, via the Popular Flying Association, to grant a Permit to Fly. (Geoffrey P. Jones Collection)

Chapter 9
OUT OF
THE FRYING PAN

EVEN BEFORE THE TRAUMAS AND disillusionment caused by the Flea fatalities, Henri Mignet was developing his tandem wing concept beyond the HM.14. Chapter Eight has described the events on either side of the English Channel that led to the famous 'ban' – actual in France for HM.14s, partial in Great Britain, where suitably modified aircraft could still gain certification.

The HM.14 was a 1933 design and in 1936 it was not surprising that developments were forthcoming from the prolific self-styled *Patron-Saint* of the amateur aviator. Through the triumphant years of 1934–1936 thousands of amateurs stretching across countries as diverse as Algeria, Argentina, Australia, Canada, Czechoslovakia, Denmark, France, Finland, Great Britain, Morocco, the Netherlands, Switzerland, Tunisia and the United States started to build examples of the HM.14 and Mignet must have received considerable feedback. The earlier HM.8 had generated volumes of correspondence, all from a relatively small number of builders overridingly from France. Following the Flea boom Mignet, with the loyal support of his wife Annette, must have had few free moments, spending the bulk of his time talking, breathing, eating and sleeping Fleas. East of Paris lies the airfield of Meaux-Isles-les-Villenoy. Mignet had moved to Meaux in September 1935 and with the support of Henri Binauld, a prominent brewer, he set up business there. On 6 November Mignet

established his company and Flea factory, *La Société dés Aéronefs Mignet*, universally referred to as SAM. SAM was not only a design and manufacturing unit, but also a flying school. On the east side of the airfield a large, square, hangar was built and it was here that SAM's four principal employees were located. These were Mignet, his brother-in-law Jean Triou (who would figure in Mignet's move to Japan in 1954 – see Chapter Twelve), Robert Robineau (builder of HM.14 No.2 and a life-long friend of Henri) and another long-time disciple, Monsieur Mabile. Later a fifth member joined the team as chief draughtsman; this was André Starck, who later became associated with a string of homebuilt designs in France.

At Meaux, Mignet could get away from the considerable attention and pressure that the HM.14 events were precipitating and he could concentrate on designing. He also took the opportunity to travel to Germany where he obtained a pilot's licence. The absurdities caused by having flown for so long in 'the joke' and the confusing requirements of the French system made Germany a far more understanding place in which to get his flying abilities recognised. This visit may well have inspired construction of the German *Himmelslause* called *Lerche* which appeared in a Leipzig aviation directory in 1937. Featuring a Nazi swastika on the fin it had a span of 6 m, a 206kg empty weight, and was powered by a seven-cylinder 45 hp radial engine. The most

Line-up outside the SAM hangar at Meaux, 1936. *Left to right:* The HM.15 prototype, an unidentified HM.14, the HM.16 'Baby Pou', the HM.17 minus main wing and HM.14 No 36.
(Geoffrey P. Jones Collection)

The first aircraft to be built by SAM at Meaux was the substantial-looking HM.19 two-seater which took the HM.14 ideas and refined them to produce a very workable aircraft. Power came from a 45 hp Salmson radial.
(RSA, via Jacques Avril)

The HM.19 outside the SAM hangar at Meaux, wearing its test registration F W-046 and the SAM motif. The HM.19 was the first product for the little company.
(Geoffrey P. Jones Collection)

First Mignet design after the HM.14 was the HM.15 seen here carrying the Mignet legend *L'Autre Aviation* on the rudder as well as the name *Pou du Ciel*. It was essentially a revised and refined HM.14, but was also capable of carrying a passenger, in the rear fuselage.
(RSA, via Jacques Avril)

significant aircraft built at Meaux was the first 'official' Mignet two-seater, the HM.19. Powered by a 45 hp Salmson radial it was of wood and fabric construction with the two occupants sitting side-by-side in the cabin. As a sign that officialdom was being allowed to creep in, the HM.19 carried the test registration F W-046.

As the designation HM.19 suggests, Mignet had produced other designs after the HM.14. The HM.15 was a development of the HM.14, but featured many modifications and refinements. It boasted an enclosed cockpit and power from a 35 hp Poinsard, the wing positions were adjusted and great attention was paid to the centre of gravity. The wings featured rounded tips and the relatively large area rear wing had a pronounced dihedral at the tips. The rear wing also included a pitch control tab on the trailing edge. The HM.15 was capable of carrying a passenger. Mignet's eldest son, François, became the first Flea passenger.

One or two amateurs chose to build HM.19s,

Louis Cosandey's refined and much remodelled HM.19C HB-SPG, a regular attender at European rallies and fly-ins.
(Henk Wadman)

the most well-known example being the HM.19C built by Louis Cosandey of Fribourg, Switzerland. Powered by a 65 hp Continental A65 his HM.19, HB-SPG, has been a regular visitor to European rallies and fly-ins. In the late 1970s the aircraft gave up its 'taildragger' configuration and adopted a tricycle undercarriage, and also a new owner in the shape of Artur Morig. Cosandey has been a prolific builder of Flea variants, including the first tandem wing glider version built in 1939. His last aircraft, completed in August 1977, was the Volkswagen-powered HM.290, HB-SUP.

To complement the HM.19 at Meaux, Mignet designed and built a single-seat version, with a 35 hp Mengin engine and a smaller span. This was the HM.18 which was ready by the summer of 1936. It was in this aircraft that Mignet was to make his second visit to Great Britain, attending the race at Ramsgate on 3

August 1936. Mignet stirred the audience with displays of the HM.18's short take-off runs, steep climbs, good controllability on the ground and in the air, even dead stick landings – it epitomised everything that the HM.14 was not. Had the events of the following months not conspired against it, it was clear that SAM were on to a winner with the HM.18. The HM.18's wing positioning was such that the killer 'slot effect' would not occur, and it carried the rear wing 'tab' of the HM.19. Mignet sold the HM.18 to his British disciple, Stephen Appleby, who ferried it back to France in September ready for its display at the *15ème Salon de l'Aéronautique* in Paris in November.

While *Service Technique* assessed HM.14 No.10 Built by the Lambert brothers, in the wind tunnel at Chalais Meudon, and the Institute of Mechanics & Fluids at the University of Lille were studying a model of the HM.19 in their wind tunnel, Mignet and his team carried out their own investigations. The angular range of the main wing was increased and Mignet thought he had found a relatively simple solution until faced with a further tragedy. While flying the modified aircraft in September 1936,

Mignet flying his HM.18 at the Ramsgate Flea Race. It did not compete, but his demonstration showed many Flea builders where the future lay.
(Geoffrey P. Jones Collection)

Robineau got into the now familiar uncontrollable dive and was killed in the ensuing crash. Mignet was understandably devastated by Robineau's death, but he was determined to find out exactly what happened. Over twenty years of development and research to find the aeroplane for the man-in-the-street, his 'motorcycle of the air', were not to be thrown away; it was essential to carry on if his dream, a dream which Robineau shared, was to be perpetuated.

Amid the turmoil surrounding the HM.14, SAM at Meaux had also developed another new design, the HM.16. Known as the 'Torpedo' or the 'Baby Pou' it was a single-seater with a wingspan of only 13 feet (4 metres) and an empty weight of 220 lb (100 kg). Weight-saving

Mignet flying the HM.16 'Baby Pou' at Meaux. Mignet clearly had a great affection for this little aircraft, it was flown frequently from SAM's airfield.
(RSA, via Jacques Avril)

on the HM.16 was one of the design's major goals. On the ground the HM.16's short fuselage – only 10 ft 10 in (3.3 m) – made it look as though it would be permanently in a reclining position. The tiny fuselage tapered to a point at the tail, the rudder hinged from the end of this boat-like tail and was supported by two faired struts stemming from the tailplane. This reclining position gave the impression that the HM.16's wings possessed too great an angle of incidence but application of the throttle made the tail rise immediately and the tiny machine could become airborne in little over 150 feet (46 metres). Mignet and the HM.16 could frequently be seen cavorting through the skies above Meaux.

In Canada the HM.16 found a loyal supporter, although this was many years later. Georges Jacquemin of Streetsville, Ontario, having translated Mignet's plans for the HM.290 into English, became intrigued by the 'Baby Pou' some twenty years after the one-and-only example had flown at Meaux. Jacquemin set to

work to redraw and translate Mignet's 1936 plans under the designation HM.160, with the aim of making them available to amateur builders. It was intended that small, two-cylinder, target drone engines in the range 20–35 hp could be adapted and fitted to the HM.160. Although several sets of plans were sold, only one HM.160 variant is thought to have been completed (see Chapter Ten).

Captivated by the HM.16 Jacquemin designed three other variants of his HM.160.

The HM.161 featured a headrest and a dorsal fin, then followed the HM.162 and HM.163, one of which was an all-metal version, and finally the HM.164 which had a tricycle undercarriage using a tapered rod-type nosewheel assembly.

Another SAM product of 1936 was the HM.17, a cabin version of the HM.16 with slightly larger dimensions. It used the same hinged and braced rudder and 'pear drop'-shaped fuselage as the HM.16. Wing positions remained as the HM.14, the trailing edge of the pivoting

Right: Delightful sketch of the unbuilt HM.160 by George Jacquemin who translated Mignet's plans into English.
(Geoffrey P. Jones Collection)

Below: Based upon the diminutive HM.16, the cabin-equipped HM.17 was a slightly scaled up version. With its neatly cowled engine it was a smart looking aircraft.
(RSA, via Jacques Avril)

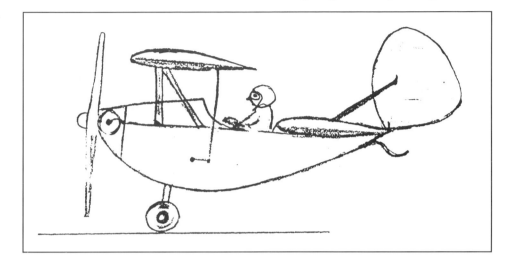

LA SOCIÉTÉ DES AÉRONEFS
MIGNET

MEAUX (S.-et-M.) FRANCE
présente ses modèles
HM. 16 - HM. 18 - HM. 19

HM. 19
BIPLACE-CABINE
DOUBLE-COMMANDE COTE-A-COTE

Envergure	6 mètres
Longueur	4 m. 80
Poids à vide	240 kgr.
Puissance	45 C.V.
Rayon d'action	400 kil.

Performances
Décollage en 70 m. (vent nul).
Montée à 200 m. en 1 minute.
Écart de vitesse 40-150 km. : h.

Ces appareils non encore connus du public français, dérivés de la formule POU-DU-CIEL 1934, sont d'une mise au point toute récente (nouveaux brevets déposés en France et à l'Etranger en 1935-1936). Ils vont être soumis à l'homologation internationale.

Leur principe nouveau d'aile *à fente commandée* alliée à la stabilité du *parachute* permet de voler sans danger en **perte de vitesse** et rend impossible la *glissade* et la *vrille*, tout en leur assurant les performances des bons avions modernes.

Cette formule qui, seule, autorise d'aussi faibles dimensions, en a rendu la réalisation particulièrement **robuste et bon marché.**

HM. 18
MONOPLACE-CABINE

Envergure	5 mètres
Longueur	3 m. 60
Poids à vide	120 kgr.
Puissance	35 C.V.
Rayon d'action	400 kil.

Performances
Décollage en 60 m. (vent nul).
Montée à 300 m. en 1 minute.
— —4.000 m. en 40 minutes.
Écart de vitesse 40-150 km. : h.

LES PLUS PETITS AVIONS DU MONDE
ÉCONOMIQUES ET CONFORTABLES

les plus sûrs   *les plus faciles à piloter*   *les moins chers*

Henri MIGNET, ayant obtenu du *British Air Ministry* l'autorisation de voler en Angleterre, s'y rendit par la route et par le bateau et put offrir la primeur de son dernier modèle en vol au public anglais, à RAMSGATE, LYMPNE et LONDRES, et voler librement sur le territoire de Grande-Bretagne.

Attestations de la Presse spécialisée :

— « L'événement sensationnel du jour, pour les connaisseurs, fut la » démonstration de M. Mignet avec sa nouvelle cabine HM-18. C'est » un véritable POU-DE-CHASSE (*interceptor Flea*). Le décollage est meilleur » qu'avec n'importe quel autre avion ordinaire et la montée se fait immé- » diatement à grand angle. La stabilité latérale semble excellente malgré » l'air agité et il effectue des virages à la verticale avec une étonnante » fermeté, tandis que, hélice calée et parachutalement, ne décelant aucun » vice caché, il évolue avec une parfaite confiance. » (*The Aeroplane.*)

— « Indubitablement, la démonstration la plus attractive de la journée » fut celle de M. Mignet sur son nouveau HM-18 à haut rendement. » (*Flight.*)

— « Le HM-18 a l'air d'un grimpeur parfait et d'une belle petite » machine qui eut un gros succès à RAMSGATE. » (Hervé LAUWICK dans *L'Aéro*.)

— « Sauf les avions de chasse les plus modernes, je n'avais encore rien » vu de semblable. Je ne comprends pas qu'on achète un avion monoplace » quand on a vu voler le HM-18. » (Edward BRET dans *Les Ailes*.)

Vue aérienne de
l'AÉRODROME PRIVÉ
de la **S. A. M.**
à 40 km. Est de PARIS
MEAUX-ISLES-LES-VILLENOY
(Seine-et-Marne)

Société à responsabilité limitée. — R. C. Meaux 13.165.

HM. 16
MONOPLACE-TORPEDO

Envergure	4 mètres
Longueur	3 m. 30
Poids à vide	100 kgr.
Puissance	25 C.V.
Rayon d'action	400 kil.

Performances
Décollage en 50 m. (vent nul).
Montée à 200 m. en 1 minute.
Écart de vitesse 40-130 km. : h.

SAM's publicity handout giving details of the company and marketing its HM.16, HM.18 and HM.19.
(Geoffrey P. Jones Collection)

wing overlapping the leading edge of the rear wing by more than one foot (0.3 metre). The large trailing edge 'flaps' of the rear wing, first used on the HM.15, were also a feature of the HM.17. These flaps made the Flea wing configuration safer, and worked in a similar manner to the complicated 'conjugated wing'

that Mignet put forward as the 'fix' required for the HM.14. Additionally these designs featured a strongly reflexed airfoil section for the rear wing which ensured that a nose-dive accompanied by any increase in speed would produce a dive-limiting tail-heavy pitching moment.

At the culmination of an extremely busy, frustrating and tragic year, Mignet was to be found in Paris in November displaying his aircraft on the SAM stand at the Paris Air Show. Here was Appleby's HM.18, G-AENV, the HM.16

The HM.19 on show on the SAM stand at the Paris Air Show, November 1936.
(Musée de l'Air)

'Baby Pou' and the larger HM.19 two seater. SAM's sales hand-out featured details of these three aircraft along with an aerial photograph of the Meaux factory. As well as details of the three aircraft it also gave quotes from three redoubtable magazines, *Flight, L'Aéro* and *Les Ailes,* all in praise of the HM.18. Edouard Bret in *Les Ailes* was quoted as saying 'Don't buy another single-seater until you have flown the HM.18'.

The final product of what proved to be the most prolific year of Mignet's life, in terms of designs, was the HM.210. SAM were on an uphill struggle to achieve orders and to put any of their designs into production and made one last valiant effort to break through with a modified and improved version of the two-seater HM.19. The all-moving rudder was replaced with a fin and rudder, additional glazing was incorporated in the cockpit area and the 40 hp Salmson radial of the HM.19 was replaced by a 70 hp Minie. Mignet put in over

500 hours of test flying on the HM.210 and it became his first design to qualify for a French certificate of airworthiness. Like the HM.19 before it, it was also tested in model form in the wind tunnel at the University of Lille.

Despite resolute efforts from Mignet, his wife and the somewhat reduced in size, but still loyal, body of partisans, failure was always around the corner. There were problems relating to the commercialisation of the designs, something that was bound not to gel with Mignet's personality. He described one of the problems at Meaux: 'The struggle to industrialise was less exciting. To think that the most dynamic businessmen are scared of progress and that the tiniest uncertainty makes them ill!' Struggling to establish a business in the light of growing antagonism being hurled at him from both officialdom and the Press, the 'star' created in the heady days of the Flea craze was now being knocked off his pedestal. Like stars of future generations, Mignet turned his thoughts to America, for conquering it seemed less formidable than Europe.

Mignet was set to start a period of nomadism that would take him around the world. Claude

Coulanges had travelled to Meaux and flown Mignet's new designs and received authority to act as North American agent for SAM. In the spring of 1937 Mignet and family followed Claude to the United States in the hope that a more understanding climate would prevail.

The final product from the Mignet drawing board of 1936 was the HM.210, a refined and updated version of the HM.19. The HM.210 was the first Mignet design to gain a full certificate of airworthiness. (RSA, via Jacques Avril)

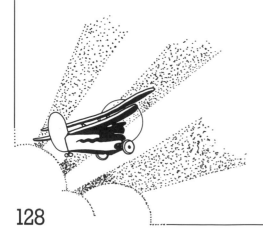

Above: If the book *The Flying Flea* was beyond your means, then the serialisation of Mignet's work in *Practical Mechanics* was another method of getting airborne. The October 1935 issue dealt with the box-like fuselage. (Ken Ellis)

Above: Cover of Mignet's second and most famous book on how to build the HM.14 - *Le Sport de l'Air*. (Geoffrey P Jones)

Below: Perhaps the best known of the extant UK Fleas is G-AEBB, maintained by the Shuttleworth Collection at Old Warden. This example was built by K.W. Owen in Southampton in early 1936. (Alan Curry)

Unusual view of the Flea displayed at the *Aviodome* in Amsterdam. Built by W. Miller in Kent in mid-1936, it carries bogus markings.
(Alan Curry)

Mignet's little HM.14 found itself being built in some unlikely places. At least one was built in Finland and is preserved at the Technical Museum in Tampere.
(Peter J. Bish)

The small size of the Flea has helped many examples to survive the last 50 years and it also makes them popular museum exhibits. G-AEJZ was built by Leslie Crosland on Humberside and was displayed in the former Bomber County Aviation Museum at Cleethorpes.
(Alan Curry)

An original HM.14 Flea, but with a Rotax engine conversion, on show at the Drage Air World Museum, Wangarratta, Victoria, Australia.
(via Geoffrey P. Jones)

Mick Ward's 1989 HM.14 Flea, powered by a Citroen Ami engine conversion. 'Hops' were planned as this book went to press.
(Mick Ward)

The 1500cc VW-powered Turmeau HT.01 bears a close design relationship to the HM.14.
(Geoffrey P. Jones)

Long shadows at Brienne cannot hide the shocking orange paint-scheme of Arthur Moerrig's tricycle-geared HM.19 HB-SPG.
(Geoffrey P. Jones)

Now part of the Yankee Air Force collection at Ypsilanti, Michigan, is Duane Rock's HM.293 N4067 which carries the military markings of Mignet's 1944 HM.280.
(Harold Sherman, YAF)

Manhandling the much-travelled Belgian HM.293 of Fernand Noiset. Powered by a 65 hp Continental flat-four, the aircraft was a well-known sight at European fly-ins during the 1970s.
(Geoffrey P. Jones Collection)

Albert Baron – one of the early post-war Flea builders – constructed this HM.293. Originally powered by a 40 hp Salmson, it is seen here fitted with a VW engine. Baron also built an HM.380, F-PKFB, the rudder of which can be seen at the right of the photo.
(Geoffrey P. Jones Collection)

Esther Duval at the helm of her HM.297. Now retired, it flew for only 2 hours.
(Geoffrey P. Jones)

HM.360 F-PSYN, a standard HM.360, plans number 128. Croses EC-6 behind.
(Geoffrey P. Jones)

Jack McWhorter's plans-built Falconar HM.360 N360CM showing the compact dimensions that the type can be reduced to; making it ideally suited to his Eustis, Florida, car-port.
(Geoffrey P. Jones)

In the white cap, HM.360 builder Jack McWhorter of Eustis, Florida, readies his Volkswagen-powered HM.360 for a sortie in 1986.
(via Geoffrey P. Jones)

R. Gauthier's Croses EC-1 which first flew in 1963, seen here at Brienne 23 years later.
(Geoffrey P. Jones)

Loyal disciple of Mignet, Emile Croses' most adopted type was the EC-6 Criquet. F-PYQG seen here visiting the PFA Rally at Cranfield, 1984.
(Alan Curry)

The Croses EC-7 Tous Terrains was designed to carry stretcher cases and capitalise on the short field performance of the Mignet configuration. The 'double' undercarriage is a notable feature.
(Geoffrey P. Jones)

The one-off EC-8 Tourisme is a three-seater built in 1973 based upon the EC-6.
(Geoffrey P. Jones)

Easily the largest Flea to date, the B-EC-9 Paras-Cargo was another of Emile Croses' ways of trying to make the type a commercial machine.
(Geoffrey P. Jones)

Makings its début at the 1987 RSA rally at Brienne was the crop-dusting version of the Croses Airplume.
(Geoffrey P. Jones)

Gilbert Landray's shapely GL-1, a modified version of the Croses EC-6, with a 90 hp Continental.
(Geoffrey P. Jones)

The tandem wing, designer Gilbert Landray, and the name GL-3 Pouss-Pou are the only real links between this 'Flea' and the early Mignet works. Nevertheless, Henri would have been more than pleased with the 1980s developments of 'his' form of aviation.
(Geoffrey P. Jones)

The Romibutter in flight. The type continues a long Belgian Flea tradition.
(Geoffrey P. Jones)

Flying advert. The HM.1000 Balerit in its first form with side-by-side seating in an open cockpit and the characteristic tandem wing.
(Geoffrey P. Jones)

Alain Mignet landing the HM.1000 Balerit, now with nose fairing, at the 1988 RSA Rally, Moulins, Central France. Sales of kits of this tandem wing type are going well.
(Geoffrey P. Jones)

Australia is another place with a loyal Flea-following. Jim Jensz of Wangaratta, Victoria, built this personalised version of the Croses Pouplume.
(via Geoffrey P. Jones)

Nedo Lavorini's second Flea project has an alloy fuselage. It is seen here aviating at the RSA 1989 Rally at Moulins.
(Geoffrey P. Jones)

Jean de la Farge showing the general layout of his 'Pulga'. Note the single-blade propeller with counterweight.
(Jean de la Farge)

The side-by-side two-seater 'Pulga' built by Jean de la Farge and powered by a 65 hp Continental engine.
(Jean de la Farge)

Too late for inclusion in the main text, Lucien Saucede flew this very standard HM.41 at Mont-Dore in New Caledonia on 10 March 1989. Engine is a Koenig SC.430.
(via Geoffrey P Jones)

Chapter 10

UNCLE SAM'S FLEAS

WITH HIS HOPES AND ASPIRATIONS SHATTERED as a result of an almost total loss of faith in his aircraft designs, Mignet and his wife Annette left Europe for the United States in 1937. Like hundreds of thousands before him, the New World seemed a land of hope – Mignet's particular hope being that far away from the stigma attached to his designs in Europe they might yet achieve popularity.

In all of Mignet's work in Europe he had been a pioneer: the first man to design an aircraft specifically for amateur construction and to sell the plans, albeit in the form of a book. America of the 1930s was perhaps the most aviation-minded country in the world – its vastness, continued pioneering spirit and rapid development of practical air transportation were some of the contributory factors. While names like Boeing, Douglas and Lockheed were engaged in a fight for supremacy in supplying the airlines of the USA, sport aviation was not being ignored. From 1929 onwards the upsurge of small companies building sport aircraft was unrivalled. While the de Havilland Moth was opening up the skies over Britain (and making itself reasonably felt within North America), in the United States companies such as Aeronca, Arrow, Cessna, Curtiss, Fairchild, Luscombe, Monocoupe, Rearwin, Stinson, Taylor, Travel Air, Waco and many others were building light aircraft. When Mignet arrived in Chicago in 1937 many of these companies were at their zenith. The idea of the homebuilt

was also 'old hat'. It is interesting to speculate how well informed Mignet might have been about the American light aviation movement in the late 1920s and early 1930s. Mignet was an avid reader and recorder of all published material that came his way, so it is probable that he had seen copies of the American magazine *Modern Mechanics* which, like *Les Ailes*, was an active hub of correspondence and comment on the subject of amateur aviation.

American homebuilt pioneers

In the United States as far back as 1926 the magazines of the day were being used for the promotion of the idea of amateur aviation. Weston Farmer, Editor of Fawcett Publications' *Modern Mechanics* suggested to Ed Heath and designer Clare Linsted the idea of a single-seat light sport aircraft that an amateur could build and operate. Farmer provided the wings from a Thomas-Morse Scout biplane fighter along with a Henderson motorcycle engine. With these basic ingredients Heath and Linsted set about designing and building a light aircraft. In 1926 the prototype Heath Parasol flew for the first time and the magazine *Popular Mechanics* published plans. Kits were also made available, sales of these reportedly reaching four figures. A few Parasols were factory-built, but it was amateur construction that created several hundred examples during the Depression and after. Jim Church of Chicago designed a mid-

A British-built example of the Heath Parasol – the world's first homebuilt to be marketed as such.
(Geoffrey P. Jones)

wing version of the Heath in 1928, calling it, appropriately, the Midwing. Church Airplane and Manufacturing Company built a series of Midwings, but their main business again lay with the sale of plans and the marketing of their new lightweight engine, the 45 hp Marathon, to power it.

Another pioneer American amateur aviator and designer, whose story is almost a copy-book version of Mignet's, was the self-taught mechanical engineer and industrial designer, Bernie Pietenpol. Born in 1901, Pietenpol spent most of his life at Cherry Grove, Minnesota,

where he died in 1984. Practically minded, as a youngster he built tractors, designed a powered wheelchair and serviced his own motorcycle. He began flying in Curtiss Jennies around 1920 but was soon relegated to following Mignet's route, in this case begging and conning flights with the National Guard at nearby Minneapolis.

Pietenpol's first aircraft was a biplane powered by a converted Ford Model T engine that he rated at around 35 hp. Everything in this aircraft that was not glued together was either bolted or riveted as the young builder did not own a drill or a welding torch. He, like Mignet, undoubtedly frightened himself silly as he combined the task of test flying with learning to fly. 'I had it in the air about twenty times,' wrote Pietenpol, 'but because I did not know how to land, I busted something every time I had it up'. A series of experiments with a First World War 50 hp Gnome rotary, then an Ace with a sixteen-valve aluminium block rated at 40 hp, left Pietenpol with the belief that his original Model T was still

Sixty years after the Pietenpol Aircamper first flew, homebuilt examples are still being built. Unlike the Flea, it is complex and relatively expensive to build. It is, however, a two-seater.
(Geoffrey P. Jones)

the best. When Ford produced the Model A from the Detroit factory, he soon acquired an example of the new Model A engine and rated it at 38–40 hp for use on an aircraft.

Pietenpol used *Modern Mechanics* as the forum whereby his experiences were shared with a wider audience – again paralleling Mignet in *Les Ailes*. The Model A engine was used on his next aircraft, the famous two-seat, parasol-winged Aircamper, which flew for the first time in 1928. The Aircamper was an attempt to produce an easy-to-build, lightweight, cheap, strong and easy-to-fly light aircraft that would be within the reach of the average man-in-the-street who wished to take up flying. Like Mignet, Pietenpol doggedly strove to keep the cost of flying to the minimum. As a result of his articles and the relative success of the Aircamper, Pietenpol started to sell plans and kits of the aircraft in 1930.

As with all powered aviation since the Wright brothers, one of the most significant factors contributing towards successful controlled flight is the availability of suitable, lightweight powerplants. Pietenpol realised this and followed and participated in the discussion that appeared in *Modern Mechanics* between 1928 and the publication of his articles in 1930. Most of American light aviation relied on the availability of cheap, but heavy, surplus First World War engines, the ten-cylinder 90 hp Curtiss OX5 being one of the most widely used. *Modern Mechanics* suggested that aircraft could not fly successfully on converted motor car engines. This statement was like a red rag to a bull as far as Pietenpol was concerned, so he and a friend set off in a pair of Aircampers on the 125 miles flight north to the magazine's office. They landed in an adjacent field and invited 'Westy' Farmer to take a ride. The invitation to write a series of articles on how to build one's own amateur aircraft followed immediately. Plans were sold for $7.50 and the fact that it was a two-seater, with a conversion plan for a readily available car engine, made it very popular. Pietenpol followed up the Aircamper with the single-seat SkyScout, which was again popularised in *Modern Mechanics*. An estimated 200 plus aircraft of both designs were completed and flown in the USA alone, although Pietenpol lost track of the number of sets of plans he sold. Kits of all the basic wooden parts needed to build the aircraft were also sold at $70 each.

First Fleas in the USA

Ed Nirmaier, a pilot and manager of Powell Crosley Airport, Sharonville, near Cincinnati, Ohio, obtained a copy of Mignet's book *Le Sport de l'Air*, in 1935. With two friends, Dan Boedeker and Herb Junkin, he set to building an example of the HM.14, starting on 3 October 1935. Exactly four weeks after work began, on 1 November 1935 the first American Flea, X-15749, made its maiden flight at Sharonville. It had cost an estimated $100 to build, not including the engine, wheels and labour. Power came from a British ABC Scorpion of 35 hp which had been salvaged from a heap of cast-off parts at the airport.

Nirmaier was personal pilot to Powell Crosley Junior, a local businessman and President of the Crosley Radio Corporation (now the giant Avco Corporation). Crosley was a former US Navy pilot and had served in France during the First World War. Mrs Page Crosley, Powell's daughter, was enlisted to christen the Crosley Flea *La Cucaracha,* reputedly with a bottle containing water sent from Kittyhawk, North Carolina, site of the Wright brothers pioneering flights. The *Cincinnati Times-Star* for 30 November 1935, reported events and quoted Nirmaier on the subject of his 'Sky Flea': 'A little time, a fair knowledge of mechanics, a little constructive ingenuity, the ability to read plans and blueprints and about $300 in cash and you can build a 'Sky Flea'.' He also considered that the aircraft might answer the Department of Commerce's search for an aircraft within the financial grasp of the 'average man'. Neither Crosley nor Nirmaier planned to put the aircraft into production, Crosley being satisfied by having brought this concept of cheap amateur aviation to the public's attention.

In December 1935 Nirmaier took the Crosley Flea to Miami to compete in the Miami Air Races, brushing shoulders with personalities from the world of US aviation who included Tex Rankin and his Ryan Monoplane. There were four accidents during the race meeting, none serious, but they included Nirmaier in the Flea. Considering the conditions the 'Sky Flea' flew well but upon landing ground-looped in the gusty wind, causing damage to the engine mountings and preventing any further flights. Andrew Hermance, Aviation Director for the

La Cucaracha, the Crosley Flea, the first HM.14 to be built and flown in the United States. It was flown by Ed Nirmaier in November 1935.
(via Don Berliner)

City of Miami and general chairman of the show committee, advised Crosley that because of the lightness of the Flea, it had been decided to award him a trophy for efficiency in construction and operation on behalf of the 8th Annual Miami All American Air Manoeuvers. This trophy is now part of the National Air and Space Museum collection in Washington, DC.

Following the crash at Miami the Crosley Flea was brought back to Sharonville and never flown again. Meanwhile, in 1936, Nirmaier was commissioned by the magazine *Popular Aviation* to write a series of articles about the construction techniques and details of his experiences while flying the Crosley Flea. This, coupled with the Miami races and the import of two HM.14s into the USA from France in 1935 and 1936 and Mignet's visit to the USA in September 1935, served to give the Flea plenty of publicity.

One of the Fleas was brought to the USA for exhibition purposes by Clyde Pangborn and flown at Roosevelt Field, New York, by him.

Going on the press photographs it was painted identically to Mignet's prototype – a popular scheme. Additionally, in New York, an Associated Press dispatch announced the arrival in America of a 'flivver' plane, brought to the country by former First World War pilot Sydney Arram. This HM.14 arrived on the MV *Manhattan* and was described as 'a one-man plane weighing 350 pounds, costing $350 and able to fly 45 miles on a gallon of gasoline – it has a 19½ foot wingspan and can be built by the purchaser from a set of parts. Its maximum speed is 75 mph and it was designed by the Frenchman Henri Mignet'.

The story of the pioneer Crosley Flea was not over. One night in 1939 a fire swept through Crosley's hangar at Sharonville, where the damaged Flea was stored. Somehow, although most of the other aircraft were destroyed, the Flea was saved and taken to the home of an insurance adjuster in Cincinnati. It was put among his household oddments and junk in a barn to become a secret attraction for neighbourhood kids until it was tracked down in August 1957. It was Pat Packard, a design consultant, vintage aircraft enthusiast and active member of the Experimental Aircraft Association (EAA) in the USA, who found the

Crosley Flea. It was extracted from the barn in a delicate six hour operation. Walt Paner, owner of the barn, was pleased to pass this aviation relic into Packard's safe keeping after eighteen years of gathering dust. Packard contacted Mignet, in Caen, France, during 1959 seeking information to help in the aircraft's restoration to flying condition. In his reply of 9 July 1959, suitably annotated with Mignet's delightful and accurate drawings, Mignet confirmed that to his knowledge the Crosley Flea was the first to be completed and flown in the USA.

Above: **Pat Packard rescues the Crosley Flea in 1957. It is now with the National Air and Space Museum, Washington.**
(via John W. Underwood)

Plans to fly the Crosley Flea again, this time with a Continental A40 did not materialise. The engine and propeller were missing when the aircraft was recovered from the barn but Ed Nirmaier was tracked down and willingly donated the original wheels that, meantime, had been used on a powered lawnmower. The National Air Museum heard of Packard's restoration project and asked him if he would donate the aircraft to the collection. Packard readily agreed to this and on 25 August 1960 it was officially taken into the custody of the USA's greatest historic aviation collection, the

Smithsonian, where it hung from the museum's ceiling for many years. In 1987 Packard took the aircraft back for further restoration and was seeking an ABC Scorpion to complete the museum piece. It is scheduled to go back on display in Washington.

'A Free Aircraft with Every Engine'

From small beginnings, the name Mignet was to continue to crop up across the United States. Prompted by the success of the Flea in Europe, in 1936 Cassell de Hibbs patented his triplane version of the Flea – perhaps a development of the HM.11 and HM.12? – and set up a manufacturing facility for the TC-1 Triplane with Universal Aircraft at Fort Worth, Texas. Their unique sales pitch was to offer a free TC-1 with the purchase of a 40 hp engine to power the aircraft; this engine cost $125. Few aircraft appear to have been bought, although nearly forty years later two were listed as current with the US civil aircraft register, including N5748N at Asheville, North Carolina.

Another important avenue in the story of the Flea in North America started to unfold on the west coast at Swan Island Airport, near

Below: **The aircraft offered free with its Universal Aircraft engine, the Cassell de Hibbs TC-1 Triplane, thought to have been based upon the Mignet HM.11 or HM.12**
(Geoffrey P. Jones Collection)

Portland, Oregon, in 1936. Frank Easton and his colleague Bud Lockwood, from the technical aeronautics course at Benson Technical College had both just graduated and were anxious to turn their often differing ideas about light aircraft into practical reality. They had read about Mignet's HM.14 in Europe and of Crosley's 'Sky Flea' in Cincinnati and, although at odds with many of Mignet's theories, mutually agreed to build a Flea exactly as detailed by Mignet. In the end a couple of minor alterations were made to the design, including wrap-around spar fittings, but otherwise the end-product was very much 'to the book'. Easton and Lockwood received help in the construction of N13384 from a couple of engineers from Swan Island Airport.

The pair followed closely Mignet's words from *The Flying Flea* including the piece about carrying out the test flying while teaching themselves to fly! They flew their HM.14 for many hours. Easton then obtained details of the mechanism for a revision of the design resulting from the work of people like Professor Louden at Toronto University and of Claude Coulanges, these modifications overcoming the supposedly treacherous diving tendencies. Correspondence with Coulanges led to Easton joining the American-Mignet project a few years later. N13384 flew on for a number of years and was flown by several pilots, all of whom considered it to be the safest aeroplane on the field at Beaverton, Ohio, where it had moved to. Easton's brother Clarence ('Clancy') stored the Flea for many years after its flying days were over, but when space was at a premium in his machine shop it was put outside

where it deteriorated rapidly. Speaking in 1987 of the aircraft, 71-year-old Frank Easton said, 'If only we could see the value of today's antiques when we were younger!'

Canadian Fleas
North of the 49th Parallel in Canada, Mignet's 'gospel' had also spread. Here the French-speaking population were ahead of the English-speakers neither requiring a tedious translation of *Le Sport de l'Air* nor having to await the Air League's version, *The Flying Flea*. One of the first Mignet aircraft to be completed in Canada was the HM.14 CF-AYM, which appeared on skis in March 1936, built at St. Hubert, Quebec, but which was involved in a fatal crash four months later. In the small ranching and wheat farming community of Amisk, Alberta, to the south east of Edmonton, one of the most active and numerous Flying Flea groups in Canada was founded by Howard Solbank. The members of this Group built their own HM.14, registered in July 1937 as CF-BII and fitted it with a Blackburn Thrush. In 1966 the wing from this Flea was still hanging in Solbank's garage at Amisk.

Above: **Thought to be the first Canadian HM.14, CF-AYM fitted with skis. It was built in 1936 at St. Hubert, Quebec, but was later involved in a fatal crash.**
(Geoffrey P. Jones Collection)

Left: **Engine runs on *Spirit of Canada*, HM.14 CF-BIH, built by O. Demine at Montreal in 1937.**
(Geoffrey P. Jones)

Built by the Central Technical School, Toronto, Flea CF-AZD was overtaken by the restrictions placed upon the type by the Canadian Department of Transport and did not fly. (via Jack McNulty)

Chris Falconar, as a young boy during the winter of 1934–1935, can still remember being taken to Eaton's, Montreal's big department store, where there was a Flea on display along with balsa models of the aircraft that were being snapped up by youngsters, including Falconar. Chris in later life was to become a Flea builder and an important part of the Flea story in North America. Other pioneer HM.14 builders in Canada were O. Demine from Montreal who completed his in 1937 with a Poinsard engine, it was registered CF-BIH and christened *Spirit of Canada*. The Toronto Central Technical School built CF-AZD and R. Thatcher of Timmins, Ontario, built another, CF-BGT.

American-Mignet Aircraft Corporation

Mignet was no stranger to the USA. In 1935 he had been invited to visit and he arrived in September of that year in New York. He had brought with him HM.14 No. 8, powered by a Poinsard-built Mengin engine of 32 hp. In May 1937 Mignet and his wife Annette arrived in the USA to stay – or so they hoped – and before long had formed the American-Mignet Aircraft Corporation at Pal-Waukee, a small rural aerodrome to the north of Chicago. The Mignets set to with the production of the prototype HM.20.

Claude Coulanges had been instrumental in forming a Flying Flea club in 1936 in the Chicago area under the auspices of the Army and Navy Club. After a visit to Meaux he became the Mignet agent for North America. Coulanges was one of the instigators of American-Mignet and with W. Logan was one of the main stockholders. Together they had approached Mignet (having been impressed with the handling and performance of the HM.19) with the suggestion that Mignet leave France. With the troubles of the HM.14 and the lack of breakthrough for any of the SAM designs, Mignet took little persuading to make the move to the USA.

At the inaugural meeting of American-Mignet two reports were presented, one the official report compiled by *Service Technique*, the other from an expert who worked for *Service Technique*. Both detailed Mignet's designs in general and the HM.19 in particular. The report from the independent expert was full of praise, the official paper 'was ostentatiously torn up and thrown in the wastepaper basket with the scorn that it deserved'. Through correspondence that had been taking place between Coulanges and Frank Easton, this third and important addition to the American-Mignet team moved to Pal-Waukee. Despite

Claude Coulanges (left) with Frank Easton at Pal-Waukee in front of the HM.21 NX18226.
(via Pierre Mignet)

what has been stated in many articles on this subject, Easton was never American-Mignet's chief engineer, he was in charge of the workshop and did the preliminary test flying

A happy group in front of the HM.20 after its successful first flight. *Left to right:* Claude Coulanges, Mr Logan, Annette and Henri Mignet, Frank Easton.
(Geoffrey P. Jones Collection)

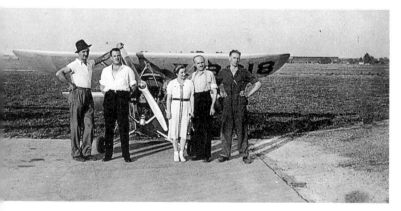

of the aircraft. Later he became responsible for checking-out other pilots on the company's products.

American-Mignet's aircraft embodied the familiar tandem wing, no ailerons and just the joy-stick for control in all three axes. They were also the first Mignet types to be constructed with a steel tube fuselage frame covered with fabric with wings of conventional wood and fabric construction. First American-Mignet product was HM.20 NX18218, which flew for the first time on 16 August 1937. The HM.20 was a single-seat, taildragger version of the HM.19.

Fifty years on, it is an interesting exercise to speculate on what the eventual fate of this aircraft was. An auction of aircraft at Boise, Idaho, in November 1986 included Lot A35, a steel-tube fuselage frame from a single seat 'Flea' (quite possibly an HM.20) covered in rotting green canvas, still on its undercarriage legs and with tail, but without wheels or engine. The wings were characteristically Flea-like, both spars were intact and the ribs of one were there. Lot A35 went to Bill Sterling who runs the local Surplus and Salvage Center. Bill describes the remains as 'junk', but could these be the remains of NX18218 from Pal-Waukee?

Uncertainty arises because Frank Easton developed his well known ME2Y Flea from the HM.20. Writing about this in 1987, Easton said, 'The ME2Y is a rebuild of the old HM.20 with many changes in rigging, controls and landing gear'. There was another version of the HM.20, built at Pal-Waukee by American-Mignet, after Mignet himself had returned to France. Some believe that this second HM.20, registered NX20473, was in fact the HM.24 and photographs of this aircraft at Pal-Waukee in 1941 show Easton standing in front of this aircraft. NX20473 may be the aircraft from which Easton remodelled his ME2Y, so if this is the case then the eventual fate of the original HM.20 is unconfirmed.

Easton's ME2Y N43993 became a common sight at EAA fly-ins at Milwaukee and Rockford in the 1950s and 1960s, before it moved venue to its current Oshkosh home. Writing at the age of 71 in 1987 Easton recalled his ME2Y and Fleas in general: 'Even the old HM.14 with its limitations, was not nearly as dangerous as it was reported to be. That is one of the reasons why I want to complete the high negative *décalage* [deviation from the horizontal] stability tests in which I am currently deeply

Frank Easton (left) with NX20473 at Pal-Waukee in 1941. This was similar to the HM.20 and is thought by some to have been the HM.24. It is most likely to have formed the basis for Frank's later ME2Y.
(Earl Reinert via John W. Underwood)

involved and which I started many years ago. The HM.14 was condemned for only about two degrees negative *décalage*. I have flown my ME2Y with hands-off trim for many hours with closer to a minus five degrees equivalent *décalage* – inclusive of five degrees positive flap on the rear wing. I hope to test the ME2Y with up to eight degrees negative *décalage*, possibly including ten degrees of flap. But here

Frank Easton's remodelled ME2Y N43993 is still in existence, but has not flown for some time. (Leo J. Kohn)

I go, is this just an old man's long term dream revised? I sure can dream young, but I haven't flown the ME2Y for several years and if it were to start to 'tuck' too quickly, I could be in trouble. I better say no more. I could chicken out with less than half the test completed.'

The HM.20 started life as a taildragger with

December 1937 at Pal-Waukee and the HM.21 NX18226 is rolled out for the first time. Note the characteristic air intake on the nose of the 71 hp Rover engine.
(RSA, via Jacques Avril)

a 40 hp Continental engine, but about 1940, still with its tail wheel in place, it was converted to an experimental tri-gear configuration by Easton. The onset of war and personnel changes within American-Mignet stopped Easton's development of the HM.20 and he decided to move on.

Next in line from the Pal-Waukee facility was the HM.21, a rework of the HM.210 from SAM at Meaux, but now using a steel tube fuselage and 'wooden' wings. Powered by a 71 hp Rover engine with a characteristic air intake on the starboard side of the nose, it was a cabin two-seater. NX18226 was completed and flown for the first time in December 1937 amid the cold and the snow of Illinois. With sound financial backing, excellent facilities, the open-minded American attitude, an enthusiastic team and now two tandem wing aircraft to prove and demonstrate Mignet's heart-felt convictions about light aircraft, the start of 1938 saw Mignet's American dream coming to life.

Whatever the HM.22 was, it never materialised into hardware and must have been a design project from the 1937–1938 period. All the stops were out at Pal-Waukee to build the third of the trio of aircraft for which Mignet was responsible. This was the biggest of the three, the HM.23, following the same constructional pattern but featuring a reverse tricycle undercarriage, the tail wheel being moved forward to a position mid-way along the fuselage and underneath the rear of the cabin. This arrangement was presumably to help with one of the shortfalls of the tandem wing concept, the cross-wind landing. Like the two previous aircraft that were built at Pal-Waukee, the HM.23 also had a full-span flap on the rear wing, to help with trim and slow-speed handling. The HM.23 also went for a more conventional engine than the HM.21, choosing the Continental flat-four of 50 hp. The HM.23

Above: A proud Henri Mignet with his American 'family' in the summer of 1938. *Left to right* the HM.23, the HM.20 and the HM.21.
(Geoffrey P. Jones Collection)

Left: American-Mignet HM.23 NX18240 clearly showing the trailing edge on the rear wing.
(RSA, via Jacques Avril)

Below: Line up of the three American-Mignet aircraft at Pal-Waukee with their workshop (with the chimney) in the background. Left to right HM.21 NX18226, HM.23 NX18240, HM.20 X18218.
(Geoffrey P. Jones Collection)

The HM.23 showing its reverse tricycle undercarriage and relatively deep fuselage. (Musée de l'Air)

first flew in June 1938 as NX18240. American-Mignet could now proudly display their product line on the wide-open spaces of Pal-Waukee with the large Goodyear airship hangar as a back-drop for one of the frequent photo-sessions that ensued during the summer of 1938.

Although Mignet was to make a premature departure from the United States because of the worsening situation in Europe that was shortly to lead to the Second World War, American-Mignet was to continue in existence until at least 1941. If one studies the Civil Aeronautics Authority (now Federal Aviation Administration) records for HM.23 NX18240 it was registered to American-Mignet Aircraft Corporation, Room 1020, 120 South La Salle Street, Chicago, Illinois, in 1940 and 1941, but also 1946. For the latter reference the address had changed to Pal-Waukee Airport, Wheeling, Illinois.

North American Disciples
While Mignet was active at Pal-Waukee he was able to visit other parts of the United States and

although the HM.14 was a 'dead duck' in Europe, in the States a few builders pressed on with the construction and flying of their aircraft, the American magazine *Popular Aviation* keeping its readers up to date. Three such projects from this time may have come to light headed by Mike Lajcak with his otherwise conventional HM.14 fitted with a neatly cowled three-cylinder engine giving the nose more the appearance of an Aeronca C.3 than a Flea. Registered N20499, Lajcak flew it regularly between 1938 and the start of the war. A less sophisticated-looking HM.14 was built by Alvin Schubert at Galesville, Wisconsin. Power came from a Harley-Davidson conversion but under the fuselage skin was a most unusual geodetic-type construction. This example flew from about 1938/1939.

The era 1937-1938 when Mignet was in the United States was just the start of the story of the Flea in North America, thanks to people like Frank Easton, who were to become part of aviation folklore as sport and homebuilt aviation made its meteoric rise in the 1950s. As with several other areas of Flea history, the main character always seemed to interreact and stimulate one another to further endeavours – just like the great designer himself. The main catalyst for the revival of the Flea came from

Right: Demine seen taxying his Poinsard-engined HM.14 which was registered, as CF-BlH, in 1937. (Musée de l'Air)

Below right: Alvin Schubert's HM.14 was built at Galesville, Wisconsin, in 1939. Power came from a converted Harley-Davidson engine. (via Leo Kohn)

Below: Mike Lajcak ground running his HM.14 N20499. Built in 1938, it flew regularly until the start of the Second World War. (Robert F. Pauley)

Below: The Pontius Model II NX68936 was based upon the HM.16 featured a plywood-covered fuselage. (Geoffrey P. Jones Collection)

north of the border, from aeronautical engineer George Jacquemin of Streetsville, Ontario, Canada who first became associated with Fleas when he translated the plans of the HM.290, and later those of the diminutive HM.160, into English for the North American market. Jacquemin went on to translate the HM.290 plans in similar manner (see Chapter Eleven). Chris Falconar, mentioned earlier, met Easton at the EAA Milwaukee fly-in in 1958 and flew in his ME2Y N43993. Through his company Falconar Aviation, plans for the HM.290 and its developments were sold around the world, including many in the United States and Canada. The type was never to become a major seller, but aircraft were completed and flown from 1960 right through to the 1980s. Plans for the HM.290 and HM.360 are still being sold by Chris Falconar.

Jacquemin's translation of the HM.16 'Baby Pou' plans became the HM.160 in Canada. Only two examples of this type has ever neared completion in North America as far as can be

ascertained. One was the HM.162 built by Louis Dagne at Lake Park, Florida. Registered as N1841 it differed from the basic HM.160 in having a tricycle undercarriage, a redesigned rear fuselage with a head rest and fairing along with a fin and rudder. Dagne designed and built his own two-stroke, four-cylinder radial engine for the aircraft. Although it completed a comprehensive series of taxi trials and high speed runs, the builder confesses that it has not actually flown. This is not due to any trepidation about Mignet's designs but worries that the engine would not be sufficiently reliable. N1841 may yet fly, however.

The second HM.160 was built by John Pontius at Holister, California. Registered NX68936 and fitted with a Nelson engine, it was completed in 1963. Reports suggest that Pontius has built and flown two further Fleas.

It is here that Pat Packard, discoverer of the forgotten Crosley Flea, re-enters the fray when he wrote a feature for the EAA's superb house magazine *Sport Aviation* in June 1959. This inspired at least one EAA member with memories of the Flea 'fever' of the 1930s to find out more about post-war developments in France. Ralph Wefel of Canoga Park, California, got details of the HM.360, the prototype of which had flown at St.-Lô in France in June 1959, via Packard whom Wefel later blamed for 'being responsible for his misery in choosing and building his HM.360'. Registered appropriately N360HM and named *Mon Petit Ami* Ralph's HM.360 was completed by September 1963. It was later donated to the

Happiness is Flea-shaped. A very satisfied looking George Pankau leans on the propeller of his HM.290 built at Dundee, Mississippi.
(Geoffrey P. Jones Collection)

Ralph Wefel's HM.360 N360HM *Mon Petit Ami* is now held by the EAA Museum.
(John W. Underwood)

EAA Museum at Oshkosh, Wisconsin, but recent pressure of space has placed it into store.

Another less well known American Flea fanatic is Joe Travis of Kendallville, Indiana. Frank Easton's ME2Y was being re-covered near Travis's home and upon seeing it he was inspired to investigate this strange type of aircraft further. He spent many years after this first encounter designing and building his own

version of the Flea: the Travis STW-01. It was a single-seat cabin version with a fin and rudder, featuring a neatly cowled Continental engine driving a McCaulley propeller. Painted in a smart mustard and white scheme it was only a few weeks away from its first flight when it was tragically destroyed in a garage fire.

Travis's second aircraft project was a non-Flea, the Travis Red-Bare-Un STW N26148. More recently Travis was 'bitten' by the Flea bug again and in 1985 he started work on the JT-03. This is a step back to the HM.14, following the classic layout completely, but using a steel tube fuselage structure with a wood and fabric rudder and wings. A converted Volkswagen of 1300cc will power the JT-03.

Of the HM.290 series aircraft builders in the United States and Canada, Phil Howell of Christiansburg, Virginia, has built one of the most widely flown and interesting examples of the type. His spur to build a Flea came from a smouldering interest in a slow-flying, safe homebuilt type which was stimulated by adverts in the American monthly *Air Trails* in the late 1940s and early 1950s showing the latest Mignet variants. It was not to be until 1965

Joe Travis's STW-01 completed but unflown – a very neat looking machine. Sadly it was destroyed in a garage fire before it could fly.
(Joe Travis)

Back to basics. Joe Travis's JT-03 Flea showing the tubular steel construction used for an otherwise entirely by-the-book HM.14.
(Joe Travis)

that things took a more concrete direction when Howell was given the Falconar drawings for the HM.290 and the HM.293; he opted for the latter with the longer wing. He planned to instal a converted Volkswagen engine and also to move the firewall forward, to give him more leg room, and fit a tricycle undercarriage. During construction it was decided to install a McCulloch 0-100-1 engine instead of the VW, fitted with a modified Ford carburettor and driving a wooden Hegy propeller. Registered as N2931 it first flew in September 1970. Phil takes full advantage of the design's folding wings, keeping the aircraft in a basement garage and towing it to and from the airfield at speeds of up to 50 mph (80 kph). It is one of the few Fleas over the years to appear at the EAA's famous Oshkosh fly-in.

Proudly wearing French roundels and the colour scheme adopted by Mignet for his HM.280 for the famous military evaluation of 1944 is HM.293 N4067 built in the late 1960s by Duane Rock of Benton Harbour, Michigan. Powered by a 1200 cc Volkswagen conversion, it was sold in 1973 to Robert Carver of Ohio and then to Joseph Szempias of Toledo, Ohio. On 1 August 1984 Szempias donated the aircraft to the Yankee Air Force at Ypsilanti, Michigan and it has remained in their collection ever since.

Several other Fleas are currently under construction in the USA. Elton Barnum from Marquette, Michigan has 'one of the most senior home-built projects in my area'. He bought a set of HM.290 plans from Falconar and concludes 'It'll be an antique when it first flies!' Albert Osterman from Springfield, Oregon, regularly corresponds with Barnum on the progress of their respective projects. Osterman is also building a HM.290. 'Its 90 per cent complete . . . with only 90 per cent to go!' he says. The Summit Academy, Waynesville, North Carolina is also home for a HM.297 project where it provides a focal point for the children at the Academy who have learning disabilities. Brian Sportsman did much of the early

Phil Howell flying his tri-gear HM.293 N2931. (Howard Levy)

construction on this HM.297 before donating it to the Academy.

In Canada another tri-gear HM.293 was completed in 1974 by Fred Bishop of Burlington, Ontario. This was C-FERN, taking him thirteen years of hard work to complete. It flew for many hours, powered by a Continental, until it was involved in a landing mishap when the nosewheel collapsed. More recently the aircraft was sold to Rene Mauch of Hemmingford, Quebec, who hopes to have C-FERN back in the air again before too long. Mauch saw Mignet flying in France when he was a boy of

Fred Bishop's HM.293 C-FERN first flew in 1974. It was retired after a landing accident. (Jack McNulty)

ten and hankered after a Flea ever after. John Sayle's HM.290 CF-RFH first appeared in 1963, powered by a 70 hp McCulloch conversion. It was later donated to the Canadian Museum of Flight and Transportation at Surrey, British Columbia by EAA Chapter 85 and is currently under restoration for exhibition. HM.297 C-GUQG was started initially in Canada by a German but was sold due to failing health to Claude and Esther Hamel who completed the aircraft in about 1977 at Chicoutimi, Quebec. Fitted with a 40 hp Continental A40 it is comprehensively equipped with an altimeter, turn and slip, RPM gauge, oil pressure and temperature gauges, compass and radio and features a striking yellow and black finish. Now owned solely by Esther Duval (née Hamel) and her husband Laurent it flew only for a short time in the hands of test pilot Yvon Tremblay and is now kept near Montreal.

One of the most exciting new developments on the Flea front in North America in recent years resulted from a visit to the 1984 RSA International Air Rally at Brienne-le-Château, France, by two Californian pilots and homebuilders, Norm Regnier and Jim Eich. Regnier had already built a replica Curtiss Pusher and Eich several gyrocopters. Reminiscing about their French trip they decided to build themselves a Flea and obtained plans for the HM.360. Preferring to work with aluminium tubing they decided to build their HM.360 using this medium and to cover it with Dacron, fitting a Rotax 377 engine. Concern about cross-winds at their El Mirage desert strip led Eich to devise a mixer mechanism for the controls that meant a split in the centre of the front wing to provide roll control with normal sideways movement of the control column, but retaining the pitch control with the angle of attack, both port and starboard halves of the wing operating together.

By August 1985 the pair were sharing concern about the centre of gravity of their project and during high speed taxi trials it proved to be tail heavy. As the whole aircraft weighed only 207 lb (94 kg) empty there were no problems in deciding to move the engine and the pilot forward. By November Regnier and Eich were obtaining some success but were by then toying with the idea of moving the main wing backwards and the rear wing forwards to get the centre of gravity close to

the pilot's seat. The Mk1 was abandoned and instead a Mk2 version was started with the fuselage built as an all-metal monocoque, using the wings of the Mk1. With this aircraft it was back to El Mirage Dry Lake in April 1986 for further tests. With Regnier at the controls it flew well, but landings with the heavier Eich on board were not sufficiently controlled so further unsuccessful experiments with the propeller and muffler system in the hope of increasing the available power concluded with the purchase of a bigger Rotax 447 of 40 hp and a new propeller. By April 1987 the Regnier/Eich Metal Flea Mk2 was making nice three-point landings with Eich on board and not so good 'wheel landings' with Regnier.

In 1987 Regnier and Eich were not the only ones building Fleas in the United States. At the EAA's prestigious new Air Museum Foundation at Oshkosh (their marvellous Air Academy, started in 1984 to stimulate young people to become part of the next generation of pilots)

The Regnier/Eich Metal Flea Mk 2 with its Rotax 447 cc engine and final configuration. The split front wing is apparent.
(Norm Regnier)

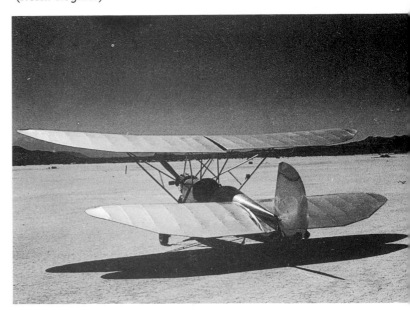

the forty students enrolled for the summer 1987 season had a project to work on – what else but a non-flying replica of the HM.14 Flying Flea. By the summer of 1988 this project was complete and ready for display in the Museum.

Another 1980s US Flea builder is Jack McWhorter from Eustis, Florida. A chat with Phil

Howell got him started: 'I debated several years before building my Flea – this was mainly due to the incorrect information I got from armchair experts and side-walk superintendents, all of them self-appointed and none of them correct. On talking to Phil Howell and seeing his Flea fly I was sold'. He bought HM.360 plans from Falconar in 1975 and spent 11 years completing his project. VW and McCulloch engines have been fitted and although a slight landing mishap to the aircraft, N360CM, in early 1989 forced the project back into the workshop, this 65-year-old was soon flying again, trailing the folding-wing HM.360 the short distance from his home to his private dirt strip. McWhorter concludes, 'This Flea does everything it's supposed to do – it's a very safe aircraft'.

Nineteen eighty-seven saw the Allen Aircraft Company of Petersburg, Virginia, launching their Gemini 350. This is a four-seat turboprop-powered ultra-short take-off and landing aircraft designed and built as a result of the US Department of Transport's request for proposals for innovative means of reducing accidents and increasing the safety of aircraft.

While this is not a Flea as such, there are many design similarities. Britain's weekly *Flight International* described the aircraft: 'The Gemini obtains its STOL capabilities – Allen calls it near-VTOL – by thrust vectoring. The pilot can pitch the fuselage to a tail-down position while the tandem wings remain in level-flight attitude, allowing the powerplant installed on the wing centre section to provide vectored thrust during take-off and landing. The aeroplane is of all composite construction. The rear wings are without tabs or elevators, and are mounted high on the vertical tail.'

Will another modern version of the tandem wing Flying Flea enter production before the Twentieth Century is finished? Mignet and many others would have liked to think so. It would be a wonderful epitaph.

North American Fleas		
Canada		
Registration	*Type*	*Notes*
CF-AYM	HM. 14	Built by Bill Kahre, Bob Coupland and G S Lace, Registered 18/3/36 to G E Millette, fitted with skis. Fatal crash July 1936 at St Hubert, Quebec.
CF-AZD	HM. 14	Built by Central Technical School, Toronto, ABC Scorpion, Dept of Transport restrictions came in before it was flown. Engine used in Heath Parasol CF-BLS, 1939.
CF-BGT	HM. 14	Built by R Thatcher, Timmins, Ontario, Aeronca E-107A, Registered 28/8/37, damaged on test flight 18/10/38.
CF-BIH	HM. 14	Built by O Demine, Montreal, Poinsard, Registered 19/10/37.
CF-BII	HM. 14	Howard Solbank and group, Blackburn Thrush. Registered July 1937.
CF-???	HM. 14	Displayed at Eaton's Department Store, Montreal, winter 1934/1935.
CF-RFH	HM. 290	Built by John Sayle 1962, 70hp McCulloch. With Canadian Museum of Flight and Transportation, Surrey, BC.
CF-SIO	HM. 290	Built by Jack Johnson, St Albert, Alberta, 1967. Destroyed in grass fire.
C-GUQG	HM. 291	Completed by C & E Hamel, Quebec, Continental A40.
C-FERN	HM. 293C	Built by Fred Bishop, Burlington, Ontario.

USA

X-15749	HM. 14	Crosley Sky Flea, under restoration by Pat Packard for NASM, Washington.
N13384	HM. 14	Built by Bud Lockwood, Frank Easton and friends at Portland, Oregon, 1936
N20499	HM. 14	Built by Mike Lajcak, 1938
–	HM. 14	Built by Alvin Schubert, Galesville, Wisconsin, 1939. Harley Davidson.
NX18218	HM. 20	First aircraft built by American-Mignet, Pal-Waukee.
NX18226	HM. 21	American-Mignet built.
NX18240	HM. 23	c/n 3, American-Mignet built.
NX20473	HM. 24	American-Mignet built.
N1841	HM. 160	Built by Louis Dagne, Lake Park, Florida. Not yet flown.
N7541U	HM. 290	Built by H D Love, Rolla, Missouri, 1968.
–	HM. 290	Built by George Pankau, Dundee, Mississippi.
–	HM. 290	Built at Houston, Texas, early 1960s.
–	HM.290	Albert Osterman, Springfield, Oregon. Started mid-1980s.
N2931	HM. 293	Built by Philip Howell, Christianburg, Virginia, 1970.
N4067	HM. 293	Built by Duane Rock, Benton Harbour, Michigan, 1970. Now with Yankee Air Museum, Ypsilanti, Michigan.
N30120	HM. 293	Built by Richard F van Loh, Wasau, Wisconsin.
–	HM.293	Elton Barnum, Marquette, Michigan. To Falconar plans, construction still underway. Barnum started another 'Flea' proir to this, but sold it off.
–	HM.297	Started by Mr Ramsey at St Joseph, Missouri, sold to Brian Sportsman of Riverside, Missouri, and now with Summit Academy, Waynesville, North Carolina.
N360CM	HM.360	Built by Jack McWhorter, Eustis, Florida.
N360HM	HM.360	Built by Ralph Wefel, California, 1963. Now with EAA Museum.
–	HM. 360	Heavily modified version now in its second phase by Norm Regnier and Jim Eich, El Mirage Dry Lake, California, Rotax 447, first flew April 1986.
–	JT-03	Joe Travis, Kendallville, Indiana. Steel tube version of HM.14, nearing completion 1987, 1300cc Volkswagen conversion.
N43993	ME2Y	Rework by Frank Easton of either the original HM.20 or the HM.24
NX68936	Pontius II	Based upon the HM.16 and built by John Pontius.
–	STW-01	Joe Travis, Kendallville, Indiana. Burnt before flight, 1967.
N5748N	TC-1	One of two still registered 1974.

Chapter 11

THE FLEA GOES TO WAR

WAR CLOUDS GATHERING OVER EUROPE seemed a long way off to most Americans. For Henri Mignet, happily working at the American-Mignet Aircraft Corporation at Pal-Waukee, these clouds appeared ominous. Always keeping himself well informed about world affairs, he became worried by the turn of political and military events and was faced with the momentous decision of whether to stay in the United States or return to his native France.

Family and patriotic ties resulted in his decision to return to France. He had been impressed by both the American attitude and also the companionship of those he had worked with – experiences that were to remain a significant memory with him for the rest of

Back home. Henri and Annette in France 1939. (Pierre Mignet)

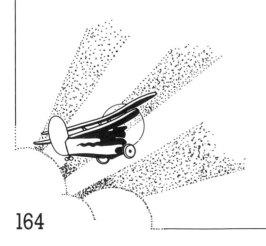

his life. He later wrote, 'Without disregarding the often unpleasant struggle for survival, I admire greatly this young, energetic, optimistic, full-of-go, taken-as-a-whole and profoundly honest people. And while the Frenchman whimpers, "All this newness bores us. What we have suits us very well and is quite good enough", the American shouts, "Something new. Quick, let's get it into production, it could be a product with a big future." ' He felt this spirit was epitomised by Continental, the engine manufacturer, who dared to inscribe on the plaque of its engines *Powerful as the Nation*.

Britain and France declared war on Hitler's Germany on 3 September 1939. The war was to have the effect of stopping the possible production of Mignet's aircraft at two locations. In the United States, with the three prototypes at American-Mignet having flown and been subjected to extensive development, the company was preparing for production. Although the United States did not actively enter the war until 8 December 1941, the events in Europe had a disruptive effect on private aviation. The last thing that many private aviators were going to do was to buy a new aircraft at such a time of uncertainty. The war *was* good news for light aircraft manufacturers who could find a military application for their products as trainers, liaison types, observation aircraft, etc. American-Mignet's three prototypes did not offer the basis for a swing to massive military use and the company ceased to exist from 1942.

Despite Mignet's departure, at Meaux near Paris *La Société des Aéronefs Mignet* (SAM) continued to exist. The last aircraft Mignet had designed before his departure was the HM.210. This had been designed partly with a rôle as an Army observation aircraft in mind. It was a two-seater, of all wooden construction powered by a 70 hp Minie Horus engine which gave it a quite exceptional performance. The prototype (described in Chapter Nine) was the first of Mignet's aircraft to achieve a Certificate of Airworthiness following over 500 hours of test flying. The HM.210 was asked to participate in the *Armée de l'Air* (French Air Force) manoeuvres in 1939 at the request of Colonel Eon, who was looking for a suitable observation machine. These trials were successful and plans were in hand at Meaux for the series production of twelve HM.210s. Several aircraft

had already been started when the German invasion of France, starting on 14 May 1940, terminated all indigenous aircraft production.

On Mignet's return to France he was inducted into the Army, where for a few months he worked in Paris as a post orderly. Mignet's third and last son, Vincent, was born in 1939, perhaps another significant reason for the Mignets' decision to return to France. The family, now with three sons, François, Pierre and baby Vincent, were able to return to the family home at Saintonge to live through the ignominy and danger of the war and the occupation.

With five mouths to feed Mignet's new 'production' was carrots and potatoes. Their area was, fortunately, little troubled by the occupation and there was plenty of land on which to grow crops. As might be expected, Henri's thoughts could not be kept from new developments of his tandem wing aeroplanes. With the help and encouragement of his friend Jean-Daniel Allard, who together with his wife, Giselle, frequently cycled the 80 miles from their home in Bordeaux to see Henri and Annette, he continued to work on aircraft designs throughout the occupation. Several scale models were built and it must be assumed that in Mignet's logical system of numbering his aircraft designs these were the HM.25, HM.26, and HM.27. Details of these, however, remain a mystery.

With the war drawing to a close, at least in France, and the Allied forces pushing the occupying forces eastwards through France towards liberation and eventual defeat, the most tragic irony of Mignet's life was to occur. Pierre Mignet takes up the story: 'The Liberation came with its procession of heroes and bandits. In the area of Saintonge where we were living, the effects of the German occupation were not great – certain 'last minute liberators' enjoyed themselves to their hearts' content with the lorry loads of evacuees, torturing and massacring the recalcitrants. They removed as trophies many of the Beware Mines signs left by the Germans. Some civilians, not knowing this and thinking the areas had been cleared, had tremendous shocks!

'As part of the intrigue and deception of the groups of opposing peasant collaborators and disappointed looters, Henri's loving and faithful wife, Annette, the spirit behind the 1934-1939

Pou campaign in Europe and North America, was needlessly killed in a bout of shooting. She was an innocent victim of these opposing factions of the Resistance, killed on 10 December 1944 by her own countrymen while she was hanging washing on the line, near to Saujon in the Department of Charente-Maritime.

'The perpetrators of this wicked crime were three Dordogne-Limousin FTP underground fighters of the Violet Group, RAC Battalion. They were known and arrested, then questioned, but having threatened to talk too much, freed by the Tribunal at the court in Saintes . . . .' To have survived the deprivations of war, to be so cruelly bereaved at the eleventh hour and still to have the stigmas of the Flea fatalities must have given Mignet an unbearably heavy cross to bear. His only compensation was renewed interest in his designs by the regrouping French military.

A Flea for the Maquis
Colonel Eon, shortly to be promoted to General, who had been instrumental in the order for the HM.210 prior to the war, was organiser and head of the French underground movement in Brittany. One part of his group, who had been parachuted into an area at night, had come across the enemy but had been annihilated. Eon felt that inside informants were at work. He came up with a requirement for a more efficient way of getting his men behind the lines. At the end of 1944, he turned to Mignet to try to enlist him for a very special project.

'I need a tiny plane that can take off from a none-too-straight road, land in a clearing and have disappeared from sight within sixty seconds of touching down. It should be able to land practically on the spot in scrub-land, even if it were damaged. It must be extremely manoeuvrable in the air, with good acceleration and fast cruise speed. I want this aircraft as my *COMMAND PARACHUTE*. Is this possible?' 'Of course it is,' replied Mignet. 'Then immediately carry on and build me such an aircraft,' was Eon's instruction. Mignet was back again doing what he was happiest at, designing and building aeroplanes. With many hours at the drawing board and frenzied work searching for materials and odds and ends that could be utilised in the construction of the new aircraft, the HM.280 was born. (More and more Mignet was using the standard French designation system of type and sub-type. The designation HM.280 in reality breaks down as the HM.28,

General arrangement of the HM.290.

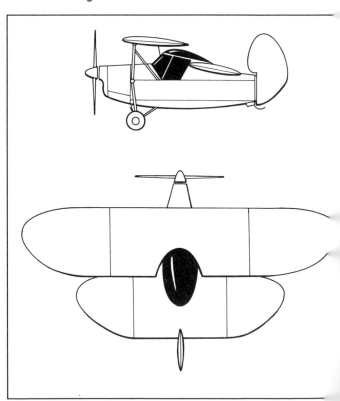

Henri Mignet prepares the HM.280 Pou Maquis for flight. Undercarriage leg is more complex because it featured steerable mainwheels. (RSA, via Jacques Avril)

first type. The next variant of this basic design would be the HM.281, and so on.) Basically a revised HM.210, it was a single-seater, with a 35 hp Mengin engine, easily foldable wings, quiet, stable in flight, very manoeuvrable, with better performance than anticipated and easily towable on the road. Wing span was only 16 ft 5 in (5 m). Another unique feature was that the main wheels were steerable.

Eon's specification was met easily by the HM.280. It was the first light aircraft operated by the *Aviation Légère de l'Armée de Terre* (ALAT – Light Aviation branch of the Army) and although much of France was still occupied by a retreating German army, Eon made arrangements with Mignet to put the HM.280 into series production for the ALAT. Production of a Mignet design was under way yet again, but shortly after the surrender of the Germans, 7 May 1945, production plans were abandoned. The story of Meaux and Pal-Waukee was repeated yet again. The prototype HM.280 Pou-Maquis was saved and became a part of the *Musée de l'Air* collection, held at Le Bourget, near Paris.

Return to peace

Despite unpopularity in many quarters and the considerable number of years since the HM.14 craze in France, there were still a large number of aviators who remembered Mignet and still supported wholeheartedly his ideals for amateur aviation and in particular, his tandem wing designs.

Many HM.14s had survived the ban and the war and it was to one of these, No.147 built in 1936, that the accolade for the first flight in France after the Liberation by an amateur-built aircraft must go. Now registered F-WFAQ, fitted with a 32 hp Mengin, it was piloted from Auxerre by Maurice Guerimet. This flight was symptomatic of the latent desire of air-minded Frenchmen to get back to flying again after the interlude of war, and was a story repeated across the country. At Rouen, Bergeret dusted off his Flea, Kohler and Bauman likewise at Belfort, Emilien Croses at Mâcon (see Chapter Fifteen), Chauvin at Jonzac, Baron and Sire at Marennes, Elie Layat at Lyon in HM.14 F-PBGZ, Jean de la Farge at Barriac-les-Bosquest (see Chapter Fourteen), Bernard Dormont at Auxi-le-Château and many more became the pioneer post-war amateur aviators. And all thanks to Mignet's vigorous search for a suitable fix to make the HM.14 a safe aircraft again. Jean-Daniel Allard, wartime friend of Mignet's, set to work on the reconstruction of the HM.210 from 1939 using pieces of the original and photographs. This aircraft was nicknamed *Puck*. Even HM.8s started to reappear, the HM.8-derived Fellot-Lacour FL-2 F-PBGV surfacing in 1946.

Anxious to contribute to this revival, Mignet started work at his new base of Chadignac on his next design. This was a revamped version of the HM.280, intended for amateur

Henri Mignet at his drawing board at Chadignac, 1946.
(Pierre Mignet)

The prototype HM.290 F-PERF, built by Pierre Mignet. It is seen here at Dax in June 1961 during one of Mignet's many French demonstration tours.
(R. Jouhaud)

construction, bearing series number HM.290, and called *Le Sport de l'Air*. Having built his prototype, Mignet set off to prove the aircraft on a 1,200 mile flight to the south of France and back. This flight was in an unregistered aircraft by a pilot who did not have an official French pilot's licence. Was this to be 1935/1936 all over again?

The new aircraft was first publicised in the 20 April 1946 edition of the French magazine *Les Ailes* and two months later in the Belgian magazine *L'Aéronef* which also announced that it was handling sales of drawings for the HM.290. Like the HM.280, the HM.290 was a single-seater built of wood and fabric. The prototype was fitted with a 30 hp Poinsard and had a span of 18 ft (5.5 m), slightly larger than that of the HM.280. With such an engine it was really only suitable for light pilots, but Mignet noted that better performance could be achieved with engines up to 50 hp. Like the HM.280, the HM.290 had easily foldable wings, these having a span of only 7 ft 10 in (2.4 m) when folded. Mignet claimed the HM.290 could lift off after a take-off run of only 160 ft (50 m) and land in double that.

Hundreds of potential builders, mainly in Belgium and France, but also further afield in Britain, Canada and elsewhere, bought plans hoping to build their own HM.290s. One of these was the British sport aviation enthusiast and fellow builder Arthur Ord-Hume. Ord-Hume recalled in a recent article for the British magazine *Aeroplane Monthly* just what a potential builder got when he bought plans from *L'Aéronef*: 'The purchaser of the plan kit received two sheets of paper. One was a very thin but extremely large sheet of paper which encompassed the constructional drawings for the entire aircraft, copiously annotated in Mignet's own neat writing. The other was a strip of that very poor quality newsprint popular on the Continent until quite recently. This comprised a translation of every word on the plan into five languages. Keying translation to plan proved quite a task but was not impossible.

'Even the border of the plan contained notes about the aircraft, its operation and how mobile the aircraft was, being possible to hangar it in a conventional garage. The top left-hand border, though, bore a dedication which must have helped a little to relieve the sadness which Mignet felt:

To the memory of Annette Mignet, who enlivened the 1934-1939 'Pou-du-Ciel' campaign, courageous little Frenchwoman, kidnapped and killed without reason on the 10th December 1944, near Saujon Charente Maritime, by three bandits of Dordogne-Limousin, known, arrested, questioned, released . . . Friend reader, known that you know this horrible thing, unworthy of a great and noble nation . . . .'

In the same month that the HM.290 was announced, Robert Guidon, the President of the Pou du Ciel Club at Valenciennes, called for the formation of a Pou du Ciel Club of France. From the interest this created a meeting was arranged for 24 November 1946, sponsored jointly by the Valenciennes Pou Club and the *Amicale d'Aviation Légère de Lyon* (Friends of Light Aviation in Lyon) with a view to forming a national group to support the interests of amateur aircraft builders. From this regional meeting came arrangements for a national meeting to be held in Paris. This gave rise to the formation of the *Réseau du Sport de l'Air* – still the guardians of the amateur aircraft movement in France today. Flea aviator Elie Layat chaired the meeting and knew that Mignet had a secret wish to be President of this new organisation. As it happened, although Mignet was present, Pierre Lacour was elected as the RSA's first President with seven other members voted to the administering council, four of them Flea-fanatics, but not including Mignet.

This was a significant snub to Mignet. Another snub was just around the corner, one that was even more insulting. Officialdom in France still remembered the problems and difficulties that had emanated from Mignet's designs of the 1930s. On 28 July 1938 a 'permit' system, not dissimilar to the Authorisation to Fly legislation adopted earlier in Britain, was

brought into being for homebuilt aircraft. This was the *Certificat de Navigabilité Restreinte d'Aéronef* (CNRA) or Restricted Certificate of Airworthiness. With the new moves towards amateur aviation in France, the Secretary General of Civil and Commercial Aviation reintroduced the CNRA system on 4 November 1946. Special clauses in the CNRA system were aimed to remove any reckless tendency in amateur builders, including the quaint term 'voluntary suicide'. The Authorities were clearly on the look-out for designs that were not going to meet their standards. With Mignet back on the scene with the HM.290 there were already grave rumblings and misgivings. Mignet's machine was subjected to tests at the *Centre d'Essais en Vol* at Bretigny, near Paris. The aircraft was subjected to + 3.5g and – 1g and, at the beginning of 1947, the CEV pronounced the HM.290, in their opinion, unsound.

Mignet's supporters were horrified by this renewed and unjustified attempt to stifle his revival. Mignet made most vigorous protests, pointing out that the HM.290 was a light aeroplane with a small engine, only intended to carry a small pilot. He had redesigned the aircraft as the HM.293, which had the same external dimensions, but was stronger and suitable for a 40 hp engine and a much heavier pilot – but too late. Blow after blow after blow seemed to follow Mignet wherever he went and whatever he did. Mignet's experience was

Albert Baron's HM.293, equipped with a Salmson radial of 40 hp, built in 1952.
(Geoffrey P. Jones Collection)

Built by M. Perrin at Geneva, HM.293 HB-SUS was test flown by Swiss Mignet 'disciple' Louis Cosandey.
(Geoffrey P. Jones Collection)

Built at Toulouse by Monsieur Rouax is this unusual tricycle undercarriage HM.293M F-PVQM. Powerplant is the ubiquitous converted Volkswagen engine.
(Geoffrey P. Jones)

to be met much later by Emilien Croses when he tried to get a full-blown certificate for his EC-7 in the early 1970s (see Chapter Fifteen).

Having been unable to obtain the justice he considered due after Annette's murder in 1944, and now receiving official rebuttal of his latest tandem-wing design Henri felt that it was time, once again, to leave for pastures new. He must gather some semblance of dignity, think things out and in a fresh and new environment continue his main delight: design work. The latter, certainly seemed impossible in France.

Fleas in post-war France

Despite these events, Mignet's impact on post-war French homebuilding was considerable and long lasting, despite the best efforts of officialdom. Amateurs were still building and flying Mignet-designed, tandem-wing aircraft, a considerable number of which were HM.293s – despite the original ruling on the aircraft. One of the first HM.293s to be completed was the work of René and Roger Lefebvre, who used the wings of an old HM.14, built a new fuselage and fitted a two-cylinder Salmson engine. They were helped in this project by young Pierre Robin, later to etch out a name for himself in connection with the Jodel light aircraft range, which gave rise to his own highly successful line of light aircraft including the modern-day Robin ATL (*Avion Très Léger* - ultralight trainer) which is in production at the Dijon-Darois facility.

In 1947 André Tisserand built a three-winged Flea powered by a 27 hp Ava at Sers in Tunisia. The third wing was in fact a stabiliser fitted high on the tail. A similar modification was also carried out to HM.14 No.52 that was built by André Thomas at Béziers. Thomas emigrated to Ethiopia and his Flea was acquired by Pierre Alquier from *L'Aéro Club du Tarn*. These three-winged versions were called Pou-PCCC and were considered more stable and safer than modified versions of the original HM.14.

Two other famous French amateur aviators were also to make their mark, thanks to Mignet and his designs, in the late 1940s. Emilien Croses has already been touched upon lightly, and will feature prominently in Chapter Fifteen. In 1948 he completed his two seat Croses EC-01 F-WCZP, powered by a 50 hp Boitel engine. Following a complete test at CEV Bretigny, it acquired a CNRA certificate. Claude Piel was the second of these notables. Progress on his first aircraft was slow. Piel used to visit the Vivien bookshop in Paris, and there in 1943 he found a copy of Mignet's *Le Sport de l'Air*. This was an eye-opener for the apprentice carpenter and a find that was to guide the rest of his career. Piel's first aircraft, the CP-10 Pinocchio, was directly inspired by the Flea, although he suppressed the wing dihedral and adopted a simpler aerofoil section – the NACA

23010 profile that was to be a trademark of many of his later designs. Before building the real thing, Piel built a scale model of the CP-10, had it tested in the Eiffel wind tunnel and then proceeded to build the full-size machine and learn to fly. As F-WFDA it first flew at Moisselles on 25 September 1948. It flew well for five hours 25 minutes before it crashed in an out-of-limits low pass on 17 January 1949. Various parts from the CP-10 crash were salvaged and used in the CP-20. History was rewriting itself again – Mignet had done the same thing in the 1920s and 1930s. Piel went on to build a varied series of aircraft, perhaps the most well known being the CP.301 Emeraude two-seater. This design is still in production, many years after Piel's death, in highly modified form, by Avions Mudry at Bernay as the CAP-10 two-seater and the CAP-20 single-seater aerobatic aircraft.

Meanwhile the HM.290 and the HM.293 designs were to go on to be probably the most widely built and flown examples of Mignet's 'family'. Their popularity spread around the world with examples being built in Belgium, Canada, France, Great Britain, the Netherlands, Switzerland, the United States and in South America. The HM.293 was eminently suited to the favourite engine of homebuilders in the 1950s, 1960s and after, the converted Volkswagen Beetle engine. This may well have been one of two reasons that go some way to explaining the type's popularity.

The second reason is to be found across the Atlantic. In 1958 aeronautical engineer George Jacquemin, living in Streetsville, Ontario, Canada, undertook the translation of the HM.290 plans into English. Along with this he prepared a comprehensive manual for its construction, including details of weight and balance. He then did a similar exercise with the diminutive HM.16, with which he had become fascinated – see Chapters Nine and Ten. Jacquemin then turned over the plans to Chris Falconar, who operated a homebuilt aircraft plans, kits and supplies business, Falconar Aircraft, based at Edmonton, Alberta. (Falconar also had such designs as the F-9 and F-11 remodelled Jodels and the Maranda RA.14 Loisir monoplane on his books, so was clearly very interested in French designs.) Later Falconar Aircraft was superseded by CDX Aviation Sales, first at Seattle, Washington, USA, and then back at Edmonton. Chris Falconar and Falconar Aviation are now back to the fore

and again selling plans of the HM.290 and HM.293 to anyone who wants them. Falconar sold HM.293 plans and materials kits with technical help in North America, but also further afield including Australia, Great Britain and New Zealand. Falconar estimates that he has sold around 250 sets of plans and about ten kits. Only about fifteen of these have actually been completed, mainly in Canada and the United States.

Thoughts on the HM.290 family

Jacquemin also worked on the HM.293 with Falconar as well on the HM.297 which had a simplified fuselage structure. Jacquemin moved from Canada to become a senior aeronautical engineer with Lockheed at their Burbank, California, plant in the 1970s. In 1979 Falconar visited him to talk about Flying Fleas. Jacquemin expressed concern about several features and, courtesy of Chris Falconar, there follows a brief transcript of that conversation, one of considerable relevance to any potential Flea builder or flyer (or even designer?) of today:

'To overcome rudder sensitivity I would recommend a fin be added as has been done to the HM.297 and by François Lederlin with his '380L [see Chapter Fifteen]. The fin area should be 60 or 70 per cent and the rudder 30 or 40 per cent [of the total vertical stabilizer area]. A large windshield and open cockpit are 'no-nos' unless the fin and rudder are much larger, especially for the short HM.290. The plans for the HM.290 show a canopy top so that relatively smooth air flows past the fin and rudder.

'A new rudder has been designed for the HM.293, the old, fully moveable, vertical tail surface having been divided in two. The front 35 per cent is fixed to the fuselage and becomes the fin with the remaining 65 per cent being the new rudder. This plan also shows a steerable tailwheel with control cable routing. To relieve stick pressure, due to loading at different speeds, power on and off, most new Flea designs incorporate a trailing edge tab or camber flap, usually on the rear wing. The HM.370 had tabs on both wings and the Lederlin HM.380L has the one on the rear wing only which deflects up and down. Louis Cosandey in Switzerland [see Chapter Nine] has one on the rear wing of his HM.293 that deflects upwards only. I recommend this one particularly for the larger and faster Mignet designs. I would also recommend the use, wherever possible, of a tricycle landing gear because of its inherent stability – the tri-gear makes cross-wind landings that much easier as well.'

Also available via Chris Falconar is the translation of some important notes scribed by Henri Mignet himself about flying the HM.290. These are also quoted as an indication of the technique involved in flying one of these aircraft.

'A conventional aircraft pilot who has never flown a Flying Flea should take off with the HM.290 only in very calm weather in order to get accustomed to the lateral control, which is somewhat different. The stability of the HM.290 satisfies the requirements of the French Certificate of Airworthiness: Norme 2004 (loading requirements CINA) in the following classes: 1) horizontal flight with full power, 2) aircraft in a dive, the stick is pulled back to the position corresponding to level flight. The aircraft levels off without further action of the controls.

'Stick free, the front wing is automatically stable in spite of its pivot being placed well forward. The suction created by the rear wing cancels the front wing pitching moment. The front wing is in equilibrium. In turbulent weather the front wing acts as a gust alleviation device, the stick moves constantly about a mean position and the aircraft does not bounce around. To go faster, it is necessary to push on the stick and pull in order to go slower. As soon as the stick is let free, it comes back to the trim position – the speed stabilises itself.

'When the stick is pulled too far aft, the pilot feels it shaking harder the further aft the stick is pulled. If the pilot insists a slight stall will occur, but the aircraft will lose only about ten feet and control will be regained immediately. With cruising power, the aircraft will not show any stall but will 'mush' a little with rudder control remaining effective. Near the ground, this gentle stall will probably damage the landing gear and the aircraft might turn over on its back if you are unlucky. This would not be a bad accident, but since the aircraft tells when the wrong manoeuvre is made, the pilot can do it only voluntarily and therefore has no excuse for such an accident. During sharp turns or turns at too slow a speed, the stick will also shake and warn the pilot. Too heavily loaded or underpowered, the HM.290 may not be able to take-off or will do so reluctantly. This, however, is not dangerous with the aircraft because its stability is greater at large angles of attack and both controls are effective right through the stall.'

That the master's style had altered somewhat in the years following the writing of both editions of *Le Sport de l'Air* must be apparent to the reader. Not only had Mignet seen much sadness since the initial, exuberant, writings, but he had also learnt a considerable amount more about aerodynamics, flying and the operation of aircraft. As his aircraft became more complex and challenging, so Mignet's writing became more precise and, with regret, less effusive and enthusiastic.

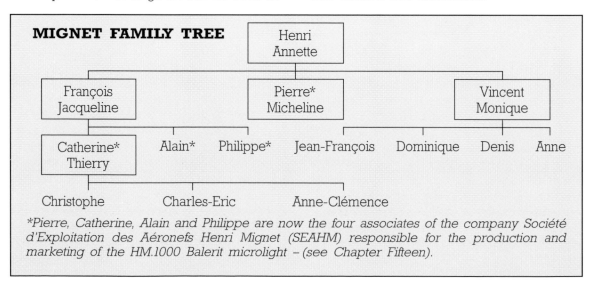

MIGNET FAMILY TREE

Henri
Annette

François / Jacqueline — Pierre* / Micheline — Vincent / Monique

Catherine* / Thierry — Alain* — Philippe* — Jean-François — Dominique — Denis — Anne

Christophe — Charles-Eric — Anne-Clémence

Pierre, Catherine, Alain and Philippe are now the four associates of the company Société d'Exploitation des Aéronefs Henri Mignet (SEAHM) responsible for the production and marketing of the HM.1000 Balerit microlight – (see Chapter Fifteen).

Amateur-built HM.290s and derivatives

France

Type	Constructor	Regn	Engine	Notes
HM.290	Henri Mignet	–	Mengin 30hp	Prototype
HM.290	Pierre Mignet	F-PERF	Poinsard 25hp	*Le Petit Bouquet*
HM.290	Perrin	–	Poinsard 35hp	–
HM.290	Poulin	–	Poinsard 25hp	–
HM.290D	Gagnat/ Delpech	F-PTXX	Volkswagen	–
HM.293	Baconnier	F-PLUJ	Ava 25hp	–
HM.293	Baron	F-PFRH	Salmson 40hp	–
HM.293	Baude	–	Poinsard 35hp	–
HM.293	A.C.M.Bauler	–	Volkswagen 25hp	Test flown by J. de la Farge
HM.293	Bernet	–	Salmson 40hp	Built in Tunisia
HM.293	A.C.Brou	F-PFKZ	Sarolea 32hp	Test flown by Boucherot
HM.293	Casterman	–	Volkswagen 25hp	Test flown by J. de la Farge
HM.293	Estang	F-PDVS	Train 40hp	Test flown by Fauvel
HM.293	Hildebrandt	F-PGYA	Volkswagen 40hp	–
HM.293	Lefebvre	–	Salmson	Assisted by Pierre Robin
HM.293	Martin	F-PKFK	Volkswagen 25hp	Now 00-32 in Belgium
HM.293	Philippe	F-PIIG	Volkswagen 40hp	–
HM.293	Rivière	–	Poinsard 25hp	
HM.293	Roch	F-PYEN	–	–
HM.293D	Dumont	F-PYFG	Poinsard 35hp	–
HM.293M	Rouaux	F-PVQM	Volkswagen	Tricycle undercarriage
HM.293W	Watteel	F-PYHD	–	Tricycle undercarriage

Argentina

Type	Constructor	Regn	Engine	Notes
HM.290	Rodolfo Maurette	LV-X90	Volkswagen	Also LV-X82
HM.294	Henri Mignet	LV-X5	Aeronca 36hp	–

Belgium

Type	Constructor	Regn	Engine	Notes
HM.290	Bassine	00-16	–	–
HM.290	Bielen	00-04	–	–
HM.290	Descamps	00-03	–	–
HM.290	Dochy	00-12	–	–
HM.290	Henssen	00-05	–	–
HM.290	Herman/ Leblanc	00-02	–	–
HM.293	Bailligand	00-96	–	–
HM.293	Branche	00-42	–	–
HM.293	Brion	00-01	–	–
HM.293	Collard	00-21	–	–
HM.293	Debaillie	00-41	Continental 50hp	Test flown by F. Noiset
HM.293	van Domme	00-60	–	–

Type	Constructor	Regn	Engine	Notes
HM.293	F. Noiset	00-11	Continental 65hp	At AELR Museum
HM.293	Rocour	00-18	–	–
HM.293	Verplanke	00-33	–	–

Canada
Type	Constructor	Regn	Engine	Notes
HM.290	Johnson	CF-SIO	Volkswagen	–
HM.290	John Sayle	CF-RFH	McCulloch 70hp	Now at CMFT, Vancouver
HM.293	Fred Bishop	C-FERN	Continental	–
HM.297	Hamel/Duval	C-GUQG	–	–

Netherlands
Type	Constructor	Regn	Engine	Notes
HM.290	Siebelink	PH-MIG	Daf B74 25hp	Not yet flown

Switzerland
Type	Constructor	Regn	Engine	Notes
HM.293	Perrin	HB-SUS	Mengin 32hp	Test flown by L Cosandey

United Kingdom
Type	Constructor	Regn	Engine	Notes
HM.293	Bill Cole	G-AXPG	Volkswagen	–

United States
Type	Constructor	Regn	Engine	Notes
HM.290	–	–	–	At Houston, Texas
HM.293	Phil Howell	N2931	McCulloch 55hp	–
HM.293	Love	N7541U	Continental 40hp	–
HM.293	George Pankau	–	–	–
HM.293	Duane Rock	N4067	Volkswagen 40hp	–
HM.293	VanLoh	N30120	–	–

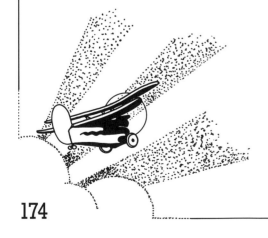

174

Chapter 12
IN THE WILDERNESS

SUFFERING MANY SAD BLOWS between 1936 and the end of the Second World War, Mignet, now a widower, had already experienced the problems of world-wide travel and attempts to put his designs into production. His two years in the USA prior to his return home in 1939 had not been successful from the point of view of seeing his designs in mass production. American attitudes and innovations had, however, regenerated his belief that success was just around the corner.

Post-war France contained too many sad memories for Mignet. He had been responsible for the first amateur aircraft constructors' movement in France, *Réseau des Amateurs de l'Air (RAA)*. With the post-war French government anxious for the country's aviation industry, including homebuilders, to re-establish itself as quickly as possible, designs large and small were beginning to appear again. To support this born-again movement the *Réseau du Sport de l'Air (RSA)* was founded in 1947 with Pierre Lacour as its first president. While RSA embodied the spirit of Mignet, he was not to be one of its officials.

Embittered, and full of personal and professional sorrow, he decided to take up an offer he had received from friends in Argentina. This was 1947, and it was to be the start of an eleven-year period of gipsy-like existence, taking Mignet around the world in pursuit of his objective – to put his designs into commercial production.

Mignet and his Flying Fleas were already well known in South America. In Buenos Aires in 1935 a group calling themselves The Circle of Henri Mignet Aviators was formed. There were an estimated twenty-plus amateurs building HM.14s in Argentina at that time, including M. Bardin, the Frigoni brothers, Roberto Gallardo and Jorge U. Pallich.

Leaving the snows and grey skies of wintertime France, Mignet travelled by sea to Rio de Janeiro and then on to Buenos Aires. He was greeted by an old friend from before the war, Yves Jean Arrambide. Here plans were finalised for creating a factory for putting some of Mignet's designs into production. This was established in one of the most beautiful and healthy parts of Argentina at a private aerodrome at the little town of Alta Garcia, to the south of Cordoba. The workshop boasted excellent tooling and equipment, everything seemed to point to success. Spirits ran high.

The first product from Alta Gracia was the HM.294, called *Butterfly*. A single-seater of wood and fabric construction, it was powered by a 35 hp twin-cylinder Aeronca engine. *Butterfly* succeeded in gaining an experimental licence and was registered LV-X5. Mignet later recalled his first year in Argentina, clearly nostalgic. 'The little Nantes Grammar School boarder, companion of Jules Verne's *Children of Captain Grant* and the solitary experimenter from the Bois de Bouleaux who became the 'Patron Saint' of amateurs was now in the

intake beneath the propeller that resembled the open jaws of an animal; Mignet waggishly painted a pair of eyes above and brought the impressive aircraft to life. With the name *Annette Mignet* inscribed on the starboard side of the cowling, Mignet toured extensively through Argentina in the HM.300 demonstrating the new aircraft to potential purchasers and backers alike.

Mignet found Argentina and its people charming, gracious and spontaneous but found a marked contrast between everyday life and South American business attitudes. Always a sensitive person, Mignet took the opportunity while in Argentina to deepen his intellectual and spiritual understanding. Buenos Aires was, and to a large extent still is, a European capital cast into the southern hemisphere, attracting many intellectuals to come and settle. Like Mignet, people were escaping something and were trying to 'find' freedom, success, or

inexpressibly charming situation of being able to fly his own plane above the endless pampas, crossing the mysterious skies of far away Argentina.'

The next product of Mignet's and Arrambide's new company, FADAM (Fabrica Argentina de Avions Mignet), was a much larger aircraft, the HM.300 which was completed by 1949. It was a three-seater, powered by a 125 hp Continental flat-four engine, and had an enclosed cabin, a welded steel-tube fuselage and wood and fabric wings – a very different beast from anything Mignet had previously designed. The engine was completely cowled and featured a large air

The products of Alta Gracia, the HM.294 'Butterfly' (foreground) with the three-seat HM.300 behind. (RSA, via Jacques Avril)

peace. Some were refugees from political, religious and social repression. Others found attitudes in Latin America more tolerant to their beliefs or political standpoints.

Henri mixed within these groups, meeting regularly in Buenos Aires and Cordoba for discussions, lectures, seminars and for the exchange of ideas. With the Andes as a backcloth, Mignet did much soul-searching here in the early 1950s and described this elitist, ordered community as being 'retired from the world, perhaps the greatest Thinkers of our day'.

While Mignet enjoyed this side of life in Argentina, a philosopher among philosophers, the seemingly always unstable and often corrupt business world perplexed and frustrated him. Although essentially a sound aircraft, like any other prototype, the HM.300 was subject to improvement and refinement and considerable improvisation. It became clear that unless FADAM made regular 'subventions' to the ministry involved, the official view of the HM.300 and its future production would remain negative, if not obstructive. Despite this, FADAM attracted investment and this influx of capital tempted one of Mignet's associates to earn a quick fortune and he started to embezzle funds. To Mignet, the idealist, it was a new and unpleasant experience.

Fortunately for Henri, his children were totally committed to his aspirations and in 1951, his son Pierre came more significantly into his life. Pierre shared his father's temperament and liked many of the things his father did. This affinity resulted in a very strong bond which Henri often qualified by use of the Arab proverb, 'When your son grows up, make him your brother'.

To Brazil

Jean Garelly, a former French Air Force pilot from the Second World War, had seen Mignet demonstrating the HM.300 at Don Torcuato aerodrome and was impressed, inviting the little Frenchman to come to his new home, Brazil, and continue his work in a partnership. With troubles and frustrations in Argentina, Henri and Pierre moved in 1951 and set-to, starting from scratch again.

New home was Santos, on the Atlantic coast to the south east of Sao Päulo. With the assistance of the charming Jean and Luc

Garelly, who became attentive and devoted friends of the Mignets, a site was chosen for the Brazilian Mignet plant at Santos' Jean Mermoz aerodrome, founded by the famous French aviator after which it was named.

Construction of the *Aviones Mignet do Brasil* 'factory' gives an insight into the difficulties that had to be overcome. Materials were imported from France for its construction – not intentionally, but by chance they acquired a consignment of wooden packing cases that had been used for the import of Saint-Gobin glassware. Their premises were in the form of a lean-to at the side of a much larger hangar with an enormous roof. Santos is on a narrow swampy coastal strip, squeezed in between the Atlantic and the mountains. When the rain falls it comes with true tropical fury. Water pouring from the adjoining hangar roof frequently flooded the Mignet workshop – there were drains and waterpipes everywhere, a tremendous nuisance. Rainfall was not the only climatic problem at Santos; the heat often meant temperatures of over 41°C causing machines as well as their operators to overheat over even the smallest piece of work.

Despite this it was to be here that design and construction of Mignet's first 'modern' aircraft started to take shape. The HM.310 was a two-seater, employing the same construction methods as the Argentinian HM.300, but was smaller, lighter and powered by a 100 hp Continental. Apparently fully aerobatic, the HM.310 flew for the first time eight months after work on the project had started, with Mignet at the controls.

Photographs of the HM.310 prototype show it carrying the registration PT-ZCA; it was also christened *Estafette*. The HM.300 built in Argentina had been large, too heavy and had too big an engine to carry three occupants economically. *Estafette* in comparison was much lighter and attention had been given to streamlining, its neat, spatted main wheels and faired undercarriage legs being more reminiscent of a modern touring light aircraft. Although the *Estafette* was beyond the price range of the average man in the street, attention to economy came through the incorporation of wing folding – first adopted on the HM.280 during the war – and this could afford savings on hangarage.

Up to 1965 the Aero Club at Santos were operating a red and white HM.310, registered

The HM.310 *Estafette* registered PT-ZCA, built by
Aviones Mignet do Brasil.
(RSA, via Jacques Avril)

as PT-AUQ. It cannot be confirmed if this was
the prototype reregistered or a second
example. Further uncertainty accompanies a
report that PT-AUQ was exported to Spain in
the 1960s.

Mignet returned briefly to Argentina with the
idea of reviving FADAM but, like many other
projects that tried to get going there at the time,
it came up against the economic and
bureaucratic problems that had dogged his
attempts a few years earlier.

Back in Brazil the HM.310 was a success as
an aeroplane, confirmed by innumerable flights
across mountains and virgin forests. No finance
could be found to perpetuate *Aviones Mignet
do Brasil*, however. Like Argentina the
economic situation was precarious and
potential backers were reluctant to launch a
new industrial concern even though the
Brazilian Air Ministry were favourably disposed
towards Mignet and his tandem-wing aircraft.

In 1953 Pierre Mignet was recalled to France
for military service. This occurrence prompted
Mignet and Garelly to consider the future of the
programme and to review improvements that
they still wanted to make to the HM.310.

Pierre Triou, Mignet's brother-in-law and
Annette's elder brother, mentioned in Chapter
One, was now living in Japan. In 1953 he wrote
to Mignet in Brazil from his home in Tokyo and
suggested that there must be opportunities in
Japan for Mignet and his designs. An energetic
and clear-sighted people, the Japanese were
in a post-war revival that was to reach
legendary proportions. The Japanese were
looking for goods to build and export and Triou
felt sure they would be attracted to the new
breed of Fleas.

To Japan

And so it was that in February 1954, with the
complete agreement and support of Garelly,
Mignet packed up his bags yet again and
boarded the MV *American-Maru* in Rio, setting
sail for Japan via Salvador (Bahia), Panama and
San Francisco, arriving in Yokohama to be
greeted by Triou and his family. Once again,
excitement and anticipation seized Mignet

despite the formidable foreignness and attractiveness of the 'land of workers'.

There had been at least one Flea in Japan before the arrival of its inventor. In 1936 the Japan Aeroplane Works Ltd of Kanazawa, near Yokohama built a very orthodox – even down to the Aubier et Dunne H-4 engine – HM.14. Registered J-BGEG it was designated the NH.1 Hibari (Skylark). It was planned to install an Ishikawajima engine, but whether this happened or even whether the NH.1 flew is not recorded.

In 1949 Tachikawa Aircraft of Tokyo had been reformed and, as soon as legislation permitted, in 1952, started production of Japan's first post-war aircraft, the parasol-winged R-52 and R-53. It soon became clear to Mignet that his belief was well-founded in Japan's commercial fervour and in their desire to expand their range of products and to gain experience in production for the light, civil aircraft market. Mignet had soon reached an agreement with Shin Tachikawa. They planned to build a slightly modified version of the HM.310 from the days in Brazil, this time powered by a Continental C90 of 90 hp.

Production of the type designated the HM.330 originally and then renamed the R-HM, was soon written into Tachikawa's expanding programme. Three airframes were planned, one for ground tests, one kept in sections held in reserve, and the third (constructor's number 03) was to be the flying prototype. Construction and progress towards the first flight of the new design proceeded far more slowly than Mignet would have wished. This was due in no small way to the language and writing barrier and the general incompatibility between Japanese and Western logic.

These problems were eventually resolved and at a major USAF base the R-HM made a somewhat hurried first take-off between a Douglas C-124 Globemaster transport that was departing and an inbound Boeing B-29 Superfortress bomber that was waiting to land. 'It all happened very quickly,' Mignet recalled several years later, 'The new plane that had only been ground-run twice, for ten minutes

Tachikawa R-HM, or HM.330, the only design built during Mignet's short stay in Japan.
(John Underwood)

each time, stationary and fully chocked, got a green light – so it was 'GO'. With full throttle it was now too late to turn back.' It was an important trial, witnessed by the dry and ice-cold Managing Director of Shin Tachikawa who was also determined to be the very first passenger in his company's promising new aircraft. The R-HM was called *Sakura* (Cherry Tree in Blossom) a name that delighted Mignet.

Henri was now well paid, living in his own new house and, perhaps most pleasing to this rejected wanderer, was, under the Japanese system of hierarchy and work, a highly respected and important figure at Tachikawa. He was now better off materially than he had been at any time since 1944. This brief spell of respectability was short-lived. The private aircraft market in Japan was no better than it had been in South America. The lack of a market and Mignet's non-renewable residency permit expiring meant that it would soon be time for him to hit the road again.

The flying prototype of the R-HM *Sakura* was registered JA3094 and was displayed at a Trade Fair in Tokyo in 1955. Tachikawa thought that they could continue the development and production programme without Mignet, but soon discovered when he left Japan in 1955 that it was more than a designer/technician that was missing, but the major driving spirit of the project. JA3094 was preserved and can still be seen to this day at the Kotsu Transportation Museum in the Kanda district of Tokyo.

The Volkswagen-engined HM.320, built in Morocco in 1956.
(RSA, via Jacques Avril)

And Morocco

Anticipating his departure from Japan, Mignet had already put out feelers around the world as to where he might try his next venture. India was considered, but negotiations came to nought. In May 1955 he left Japan for Casablanca in Morocco, a country that had seen many pre-war HM.14 builders, including perhaps one of the heaviest ever, Gilbert Mourlan, who tipped the scales at over sixteen stone (102 kg) and had built Flea No. 4 during 1935.

Here Mignet set up *La Société des Avions Henri Mignet* building a single-seater, the HM.320 and the two-seat HM.350. At the same time he started work on two new designs, the HM.360, a development of the single-seat HM.290 of 1946 and also the HM.380 two-seater.

His resultant demonstrations of both the HM.320 and HM.350 in Morocco were quite convincing.

Since 1947 Mignet had travelled the world, gained immense experience, designed and built several new tandem-wing aircraft, but with none of them had he achieved commercial success. But after 11 years his exile was soon to end.

The other Moroccan product, the HM.350, continued refinement of the side-by-side cabin theme.
(RSA, via Jacques Avril)

Chapter 13

TEMPTED HOME

MIGNET MUST HAVE BEEN PLEASED TO receive Monsieur Agesilas from the *Service de la Formation Aéronautique* (SFACT – the government-run body promoting and advising on light aviation development) in France, and to have the chance to show him his drawings and calculations and to demonstrate his latest designs, particularly the HM.350. This was a side-by-side two-seater that was a distillation of his experience in design and construction of tandem wing Fleas around the world during the previous ten years. With a mix of wood and metal construction it had larger wings than previous similar designs with 32 ft 10 in (10 m) and 19 ft 8 in (6 m) spans and a total wing area of 200 square feet (18.6 square metres). The undercarriage was of the 'cross-wind' type, a reverse tricycle arrangement that lent itself to better landings without ailerons. With its 90 hp Continental C90 flat-four engine the HM.350 would cruise at an encouraging 110 mph (180 kph). Registered F-WHQT, the prototype first flew on 5 March 1957.

Mignet described Agesilas's reaction to his latest and very much matured Flea as 'a revelation'. It seemed to Agesilas absolutely essential that Mignet return home to France to help promote the progress of French light aviation. He expressed these views in his letter published in the aviation press on 8 August 1957, saying he wanted to aid the development of this 'novelty', and now that the growing post-war homebuild movement was approaching its

silver anniversary he felt that a priority was to return the promoter of the Flea to France.

Agesilas was not the only one with this view. The French organisation *Pro-Avia* had been formed to promote the development of light aviation and a string of airfields and air routes that the private aviator could use. The leader of the *Pro-Avia* group at the time was Daniel Robert-Bancharelle who, in the 1930s, had been one of Mignet's disciples, having built his own HM.14. Robert-Bancharelle and *Pro-Avia* soon received the full support of Agesilas and SFACT and the two of them, together with an industrialist from Caen in Normandy, financed and organised the return of Henri Mignet to his native France in 1958. It was only at this stage, after 2,000 hours flying, that Mignet finally obtained a *French* pilot's licence.

As well as bringing the inventor of the Flea and the latest of his aeroplanes, the HM.350, back to France, this group of supporters also sought to give Mignet the means to work and earn his living in the way that he always wanted to. SFACT saw the setting up of a light aircraft design competition as one way of doing this, requesting entrants to design an economical two-seat-training and touring aircraft. Call it what you will, the criteria for the competition were chosen so that they conformed very closely to those of the already designed and built HM.350. It was now up to others to see what they could come up with and this they certainly did with another 54 projects

Back home. Mignet with his HM.350 prototype at Toussus-le-Noble, near Paris.
(Geoffrey P. Jones Collection)

eventually being entered for the SFACT contest by the closing date.

Mignet's HM.350 certainly got the French light aviation world talking Fleas again. Memories of the HM.14, its longitudinal stability problems affected by the position of the centre of gravity and by the gap between the wings, were all revived. The HM.350 had none of the faults of the original Flea though, but retained its extraordinary non-stall qualities, freedom from spinning and absolute safety in turns

The HM.350 at Dax airfield. Mignet's return from Morocco, with this aircraft, was the occasion for a third 'renaissance' for his designs in his homeland.
(Geoffrey P. Jones Collection)

through its two-axis control system. As well as this revival of talk of tandem wings, Mignet's biggest thrill on his return was the touching friendship of so many people and the faith of his supporters who were all united by a single enthusiasm of which he considered himself the initiator. This was a great consolation to him after so many troubled years and gave him a major boost to continue his work.

The designs for the HM.360 and HM.380 that he had started in Morocco were published from his new headquarters which were established at Saint-Lô on the Cherbourg peninsula of Northern France. *Société Manche Aéronautique* was set up primarily to produce the entry for the SFACT competition and, it was hoped, for its subsequent production. Saint-Lô was the place for the first HM.360 to be built, by L. F. Gancel, under Mignet's supervision. With Mignet at the controls this aircraft took off on its maiden flight in June 1959. Powered by a 65 hp Continental A65 engine, the HM.360 was a single-seater but was intended to have a better performance than its precursor, the HM.290. Its wing also had a larger span, of 21 ft 4 in (6.5 m)

In France several other HM.360 builders started work, including Jacques le Goubin, who built F-PKFV and fitted a 40 hp Salmson radial to it, George Andrey, and colleague from the Bordeaux area with F-POIJ, Guy Rivet, with F-PSYN, both being Continental powered. More recently has been Pierre Bousselaire with F-PYHC to which he fitted a 1600 cc Volkswagen conversion and reverse tricycle undercarriage.

In 1959, the first HM.360 became airborne,

HM.360 No.92, built by George Andrey, power coming from the ubiquitous Continental A65.
(Reginald Jouhaud)

Continental-powered HM.360 No.128 F-PSYN, built by Guy Rivet.
(Geoffrey P. Jones Collection)

An artist's impression of the HM.370. It was never built, but showed the state-of-the-art thinking on the tandem wing concept.
(Geoffrey P. Jones Collection)

plans for this and the HM.380 were being sold and *Société Manche Aéronautique* had been established, work proceeded apace on the modified version of the HM.350 for the entry in the SFACT competition. In working towards his definitive entry, Mignet reproduced details of his HM.370, a little-known project that never resulted in the construction of an actual aircraft, but showed the way that his thoughts were then being directed. The HM.370 was a clean-lined, 'beefy'-looking two-seater, constructed of steel tube with no externally visible control lines or support rigging to wings or tail. It was of similar dimensions to the HM.350 with its 32 ft 10 in (10 m) span and a 90 hp engine. The main difference was the rear wing, which had a smaller area and narrower chord than the main wing. Both wings had tailing-edge trim tabs in their centres.

Amongst the aircraft that did not win the SFACT comtition was a product of Morane-Saulnier, one of France's longest-established aircraft manufacturing companies. Their entry was an all-metal two-seater low-wing tourer with tailwheel

Competitor to the HM.390 in the abortive SFACT competition was the Legrand-Simon LS.60 two seater.
(Geoffrey P. Jones)

Mignet's competitor, the LS.60 was an unusual-looking high wing monoplane with a tailwheel fuselage enclosing a side-by-side two-seater cabin. The metal wing was one of the design's principal features, being of narrow chord, with full-span leading edge slots, large differential flaps and ailerons at the tips. A considerable dihedral on each wing and a large and high tail and rudder all pointed to this aircraft's being a superb short take-off and landing (STOL) aeroplane with excellent manoeuvrability. In any realistic competition it seemed set to give Mignet's challenge a fair run for its money. The prototype was registered F-WJSA and is still active (now registered as F-PJSA).

The HM.390 was a three-seater development of the HM.350 and was built with a steel tube fuselage frame with laminated polyester skin, its occupants being seated side-by-side in front with a single seat behind. It was powered by the ever-reliable Continental C90 enclosed in a neatly-cowled, streamlined nose. The HM.390 had spatted 'cross-wind type' reverse tricycle undercarriage with faired struts supporting

undercarriage and a 90 hp Continental C90, designated the MS.880. It featured a complex wing with lift devices that owed their lineage to the abortive MS.1500 *Epervier* ground-attack aircraft, giving the little MS.880 excellent slow flying and short field characteristics. The MS.880 was refined to become the tricycle undercarriage-equipped MS.880B Rallye two/three-seater which was in production until recently with SOCATA (*Société de Construction d'Avions de Tourisme et d'Affaires*), the light aircraft division of the giant Aérospatiale state-owned aircraft industry; over 3,500 examples have been built.

Entrants in the competition were whittled down to two finalists, the Legrand-Simon LS.60, which was the project of a group of designers and students at Bréguet's factory at Villacoubly near Paris, and Mignet's latest creation, the HM.390. These two aircraft were to be built for a fly-off.

The prototype HM.390, built for the SFACT competition. Its clean lines, reverse tricycle undercarriage and small-looking rudder are apparent.
(RSA, via Jacques Avril)

wings made of light alloy. The prototype was F-WJDY (in the test sequence, later F-PJDY once it had gained its CNRA paperwork) and it made its first flight at Saint-Lô in August 1960. A major departure from the tandem wing concept which Mignet campaigned for ever since 1933, the main wing had ailerons, these were interlinked with the control column and improved still further control effectiveness.

The final years

Mignet wanted to put the HM.390 into production as the Auto-Ciel and in fact built a second example, F-PJXI. He was being shamelessly exploited in his work and, through his dogmatic nature, was having differences of opinion with his associates. While at Saint-Lô Mignet first realised that his declining health was not as a result of the poor working conditions and cold winters, but were the first signs of the cancer that was ultimately to prove fatal. He became increasingly irritable with his compatriots and yet again became totally disillusioned.

He left Saint-Lô, still have heard nothing positive from the SFACT competition, and returned to his roots in western France at Saintonge, near Saintes. The co-ordinator and organiser of the competition, Agesilas, left France to take up a post in America, leaving those at Saint-Lô, minus Mignet, to collaborate in modifications to the design of the HM.390 in which Mignet now wanted no part. He described the situation as 'unpleasant moral and material conditions with the name Mignet effaced from his aircraft which had been modified and altered by incompetence into 'un veau à cinq pattes' a five-hooved calf.

It is reputed that after modifications to the HM.390 a report was prepared on the aircraft, concluding that 'it was a disastrous machine – a manifest failure'. Mignet was not privy to this report, of course, and having been submitted to SFACT it was then passed on to the French Air Ministry. Here, many Mignet followers believe, the aircraft was killed off. Twenty-seven years after the Air Ministry had tried its demolition tactics on the HM.14, the same was happening again. Some felt that the name Mignet was an undesirable attachment to an aircraft and that with the demise of the HM.390, the end of the Mignet line was assured. Not so – it was only the end of the beginning.

A period of convalescence and rest at the family home brought about some improvement in Mignet's health, but early in 1962 the cancer reappeared and he was given no hope by the doctors who were treating him. Mignet was too much of a fighter for such a diagnosis and, having heard about new advances in treatment in Belgium, the very next day appeared at the Belgian Centre of Medical Physique in Brussels, where he was welcomed by Doctor Seret. Mignet spent a month undergoing treatment in Brussels, which was deemed to have been effective. In April 1962 he returned home to continue work on amateur aviation projects, photography, cine films and his new found passion – tape recording sounds. Henri's son Pierre still has a large collection of the films and tapes that Mignet made at Saintonge during the last few years of his life and which are a continuing and poignant reminder of him. As Pierre put it 'It is as if he were there behind me, ready to touch me on the shoulder . . . '.

It was also in 1962 that the American Experimental Aircraft Association made a valiant effort to bring Henri Mignet and Pierre to attend their big annual international fly-in which was then held at Rockford, Illinois (now staged at Oshkosh, Wisconsin and the largest fly-in in the world). The project was spearheaded by his former associate at American-Mignet at Pal-Waukee from before the Second World War, Frank Easton, who was then living in Salem, Ohio. They also hoped to bring one of Mignet's aircraft to the United States from France. Mignet's poor health prevented the wellmeant plans from coming to fruition.

In 1962 and 1963, Mignet was working on what turned out to be his final design, the HM.400, again with a view to commercial production. He made enquiries in the Les Landes region to the south of Bordeaux about suitable workshop premises, but he could not put his heart into the project and anyone he approached would consequently not take him seriously. A two- or a three-seater, the HM.400 had an extremely wide cockpit (4 ft, 1.25 m) and could take engines of 100-105 hp. It was to have had folding wooden wings, a steel tube fuselage with laminated reinforced plastic monocoque shell, tricycle undercarriage, airbrakes and customer choice of either the Mignet simplified control system, or the more conventional three-axis controls. After thirty years of campaigning for his tandem wing designs and simplified control system, Mignet was finally to be seen bowing to established convention. In either form the HM.400 did not see the light of day, so its impact will never be known.

Mignet came to settle in Pessac, a suburb of Bordeaux, where an old friend, Jean-Daniel Allard, found him a well-positioned and comfortable flat. There was continued interest in the HM.400, but remembering his bitter experiences from around the world where promises came to nought, Mignet was disinclined to take any notice. The cancer returned, but Mignet thought a return to Brussels was not worthwhile. Instead he went to the Bergonie Foundation in Bordeaux, where for a while it was thought he might not have cancer at all. He attended a bone specialist and his family lived in hope that he would recover with the special treatment he was receiving.

It was an impossible fight. In 1965 Mignet was positively diagnosed as having cancer and his battle for life ended on 31 August. The self-proclaimed *'Patron-Saint'* of Amateurs was gone.

Henri Mignet (1893-1965) was buried in the family vault at the village church of Saint Romain de Benet, between Saintes and Royan in the *département* of Charente-Maritime. He had finally come home to the part of France he loved best.

Sampling the HM.380

One of the first homebuilt examples of the HM.380 to get underway in France was the work of François Belleville, built at Aix-les-Bains, near Chambéry in the French Alps. F-PKFN a 65 hp Continental-powered, side-by-side two-seater is one of the highest-houred Fleas still flying. It holds particularly fond memories for co-author Geoff Jones who had a chance to fly this aircraft at the 1986 RSA international rally at Brienne.

Still finished in the dark maroon in which it made its first flight 25 years ago, this 'mature' homebuilt has flown well over 1,000 hours in complete safety, and is now operated by a flying group calling themselves *Les Ailes du Lac du Bourget* based at Challes-les-Eaux to the south east of Chambéry. Helping in the de-learning and re-learning process involved in flying this Flea was group member Pierre Devaucoup.

F-PKFN has undergone two major changes in its life, a conversion to a tricycle undercarriage, in which configuration it was displayed at the 1975 RSA rally at Laval, and more recently the addition of a Croses-style rudder/tailwheel combination. By the time of Brienne's RSA rally in 1986 it had long reverted to the neater tailwheel undercarriage. From the outside in 1986, the most striking feature was *Foxtrot November's* unusual propeller. Carved from wood by its original builder, Belleville, each blade is sickle-shaped, the theory being that the tip of the prop moves forward through the air at a higher rpm, resulting in better performance in the climb.

A view of the scimitar-like propeller on HM.380B F-PKFN.
(Geoffrey P. Jones)

HM.380B F-PKFN taxying at the 1986 RSA rally at Brienne, note the rudder/tailwheel modification.
(Geoffrey P. Jones)

The trouble with this air test was that Pierre Devaucoup spoke no English and the author very little French. It was to be a check-out by sign language and practical demonstration. Access to the HM.380 for both occupants is by a hinged door on the starboard side. At first glance the machine did not look too different from any other homebuilt light aircraft. Outside through the canopy, the large pivoting wing sat above us and behind was the other wing, appearing to be like a large span tailplane.

Inside the cockpit the central control looked rather like ram's horns with grips at the top, the whole construction protruding from the base of the basic, but adequate, instrument panel. The throttle was on the central console, and from the floor between the seats projected an unfamiliar gear lever-type control which could easily have been taken for a flap lever. There *were* pedals, not for the rudder as in a conventional aircraft, but simply for the wheel brakes.

It soon became evident that manoeuvring this Flea was to be a hands only experience!

HB-YBK, a more conventional HM.380, with the original rudder, built by H. Chaix.
(Geoffrey P. Jones)

Cockpit of F-PKFN showing the unusual control yoke and the 'gear stick' between the seats.
(Geoffrey P. Jones)

HM.380 F-PKFN flown by Pierre Devacoup. This aircraft is the subject of Geoff Jones's air-test.
(Geoffrey P. Jones)

Excellent all-round visibility on the ground was welcome as people and aircraft mingled on the Brienne taxiway. Control by the 'stick' for ground handling was soon learnt, the tailwheel being incorporated neatly in the rudder which was moved by a left or right sideways movement of the control column. This column pivots part of the way down so that the pilot is effectively holding an inverted control column. Extra control on the ground in tight spaces was achieved by means of differential use of the toe pedal brakes.

Out on the runway, amid a flurry of activity an application of full power had us rolling with the Continental A65 turning over quite sweetly. Before long *Foxtrot November* was off the ground and established in a steady climb of about 800 ft/min (4 m/s). With a beam on his face, Pierre pointed to his watch, the VSI (Vertical Speed Indicator) and the altimeter from which one could conclude that the aircraft had an excellent rate of climb two-up on a relatively low-powered engine.

It was now time for the first handling demonstrations, initially at normal rpm in level flight. Control could be described as sensitive with the slightest movement of the column backward or forward disturbing the big wing above our heads and setting the HM.380 into an unsteady, undulating, flight pattern. Turning was a new experience, allowing the aileron-rudder-elevator combination of a conventional aircraft to be forgotten. As the aircraft began to feel a little more familiar one could understand how Mignet's idea would enable a novice flier to learn easily and naturally. There was a tendency for the aircraft to dutch-roll in the hands of this conventionally trained and inexperienced Flea pilot because of the unfamiliar and sensitive controls, but things soon settled down. Pierre then set about his non-stall, non-spin and unusual attitude routine!

With the language barrier ever-present the 'gear lever' between the seats was demonstrated. This is connected to a trailing edge trim surface on the rear, fixed, wing and helps to control the attitude of the aircraft, also acting as a kind of flap. This is operated in conjunction with the main control column so that with the trim back and the stick forward a gradual descent is made. Conversely, with the trim forward and the stick back the HM.380 climbs. This clearly demonstrates one of the characteristics of the Flea, that in general the front wing automatically stays level in flight and the remainder of the aircraft, including the fixed rear wing, alters in attitude.

In level flight Pierre pulled the nose up, trimmed backward and cut the power, and the Flea assumed a very high angle of attack and the airspeed indicator wound down until at

35 mph (58 kph) F-PKFN trundled through the air, nose high, on a trickle of power yet virtually no rate of descent registering on the VSI. Pierre pointed to the instruments and beamed again – a totally convincing demonstration of the aircraft's slow speed handling under minimal power. There followed similar demonstrations, but in different attitudes. Into a left-hand turn with low power, 30 degrees, then 45 degrees of bank, and all the while pulling back hard on the control column; in any normal aircraft this would have meant entry into a spin or spiral dive, but not so in the HM.380. The process was repeated to the right, with Pierre, as ever, pointing successively to the airspeed indicator and the VSI.

For the approach back into Brienne a short field landing on the grass strip was on the menu. The approach looked as though it was going to result in an overshoot, because the Flea was so high and not far from the threshold on the relatively short runway. This presented no problem to Pierre. The 'trim' was adjusted, the stick pulled right back, and a trickle of power fed on and off as required in a repeat of the slow speed handling demonstrated fifteen minutes earlier up at 3,000 feet. We came down steeply but under control, like a parachute, to a perfect three-pointer that, had it not been for traffic behind, could have seen us roll to a stop in less than 200 feet (61 metres).

The aircraft is controlled in pitch by the variable incidence of the front wing and there was a risk that the uninitiated could 'over-pitch' and semi-stall the front wing in the early Fleas. A remedy from this undesirable situation was soon introduced with restrictions on the incidence of the front wing and detailed attention to centre of gravity, powerplant etc. In F-PKFN can be found a two-seat Flea that has flown safely for over 25 years, is different in the air as far as a conventionally trained pilot is concerned, but is proven to be completely safe with excellent controllability.

Mignet did get the concept right, despite the unfortunate experiences of 1935/1936. Mignet had done a large amount of work to test the design of the HM.14 to the best of his abilities. He could not control constructional quality, powerplant suitability or pilot ability. The aerodynamic research undertaken at Chalais Meudon and Farnborough was well beyond his resources. Faced with the knowledge of the problems of the HM.14, a 'fix' was forthcoming quickly. The concept of the tandem winged aircraft with the unusual control system has been proved consistently to date, through Mignet's own subsequent designs, and those of his disciples – including his son – and his design philosophy will doubtless continue to be used by designers still to come. Mignet's tandem wing design should not be 'knocked' any more.

Chapter 14

A GLOBAL FOLLOWING

IT IS NOT SURPRISING THAT MIGNET'S wanderings on a world-wide scale have resulted in people in vastly differing countries becoming addicted to the Flea 'bug'. Even in countries he did not visit in person, the name 'Pou' or 'Flea' had an instant meaning for many with only the slightest aviation knowledge.

So far events and aircraft related to Mignet have been discussed in Argentina, Belgium, Brazil, Canada, France, Great Britain, Ireland, Japan, Morocco, Switzerland, Tunisia and the United States. While these countries showed the greatest activity, research has shown that there were many more besides where aircraft bearing the designation 'HM' have been built and flown.

Mignet's designs first started to spread outside his native France with the HM.8. Influence here was not too widespread and was in general restricted to French protectorates

and colonies such as Indo-China (present day Vietnam), the Sudan and one recorded in Océanie (French islands in the Pacific, such as Tahiti). This spread is understandable as Mignet's self-published book on the HM.8, *Le Sport de l'Air* was initially restricted to the French language. Things were to change with the advent of the HM.14 Pou du Ciel and Mignet's book on this subject, also called *Le Sport de l'Air*. This was widely printed in France, and, through the Air League of the British Empire, appeared in an English translation as *The Flying Flea*.

Fleas are known to have been built beyond these boundaries in Australia, Czechoslovakia, Denmark, Finland, Germany, Japan, the Netherlands, New Zealand, Sweden and, it is thought, even in the Soviet Union. There is every probability that this list could be enlarged upon, South Africa being a likely candidate for Flea activity. The very nature of Mignet's initial philosophy, which approached flying as a freedom of right which, if necessary, would mean disregarding authority for its fulfilment, has conspired to keep the activities of many Flea builders out of public archives and, therefore, some form of regimented chronicling.

In more recent years with development of Mignet designs, and new tandem wing aircraft such as those of Croses, at least two more countries can be added to the Mignet 'club'. These are Chile, where a Croses EC-3

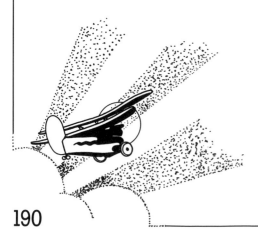

Pouplume has been built and Italy where, thanks to the efforts of Nedo Lavorini, two new metal microlight versions of the Flea have been built in the last eight years. With the upsurge in construction and flying of microlights the spread of Mignet design philosophy may only just have begun.

Argentina's 'Pulga' family

Mignet's influence in South America was considerable. It was reinforced by the visit to Argentina in 1962 of Emilien Croses and also by the emigration of French HM.14 and HM.290 builder Jean de la Farge. The South American connection gave a new sound to the generic name for Mignet's tandem wing aircraft: *La Pulga del Cielo*. De la Farge had worked with the resistance in the Auvergne for eighteen months, becoming familiar with the HM.280 Pou-Maquis. Immediately after the war ended de la Farge, living at Barriac-les-Bosquets, was one of the first amateur aviators to get back into the air, using a rebuilt HM.14. Writing about this he recalled, ' . . . the HM.14 ended badly, since I landed it upside down – no great problem so long as you keep your cool!'

When the HM.293 design became available de la Farge completed one with a 19 ft 8 in (6 m) span wing, NACA 23012 wing profile and a 25 hp Poinsard engine. It flew well but was soon sold to allow de la Farge to concentrate on the building of a similar aircraft with an 18 ft (5.5 m) span wing and a 32 hp engine. Following almost exactly in Mignet's footsteps, de la Farge took his HM.293 on a lengthy series of flights wandering 1,500 miles (2,500 kilometres) through much of France and Belgium, flying with neither official papers for the aircraft nor a private pilot's licence for himself.

One of de la Farge's uncles was the French military attaché in Argentina and Jean moved there in 1950 at the same time that Mignet was working at FADAM and trying to market and produce the HM.300 *Annette Mignet*. Mignet visited de la Farge, whom he knew of old, but de la Farge was most disappointed with the *Pulga del Cielo*, which had a 125 hp engine but was only really able to carry two people. Jean designed and built a new propeller for the HM.300 and it was then capable of carrying a pilot and two passengers. De la Farge returned briefly to France, but came back to Argentina in 1952 to settle in Cordoba, very close to where Mignet (by then in Brazil) had been working.

Working in an iron foundry, de la Farge largely ignored aviation until 1960 when he was bitten by the *Pulga* 'bug' again. He rebuilt a

French-born Argentine Flea pioneer Jean de la Farge's 1960 *La Pulga en Pacheco*, first with the now characteristic T-tail.
(Jean de la Farge)

A proud Jean de la Farge in one of his later generation 'Pulgas', 1986.
(Jean de la Farge)

A de la Farge 'Pulga' in flight showing the distinctive tandem wing-plus-tailplane layout.
(Jean de la Farge)

HM.290 with a 40 hp converted Renault car engine, producing a single-seater with an 18 ft (5.5 m) span wing with a T-tail perched on the fin and rudder. This aircraft had the centre of gravity moved from 25 to 32 per cent of the length, wing profile was a NACA 3012 and it could cruise at 91 mph (150 kph). Called *La Pulga en Pacheco* it was, like all those of the Mignet formula, completely stable in all aspects of flight.

Politics in Argentina started on the downward slippery slope (not for the first time, of course) in 1973, a slide that was to culminate in the Falklands crisis and the eventual toppling from power of The Generals. Industry and commerce suffered and yet it was in this climate that de la Farge took up the *Pulga* question again. There was a small group with similar ideas, who as well as being influenced by Mignet had also met with Emilien Croses during his visit to the country in 1962. There were twelve in the group initially and in the following years all started to build or assist with the building of several types of *Pulga*. This group has grown so that at the last count there were fourteen *Pulgas* in and around Cordoba, three in Buenos Aires and one in Asunción. It is interesting to note that homebuilding in Argentina is monitored by EAA Chapter 722, and aircraft built under this aegis are registered in the normal way; not so the *Pulgas*. The idea certainly took on and to quote de la Farge '. . . The Pou religion certainly reigns in Cordoba'.

This particular sect of the 'religion' have built updated and modified versions of de la Farge's *Pulga en Pacheco* with its tandem wings and T-tail. Jean had hoped to start a school for amateur constructors in Argentina, but the collapse of the country's financial situation prevented this and he concentrated on his own amateur construction projects. One of the greatest problems in Argentina is the availability of engines. De la Farge expands on this subject:

'The shortage of engines suitable for homebuilts forced us to smuggle Volkswagens in from Brazil along with old German BMWs. My luckiest find was a scrap 65 hp Continental which I soon restored to its former glory. With this and my new airframe with an enlarged tail I was away and even though the aircraft's centre of gravity was at 36 per cent of its length and even in some of my friend's aircraft at 40 per cent, our aircraft still flew exceptionally well and were perfectly stable.

'One of the qualities of the design is that adaptations can be made and I am currently (1987) doing a rework of my aircraft to a tandem two-seater, to be powered by a 1600 cc Volkswagen with a 3:1 reduction gear and a 10 ft (3 m) propeller. This has an enclosed cockpit and an unusual gull-type forewing, the characteristic T-tail, spatted undercarriage and should also suit a Salmson radial as well. A similar project is also a two-seater, *El Moscardon*, but with side-by-side seating and the easily folding wings that have characterised many of Mignet's designs.'

Summing up his opinion of Mignet, de la Farge writes, 'despite his vicissitudes he remains a great name in aeronautical history'.

At Alta Gracia aerodrome near Cordoba the Farinoli brothers, Serge, Pancho and Filone, fly one of Argentina's best-known *Pulgas*, a two-seater with a 65 hp Continental engine, the T-tail, a 21 ft (6.4 m) main wing span with a NACA 23015 profile, and the typical Pou short field performance. On touchdown the tail is pulled up to 10 degrees negative, which lowers the fuselage and the rear wing, enabling the aircraft to land very slowly on its tall, stalky, undercarriage. Three other similar, but single-seat, versions are also flying at Alta Gracia. The example built by Galvani also has a Continental engine. Barau's a two-cylinder home-produced 1700 cc engine, and Seti's a converted Citroen car engine. All have similar wing spans, T-tails and NACA 23015 wing sections and all are unregistered.

Despite the enthusiasm for homebuilt aviation, and in some quarters for the *Pulgas*, de la Farge sums up the situation in Argentina at present. 'Here the clubs are in a black despair, material deteriorates and it isn't possible to replace it, also the Authorities are beginning to look askance at amateur aviators. The amateur movement is suffering from the disastrous effects of the economic situation and already one of our friends from the Pou-Club has emigrated to Australia and I am thinking of going to Brazil. Here one can hardly manage to survive.'

This may be painting an over-pessimistic

The 'Pulga' built by Mr Seti and powered by a Citroen conversion showing its ease of being moved by road and bulky canopy.
(Jean de la Farge)

'Pulga' builders, Serge Farinoli and his sons, with the side-by-side two-seater behind.
(Jean de la Farge)

picture for at the EAA's 5th National Argentinian fly-in at Mercedes in December 1986 a large number of light aircraft, homebuilts and microlights turned up. None of them was a *Pulga*, but then perhaps they like to keep themselves out of the limelight beneath the foothills of the Andes at Alta Gracia, near Cordoba.

The *Pulgas* are not the only Mignet followers to be found in Argentina. At the December 1987 'Expohobby' exhibition in Buenos Aires an example was shown of one of several HM.290 variants built and marketed on a semi-commercial basis by a company called Avex. Marked as 'LV-X82' (but actually LV-X90), this was built by Rodolfo Maurette, powered by a flat-four inside a substantial-looking cowling.

Elected as Grand Champion homebuilt at the San Pedro flying convention of December 1987 was Marcelo Bonacina's immaculate 65 hp Continental-powered Croses EC-6 LV-X66. Bonacina, from Santiago del Estro, had previously built Croses Pouplume LV-X218.

Croses EC-6 LV-X66 built by Marcelo Bonacina, was the 1987 Grand Champion Argentinian homebuilt.
(Geoffrey P. Jones Collection)

Rodolfo Maurette's Avex HM.290 variant on show in Buenos Aires in December 1987.
(Daniel Gomez)

Australian loyalty

It is clear that the Flea 'bug' travelled early to Australia and a few die-hards continue to stick with the breed. Mignet's HM.14, however, seems to have circumvented Australian aviation authorities completely and knowledge of who-flew-what in this vast land is limited. What there is results from the researches of modern-day Flea-builder Bob Cornwell of Greta, New South Wales.

The earliest known Australian-built Flea is the HM.14 built around 1937 by the Rudd brothers of Melbourne. Powered by a Blackburn Thrush, it is reported to have flown well. The Rudds

were killed during the Second World War and the HM.14 was acquired by J. Friswell of Bendieo, Victoria. The engine then went on to Tom Mulcahy of Mount Emu. Tom had P. J. Pratt, well known in Australian gliding circles, build an airframe for him. Pratt is thought to have built three other HM.14s prior to this, at least one being fitted with a surviving Carden-Ford engine. The war is reported to have stopped further progress on these machines.

Post-war, Doug Bloomfield of Wangaratta, Victoria, acquired an HM.14 of unknown provenance. It is now displayed in the Drage's Air World Museum and is fitted with a Rotax engine. Bob Cornwell himself built an HM.14 over a ten-month period in 1988/1989 and it is fitted with a Chotia 460cc single-cylinder, two-stroke engine rated at 28 hp.

A modified Croses Pouplume fitted with a Rotax 277, has been built at Wangaratta by Australia's most avid Flea-maniac, Jim Jensz. At Kapunda in Southern Australia, Gordon Laubsa has built an HM.293, fitted with a 1500cc Volkswagen. All of the above aircraft have no official identity, despite the fact that Australia has a flourishing homebuilding movement

Belgian cousins

Belgium has seen considerable activity from Flea aviators. Since 1946, when the plans of the HM.290 were detailed and sold through the Belgian magazine *L'Aéronef*, there has been a steady stream of Mignet-designed and Mignet-derived aircraft projects. No book on the Flea would be completed without mention of the Belgian aviator Fernand Noiset. During the

1960s and 1970s Noiset toured extensively in mainland Europe with his 65 hp Continental-powered HM.293 OO-11. With this relatively large engine the aircraft was extremely spritely, a fact that Noiset took great delight in demonstrating to air rally crowds on his travels through France, the Netherlands and Switzerland. Over the years his aircraft became adorned with an increasing number of stickers from rallies, flying clubs and towns that he visited – he had completely covered the starboard side of the fuselage and was well on the way to covering the port side when due to ill health he gave up flying, and retired OO-11 to the AELR Museum.

At the dawn of the microlight era, the Belgians G. François and R. Mossoux designed and built a hang glider with a Mignet-type tandem wing. This was motorised at the beginning of 1979 with a McCulloch M101 engine mounted on a pylon behind the rear wing. With an empty weight of just 88 lbs (40 kg) the Butterfly, as it was called, was one of the lightest of the microlights.

Flown by René Thierry, the Butterfly took part in the September 1982 London to Paris microlight air race, continuing to fly and to land safely in bad weather when all the other participants were safely on the ground. This echoed Mignet's December 1934 demon-

Romibutter OO-504 built by Michel Rocourt in the static park at Brienne 1987.
(Geoffrey P. Jones)

strations of his prototype HM.14 in very windy conditions at Orly. The design of the Butterfly was changed and diversified during the early 1980s, the 1984 version, the Lascaud Butterfly, being detailed in Chapter Fifteen.

In Belgium the Butterfly concept saw a resurrection in 1987 with the Romibutter, built by Michel Rocourt at the *Aéro Club de Hesbaye*. Using the wing, tail and fuselage design, Rocourt enclosed the fuselage and instead of a pusher engine installed a conventionally-placed Rotax in the nose. Registered OO-504, in smart red and white scheme with spring steel undercarriage, the aircraft was first displayed at the RSA's annual international rally at Brienne in France in July 1987.

Italian emergence

For a country with no history of post-war homebuilding until about ten years ago, it is somewhat surprising to find a keen advocate of the Mignet philosophy in Italy. Nevertheless Nedo Lavorini, from Monsummano, has designed and built two versions of the Flea in the last ten years. Both are what could be

The first Lavorini Flea of 1981, with a very HM.14-like fuselage shape.
(Geoffrey P. Jones)

termed unofficial, in that both have yet to be registered. The first Lavorini Flea, built of light alloy and powered by a 1600 cc Volkswagen engine, had a fuselage very similar in shape to the original HM.14. At the 1981 RSA rally at Brienne, Lavorini put his first Flea through its paces at the crack of dawn and by the time most people had roused, he had wrapped up his little aircraft and retired for the rest of the day!

Brienne 1987 saw the début of the Lavorini Flea MkII, although no flying was done. His second aircraft continues the use of metal in its construction, although this time the configuration is more unusual, the aircraft sitting low on the ground, with a pointed nose housing the enclosed cockpit and the pusher 25 hp KFM engine with the propeller turning just behind the trailing edge of the main wing. Like the HM.14, there is an all-moving rudder. Lavorini first flew the MkII in May 1987.

Netherlands revival

Another European country with little history of homebuilding until recently is Holland. Like West Germany and Switzerland, HM.14s were built there in 1935/1936. One was the work of E. J. D. Nagelgast. It was registered PH-EDO and when completed in 1936 was taken to the Dutch Government Test Centre for complete analysis. As a result of this no further HM.14s could be flown – at least officially – because the aircraft was pronounced to be 'too dangerous'. Another Dutch HM.14 was built at this time by H. J. Kampen, although this never flew.

All things change, and in 1987 the first post-war Flea was nearing completion in Holland, the work of Dick Siebelink at Haren. In 1979 he received permission to build a HM.290, using copies of the original plans from the 1946

Very different is the Lavorini Mk II Flea, which made its début at the 1987 RSA Rally at Brienne.
(Geoffrey P. Jones)

First post war Flea in the Netherlands HM.293 PH-MIG is nearing completion at Haren.
(Geoffrey P. Jones)

West German technology

Despite the country's general dearth of homebuilts, a few Fleas have materialised in Germany. HM.14 D-EMIL is displayed in the Auto und Technik Museum at Sinsheim, marked 'Aero-Club Brandenburg' as evidence of the Flea craze breaking into Hitler's regime. Herr F. L. Neher built an HM.14 at Stuttgart and this sported the swastika on the rudder. A similarly adorned HM.14, christened the *Lerche* (Lark), fitted with a 45 hp radial engine, was featured in a Leipzig publication in 1937. More recently the country has seen the construction of a 'plastic' Flea. Herman Frebel, utilising West German glider technology in the use of composite materials, has designed and built a modern-looking tricycle-undercarriage Flea-concept aircraft. This is the single-seat Frebel F.5 D-EAPT, which made its first flight in 1978 powered by a Volkswagen conversion. The fully pivoting main wing is supported on two sturdy-looking struts, the rear wing featuring a small 'tab' with a fin and rudder combination at the rear. After extensive developmental flying, plans were mooted in 1981 for a two-seater and to market plans for amateur construction. This has yet to materialise.

edition of *L'Aéronef* but under the supervision of the *Rijks Luchvaart Dienst* (the Dutch equivalent of the CAA or FAA). The aircraft is fitted with a converted DAF B74 car engine and is nearing completion, now registered as PH-MIG.

The very advanced, plastics-structure Frebel F5 was seen as the precursor to a two-seat production version.
(Geoffrey P. Jones Collection)

Chapter 15
FULL CIRCLE

HOW PLEASED HENRI MIGNET WOULD HAVE been, had he lived for a few more years, to witness the rekindling of his aspirations of the 1930s. Mignet was, in his own words, 'under the spell of the air', and he firmly believed that 'true amateur aviation is not a question of money'. Excellent ideals, but ahead of their time as a further fifty years of aviation experience has unfolded since Mignet first wrote those words.

In the late 1970s and early 1980s, the world witnessed an unprecedented upsurge of interest in sport aviation – an interest embodied in those quotes from Mignet and in line with what he had always advocated. Chanute, Lilienthal and Pilcher all used hang gliders for their experiments in the late nineteenth century and, thanks to research by Francis Rogallo for America's National Aeronautics and Space Administration the sport of hang gliding was to achieve a renaissance.

Rogallo's fabric wing, (developed as an alternative to the use of parachutes in returning spacecraft to earth), together with the availability of cheap, strong and lightweight materials completed the equation. With rapid refinement a few experimenters attached small domestic and light industrial use engines to their hang gliders and suddenly the sport aviation world was talking about the rebirth of the light aeroplane and of 'bicycles of the air'. Microlights (ultralights in the United States and ULMs – *Ultra Léger Motorisé* – in France) had arrived, bringing with them true amateur

powered sport aviation.

Few controls existed at first over who could fly these early microlights, over who could design and build them, or over the materials used. The inevitable happened. It was 1936 all over again with the newspapers full of microlighting accident 'news' stories that were, unfortunately, headed by several fatalities. In the United Kingdom, under the auspices of the British Microlight Aircraft Association, controls were introduced on piloting training and standards, airworthiness requirements and general guidance on this new form of sport flying. The same situation occurred around the world, including in France albeit less restrictively. Once again 'freedom of the skies' disappeared as the knot tightened.

Microlights were to mature from hang gliders with an engine strapped on with directional inputs coming largely from weight-shift to small lightweight aeroplanes with 'traditional' looking layouts and three-axis control. These developments were to see the return of the name Mignet. With the return of the famous name came the return of the famous tandem wings at the core of the Henri Mignet concept – the story had gone full circle.

The brainchild of Henri's eldest son, Dr Pierre Mignet, who lives in the town of his father's birth, Saintes, is the HM.1000 Balerit. After his father's death and a long period of sadness, Pierre started delving into Henri's notes, books and drawings. With considerable

In father's footsteps. The HM.1000 Balerit in flight. Location of the propeller can be seen to advantage with this view. (Geoffrey P. Jones Collection)

The Balerit Hydro float-equipped production version in a somewhat restricted flying area! (Avions Mignet)

Just as the HM.14 *Pou du Ciel* was roadable, so the HM.1000 Balerit is also capable of easy ground transportation. (Geoffrey P. Jones)

material and help from an old family friend, Pierre Alguier (builder of HM.14 No.49 in 1935) he designed and worked on the construction of an HM.384 development, the HM.385 Occitainie in the 1970s. With the advent of the microlight 'revolution', Pierre immediately saw close comparisons with his father's 'crusade' with the HM.14 so abandoned the HM.385 and together with his nephews Alain and Philippe and his niece Catherine, formed *Société d'Exploitation des Aéronefs Henri Mignet*. Their aim was to design and build a 1980s version of the Flea, but in the now popular microlight or ULM category.

Balerit is the popular name in Saintonge of the little Crecerelle Falcon, a bird which has long, slender wings, can glide well and can take to the air powerfully and rapidly –an appropriate name for the newly reborn Flea which possesses similar characteristics. Design work on the HM.1000 started in 1982 with the prototype first flying on 9 April 1984. By July 1985 the first pre-production Balerit was under construction. It flew for the first time on 21 November. An initial production batch of ten aircraft followed.

In true Mignet tradition the Balerit has a tandem wing configuration with control being effected on two surfaces, the pivoting forward wing and the rudder. The rear wing is fixed and there are no conventional roll surfaces. Balerit seats two side-by-side, a cockpit and nose fairing now enclosing the originally open framework. Power comes from a Rotax 503 Bombardier engine of 46 hp driving either a two- or three-bladed wooden propeller via a belt. Structure of the HM.1000 is light alloy tubing but with a carbonfibre, horn-balanced rudder, wood having long been usurped as the cheapest and lightest material. Overall empty weight comes to just 386 lb (175 kg) – about 50 lb heavier than the typical HM.14.

Embodying Henri's concept of a totally transportable aircraft that could be easily towed behind a car or even a motor scooter, the Balerit's wings are built up in three sections: a centre section (fixed to the fuselage frame) and two outer panels. These fold inwards on top of each other so that the span decreases from 24 ft (7.3 m) down to 8 ft 3 in (2.5 m). With the nose wheel detached the front of the fuselage frame can then be attached to a tow hook on a car for towing home, at speeds up to 50 mph (80 kph), on the aircraft's main

wheels for storage in a conventional garage. Folding the wings and converting the aircraft into a trailer takes less than five minutes. An example of the Balerit has already been fitted with floats. In 1986 the pre-production HM.1000 achieved second place in its class in the *Grand Prix de Paris*.

In the air the Balerit can be flown sedately or spectacularly. When Pierre Mignet first brought the Balerit to the RSA international rally at Brienne-le-Château in July 1985 it was the latter form of flying that captured the crowd's imagination. The Pou concept had always been claimed to give aircraft excellent short take-off and landing (STOL) performance and with Pierre flying the Balerit off the short grass strip at Brienne nowhere was this better proved.

The Croses Family

To Emilien Croses, based at Charnay-les-Macon, just to the north of Lyon, must go the title of Mignet's number one faithful friend and disciple.

Croses first started 'flying and building aircraft in 1936, when like so many Frenchmen of similar ilk, he built an HM.14 *Pou du Ciel*. This was followed by an HM.293 and then his own first design, a tandem, two-seater, the Sarolea. His second aircraft was the Croses EC-1-01 in 1948, a side-by-side two-seater fitted with a 50 hp five-cylinder Boitel engine. This aircraft (F-PCZP) was subjected to official Air

**Dedicated Mignet disciple, Emilien Croses with his mammoth EC-9
(Geoffrey P. Jones Collection)**

Emilien Croses' EC-1-02 F-PIHL in its original form with conventional tail arrangement.
(via Geoffrey P. Jones)

ministry tests at the *Centre d'Essais en Vol* at Bretigny to enable it to be granted a 'Permit' under the CNRA registration system. In 1956 Croses improved this design in the EC-1-02 (F-PIHL) fitted with a 65 hp Continental engine. This aircraft is still flying though in substantially modified form.

Croses, and in more recent years his son Yves, have between them designed and built a complete range of Flea-type aircraft.

The smallest of these epitomized the philosophy espoused by Mignet with the HM.14. This was the Croses EC-3 Pouplume (Flea Feather) which took about 600 hours to build and flew for the first time in June 1961. This aircraft was arguably the world's first microlight and was built to compete in the International Concours of Bourges, 6.2 miles (10 kilometres) around a closed circuit having an engine of less than 175 cc. Powered by a tiny converted 10 hp Monet Goyon motorcycle engine it weighed in at only 243 lb (110 kg) empty. With pilot and fuel the EC-3 has a take off weight of 485 lb (220 kg) and is capable of lifting its own weight and not surprisingly was the easy winner at Bourges. Following true Flea tradition, the EC-3 was built of wood, the wings being fabric covered and the fusealge ply covered. The rear wing was fixed and the forward wing

pivoted with a large rudder supplying directional control.

Initially Croses fitted a 150 cc engine in the EC-3, but realised that this was too small. Even with a 230 cc Monet Goyon the economical cruising speed was a mere 31 mph (51 kph). The prototype, registered F-PKFA, was a true 'motorcycle of the air'; its wheels came from a Vespa motor scooter. The tailwheel was incorporated in the rudder.

Croses EC-3 Pouplume with a 10 hp Monet Goyon conversion and motor scooter wheels, first flown June 1961. Arguably this was the world's first microlight.
(Geoffrey P. Jones Collection)

F-PIHL Croses EC-1-02 in its latest version at an RSA Rally at Brienne.
(Geoffrey P. Jones)

Like Mignet before him, Croses travelled to South America and at the end of 1962 visited Argentina. In Buenos Aires he met Santiago Sabouret, Marcelo Bonacino and Alif Chaikh whom he helped with the construction of the first South American Pouplume. Registered LV-X28, this example was soon completed. The foursome set up Macon Ltd with a view to mass-producing the Pouplume in kit form for sale to amateur builders in both South and North America. The Pouplume was redesigned to accept engines as powerful as 65 hp. Croses has also built a larger side-by-side, open cockpit version of the Pouplume; when seen in 1987 it was fitted with a Rotax engine. As is evident from Chapter Fourteen, from the difficulties homebuilders have faced in South America and in particular Argentina, the chances of the Macon venture succeeding were slim. Pouplume LV-X28 is still extant, owned by Marcelo Bonacina who subsequently built one of Croses' later designs, the EC-6.

Croses' designs led eventually to the aircraft that has proved to be his most popular and well known homebuilt type, the EC-6 Criquet (Locust). The EC-6 is a side-by-side two seater which stands high off the ground giving excellent forward visibility, good ground handling and, like so many Flea-types, exceptional short field and climb performance. Prototype EC-6 was registered F-WNGA and, powered by a 90 hp Continental C90, first flew on 6 July 1965.

Still made of wood and fabric, Croses having

Around forty Croses EC-6s have flown so far, making it a very popular type. F-PYFV, illustrated here, has visited Britain on two occasions.
(Geoffrey P. Jones)

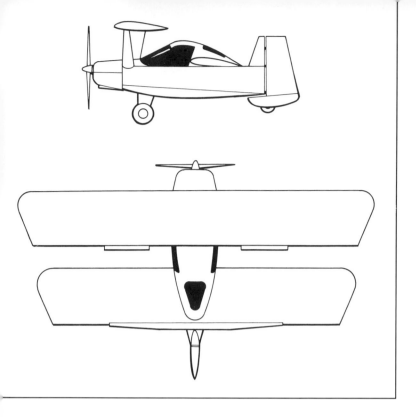

General arrangement of the EC-6.

stuck to the materials employed by Mignet until his most recent designs, the EC-6 showed the first signs of shaking off the somewhat staid and out-dated looks that had characterised Flea designs up to that time. The most prominent of these characteristics are the cantilever main undercarriage legs, like those on a modern Cessna but made of wood and wrapped in glass-fibre, and the V-form cantilever struts that support the forward wing. As with the Pouplume, the EC-6 has its tailwheel neatly

incorporated in the base of the rudder. A concession to the original Flea tandem wing formula are small flaps set into the trailing edge of the rear wing, which are used as pre-set ailerons to assist with cross-wind handling.

Construction is claimed to be easy with attention being given to time-saving items such as the wing ribs being cut from thin ply and not requiring the usual cut-outs to lighten the structure. At least sixty EC-6s have been built, or are underway in France. By 1988 271 Croses aircraft of all type were recorded as being under construction of which 68 are known to have flown.

EC-6 operators will not quote a stall speed for the Locust because, like most Flea designs from the earliest days of Mignet's ideas, it will not stall. This is a topic that present-day Flea aviators all over France will expound upon at great length. Other design attributes that will come out in such an oratory include the fact that it will not spin and that it is a very safe aircraft in all flight regimes. Croses is still mystified as to why no British builder has so far attempted to construct one of his aircraft, particularly the EC-6. The scars of the 1930s must still be there. Emilien sums up the apparent snubbing of his designs with a stoic, 'It is not for nothing that the English are the English.'

Composite materials as a mode of construction for light aircraft first came to the fore in the early 1970s. The first homebuilt aircraft to use these materials was Claude Piel's CP.80 Zef, a single-seat Formula One racer. The prototype Zef first flew in 1973 – almost two years before Burt Rutan's prototype Vari-Eze canard first flew in the United States. (Piel was greatly influenced by Mignet in his early days – see Chapter Eleven.)

Croses, well tuned to developments in the world of aviation saw the potential for this method of construction and in the years 1973 to 1975 worked on an all-plastics single-seat version of the EC-6. This he called the Croses Mini-Criquet. To date only the prototype, F-PVQI, has been built, with the assistance of George Flicot and M.Millet. It first flew from Abbeville in 1975. F-PVQI's fuselage, engine cowling, fin, wing spars, upper wing support

The futuristic 'plastic' Croses Mini Criquet was built in the early 1970s at Abbeville. (Geoffrey P. Jones)

struts and main landing gear legs were made from polyester resin and glass-fibre. The wing ribs and other components were made from a material called Klegecel.

Despite the diversion of the Mini-Criquet, Croses' attentions were still to be largely focussed upon the basic Flea concept and on refining the EC-6. With a 100 hp Continental, the first of these was the B-EC-7 Bujon or Tous Terrains. The 'B' suffix denotes the involvement of M. Bujon in design and construction. The B-EC-7 was essentially an enlarged EC-6 capable of carrying three people or alternatively a pilot and one stretcher case. Living close to the Alps, Croses was always looking for practical commercial uses for his designs and the B-EC-7 was seen as ideally suiting the medical evacuation role in the Alpine environment. The B-EC-7 offered excellent STOL characteristics,

The large Croses B-EC-7 Tous Terrains was designed to capitalise on the type's excellent short field performance and can be equipped for carrying stretcher cases alongside the pilot. (Geoffrey P. Jones)

very low handling and approach speeds, a rugged, all-terrain, four wheel main undercarriage and was economic to operate.

So far only the prototype B-EC-7, F-PPPM, has been built and in 1987 was being operated

The cockpit of the B-EC-7 Tous Terrain F-PPPM showing the large control yokes. (Geoffrey P. Jones)

Similar to the EC-7, but not featuring the heavy duty undercarriage is the one-off EC-8 Tourisme F-PTXC.
(Geoffrey P. Jones)

View of the cabin of the B-EC-9 Paras-Cargo.
(Geoffrey P. Jones)

from Lognes airfield, near Paris. Croses has attempted for many years to obtain a full French equivalent of the British Certificate of Airworthiness for the type, so that it could undertake aerial work. Although the French authorities successfully completed a stress and design analysis, they would not grant a Certificate until it could demonstrate a recovery from a spin. It was 'Catch 22' for Croses. While a spin is theoretically possible it is not within the designed performance envelope of the aircraft. Indeed, one of the main selling points of the EC-6 is that it cannot spin or stall. In tests on a large scale model it was proved that a recovery from a spin could be made. Croses had plans for a full size EC-6 to be slung under a helicopter to spin the aircraft on its axis and release it with no forward speed in order to induce a spin, but this has not been carried out.

Similar to the B-EC-7 but without the rough-field landing gear was the next Croses design, the EC-8 Tourisme. As the name suggests it was intended as a three-seat tourer and equated roughly to the Robin DR.220 2+2 with its 105 hp Continental and the SAN Jodel DR.1050 with its 100 hp Continental. Jacques Langlois built the first EC-8, F-PTXC, which

Dominating the 1978 RSA Rally, in size if no other way, was the Croses B-EC-9 Paras-Cargo F-PYBG. (Geoffrey P. Jones)

made its first flight on 27 May 1973. To date it is the only example flying, but others are known to be underway.

Among all the accolades due to Emilien Croses, in his pursuit of popularising and proving that tandem wing Flea formula aircraft can be working aircraft as well as machined for enjoying the sport of the air, goes the distinction of having designed and built the largest Pou ever. His B-EC-9 Paras Cargo drew on all his experience and was unique in its attempt to produce an aircraft capable of cargo transportation yet built by amateurs. The B prefix acknowledged, again, M.Bujon, who assisted Croses in its construction.

Built from Croses' established wooden construction methods, the prototype F-PYBG was powered by a 180 hp Lycoming and had the four-wheel rough-field landing gear arrangement of the B-EC-7. Another feature was the large roller-type access door on the port side of the fuselage. Loads envisaged included parachutists, general cargo, stretcher cases, farming equipment and camping gear.

F-PYBG made its public debut in July 1978 at Brive in South West France, the venue of that year's international RSA rally. The lumbering aircraft joined overhead and most visitors to the rally did not really believe what they were seeing. Yet the aircraft was obviously totally manoeuvrable and apart from its odd and gargantuan shape, was quite at home in the busy airfield environment.

Mignet's two-control system of pivoting fore wing and rudder was used on the prototype, but as with most Fleas following the HM.14, tab control surfaces on the trailing edge of the rear wing were also fitted. Croses proposed that subsequent examples could have either the Mignet-style controls or the conventional three-axis system and that the B-EC-9 be offered to amateurs in plan or kit form.

The cockpit was nothing but spacious, with two steering-wheel type control handles poking out from the foot of a curved, sloping wooden instrument panel containing just the basic flight instruments. The throttle control knob was located centrally and the floor pedals were the wheel brakes. Extending down from the cabin roof between the two seats were twin levers, like throttles in a multi-engined aircraft. These were controls for the trim tabs on the trailing

The one-off EC-10 built by Jean Claude Balancard and partners at Roanne.
(Geoffrey P. Jones)

edge of the rear wing.

Considering the Paras Cargo's size, its ground handling was good. Although there was little clearance between the bottom of the fuselage and the ground, once the pilot had landed that was where it would stay as it was totally stable due to the extremely wide track, twin wheel undercarriage. Undercarriage track in fact came to almost half the wing span. Aspirations for this concept came to nought, although the prototype can still be found at Macon airfield and recent reports suggest it may be readied for further flying.

Jean Claude Balancard and partners from Roanne are flying the only example of the EC-10 Criquet, F-PXKK, which is a composites version of the EC-6, which first flew in 1975. Other one-off variations of the EC-6 theme include the Croses Noel CN.01, F-PYHQ built at Ussel which has a different rudder shape and tail wheel mount.

Landray Variations
Designations so far used for all Croses' designs have been taken from the designer's initials.

A Croses LC-6, following the variations of Gilbert Landray.
(Geoffrey P. Jones)

Gilbert Landray's first Flea-type design was a modified Croses EC-6, the Landray GL-1, powered by a 90 hp Continental.
(Geoffrey P. Jones)

Many examples of the EC-6 Criquet were, however designated LC-6. The 'L' derives from the surname of France's number two living Pou exponent, Gilbert Landray, who now lives at Crosne to the south of Paris. In the 1970s Landray built an EC-6 and, like so many homebuilders, varied the basic design to suit his own idiosyncrasies. It incorporated some composite components, had a sleeker, flatter-bottomed, more streamlined fuselage, a redesigned cockpit area, an additional pair of fore-wing stays and a neatly spatted undercarriage. Landray's version of the EC-6 was designated GL-1 and, like the B-EC-9, made its public début at the 1978 RSA rally. Subsequently Croses Criquets incorporating some of these modifications have been termed LC-6s. Both the LC-6 and the GL-1 are powered by the 90 hp Continental and are fast touring types capable of 120 mph (200 kph).

Gilbert Landray was an impressionable teenager when Henri Mignet was hitting the headlines in the mid 1930s. Landray was born in 1920 and learnt to fly soon after his seventeenth birthday in 1937. Since that time he has devoted himself to Mignet and his philosophy of flying. Landray recalls several meetings with Mignet and found the man was as charming and pleasant as his writings, just as he had imagined him to be. He found him a straightforwardly simple yet totally distinguished man and is proud to have known him. Mignet was very *vieille France* – the traditional old-fashioned Frenchman.

Most of Landray's flying has been in Flea-type aircraft. Since his GL-1 (F-PXDV) first flew in 1974 he has become even more prolific than Croses in his output of new and original tandem wing homebuilt aircraft. The GL-2 was a step back to the simplicity of the HM.14, being a single-seat, wood and fabric aircraft of small dimensions, affectionately called the Ami-Pou by virtue of its powerplant, a converted Citroen Ami 8 motorcar engine.

Complete departure from the norm was seen in the GL-3 Pous-Pou (F-PYIL) which was first seen in 1981 at the RSA's annual rally at Brienne-le-Château. Adopting the increasingly fashionable idea of using pusher powerplants in homebuilt aircraft – a trend much spurred on through the Vari-Viggen, Vari-Eze and LongEz families from American designer Burt

Still tandem wing, but employing even more radical thinking than Mignet, Gilbert Landray's GL-3 Pous-Pou F-PYIL.
(Geoffrey P. Jones)

Rutan – Landray designed this, the first tandem wing pusher. Again a Citroën conversion was used and to keep this and the propeller high off the ground at the rear of the aircraft a tricycle undercarriage was fitted. Wood and fabric construction was used for this revolutionary single-seater. The problem of rudder mounting associated with the pusher layout was overcome by positioning twin rudders on the rear, one each side of the engine. The enclosed cockpit had the strut-braced, pivoting, forewing mounted above it.

The GL-3 was soon emulated by Georges Briffaud with his single-seat GB.10 Pou-Push F-PYOJ, powered by a two-cylinder 438 cc Hirch. The GB.10 first flew on 23 June 1983 and, like the GL-3, featured twin tails, but this time mounted on the tips of the rear wing, more in the Vari-Eze mould.

Not satisfied with the power of the Ami-Pou, Landray decided to try another commonly available and lightweight car engine, the 650 cc/27 hp Citroën Visa. Hence the Visa-Pou was born, a basic ultralight that was in the French ULM category for weight and performance, the same as the HM.1000 Balerit described earlier. Landray was awarded the SFA prize (Coupe Allard-Henri Mignet) by the RSA when the Visa-Pou made its début at Brienne in 1983. Subsequently the Visa-Pou has been flown extensively by an assortment of pilots including several test pilots, all finding the aircraft a pleasure to fly and virtually faultless.

Unveiled in 1986 was Landray's most recent Pou design, the GL-6, a side-by-side two-seater. Again the automobile industry supplied the engine, this time the well tried and well proven 1800 cc Volkswagen. With wood and fabric the main structural ingredients the GL-6 features a robust undercarriage with the pivoting forward wing mounted on four struts stemming from the top of the fuselage. Like the Visa-Pou the GL-6's rear wing is only a couple of feet shorter than the main wing and both wings have a slight dihedral at their tips. Like most modern Fleas it also has a rudder and a fin for better directional stability.

The Briffaud GB-10 Pou-Push is one of a seemingly endless number of Flea variants, although only the tandem wing gives any lineage.
(Geoffrey P. Jones)

Named from its powerplant, the Landray Visa Pou, features a Citroën car engine conversion. (Geoffrey P. Jones)

Gilbert Landray's latest offering, the GL.06 which is firmly in the microlight category, yet seats two. (Geoffrey P. Jones)

Croses again

After the B-EC-9 the Croses 'design bureau' was quiet for a while. Then Emilien's sons, Yves and Alain, completed a ULM version, the Croses Airplume. Taking advantage of composites and the new lightweight engines, the Airplume was conceived in the true traditions of Mignet as a cheap, easy to build, easy to fly, fun aeroplane. Construction of the prototype started at Yves' workshop in Lyon in October 1983 and the Airplume flew for the first time on 3 April 1984 in plenty of time to make its début at that year's RSA rally at Brienne. Power was a 33 hp Cuyuna engine, giving a cruise of 60 mph with 'two up' as well as excellent short-field performance off grass or concrete.

A tandem two-seater, the Airplume is intended for sale to amateurs in kit form, the basic bathtub-like fuselage looking not unlike a fibreglass canoe until it is fitted out. In the first year of sales 26 kits were sold, confirming that despite drawbacks that may be levelled at the tandem-wing design, in France the popularity that it attracted from 1935 onwards has never really disappeared. Later 'production' versions of the Airplume have generally used Rotax engines for power. In 1987 the first crop-duster version was unveiled with the front cockpit substituted by a chemical hopper. Spray bars carrying atomisers were fixed to the sides of the fuselage.

Since the .Airplume the Croses have produced yet another tandem-wing design, the 'Criquet Léger', basically a lightweight version of the EC-6 but with open cockpit and powered by one of the excellent power-to-weight ratio Rotax engines that dominated the world of

Second generation, Yves and Alain Croses have produced the Airplume tandem wing, with distinctive bathtub-like fuselage.
(Geoffrey P. Jones)

microlighting in the late 1980s. The Criquet Leger was first demonstrated in public at the RSA international rally at Brienne in 1987.

For Emilien Croses' outstanding work in the field of homebuilt aircraft the RSA honoured him on 31 July 1988 with their coveted George Beraud Diploma. At the RSA's annual rally at Moulins. Croses was awarded the diploma by RSA President Louis Cariou. A previous recipient of the Diploma had been Claude Piel.

More disciples

1984 was a classic year in the recent history of RSA rallies. Being the *Henri Mignet Le Sport de l'Air Cinquantenaire,* fifty years since the famous book that started it all was published. The RSA Centre Loire organised the construction of a replica of Mignet's HM.14 No 1 and in the RSA hangar at Brienne built a tableau to represent Mignet's camp site in the Bois de Bouleaux, complete with motorcycle and sidecar, tent, bushes and the HM.14. Out on the airfield were eight Croses designs, eight Mignet designs and derivatives, the new Briffaud GB-10 Pou-Push, the Airplume, Balerit, Visa-Pou and two (yet to be described) new ULMs, the Butterfly and the Piel Onyx. This was a total of 22 Flea-type aircraft, all airworthy – probably the largest gathering of such types in one place that there has ever been.

Mignet's son, Pierre, was there, his brothers François and Vincent along with two of their

Replica of the HM.14 prototype, built by RSA Centre Loire and seen here on show at the 1985 Paris Air Salon.
(Ken Ellis)

The Onyx, designed by Claude Piel, father of the Emeraude and other classic aircraft and influenced considerably by Mignet.
(Geoffrey P. Jones)

The Lascaud Butterfly microlight, using the pivoting wing control system and tandem wings pioneered by Mignet.
(Geoffrey P. Jones)

sons. Helping in the celebrations was Pierre Lacour who had been the first president of the RSA when it was formed in 1946 after the war. For those wanting the famous book, *Le Sport de l'Air,* a reprint was launched by the RSA. Published in 1985 it was the fifth edition of the book, containing all the original text, plus several new chapters describing Mignet's later designs plus other developments.

Those other Fleas? The Piel CP.150 Onyx comes from the drawing board of Frenchman Claude Piel. Piel's name in light aviation ranks alongside that of Mignet, Joly and Delemontez (creators of the Jodel). The Onyx was to be Piel's last design, for he died in 1982. George Gangloff built the prototype. Like so many of the recent Flea-type designs the Onyx is in the ULM category and vaguely resembles a less streamlined, smaller, open cockpit version of the Briffaud Pou-Push. The forewing pivots

The Lascaud Bifly a development of the Butterfly. Kits or complete aircraft are offered.
(Geoffrey P. Jones)

The Roy GR.01 features aerofoil-shaped rear fuselage and a conventional tail with fin, rudder, and elevators.
(Geoffrey P. Jones)

above the cockpit and the larger, swept, rear wing has stabilators at its tips. Power comes from a small 12 hp Solo pusher mounted in the rear. Piel's son, Jean Claude, has set up Aéropiel, to market kits and plans of the Onyx. It is only marginally in the Flea category because of its three-axis controls.

Smaller than Mignet's original HM.14 is yet another ULM Pou, the Lascaud Butterfly. To match its tiny size it has a tiny Stihl chainsaw engine rated at 8 hp. The engine is located behind the forewing and in front of the rear wing. The pilot is 'seated' in a suspended canvas frame under the fuselage structure. Empty weight is only 143 lb (65 kg). This is a version of the Belgian Butterfly referred to in Chapter Fourteen and has now been complemented by the Bifly with similar wings, and enclosed fuselage and conventionally placed 275 cc JCV engine in the nose. In 1987 a complete kit for the single-seat Bifly was retailing for £2,800 including the engine. A completed and tested Bifly would cost £3,700.

Guy Roy has always been fascinated by Mignet and his aircraft. He first built a HM.381 two-seater, F-PLUJ, that flew for the first time on 13 December 1963. In the construction of this aircraft he was privileged to be helped by Henri and Pierre Mignet. Roy went on to design and build his own modified version loosely based around the Croses EC-6 in size and shape. This was GR-01 F-PSYT with its distinctive aerofoil-shaped rear fuselage and a striking red and white colour scheme. So far it is the only example to have been built.

Well known for many years in the European homebuilt aircraft fraternity is François Lederlin from Grenoble. In the early 1960s, wanting to build his own aircraft, he wrote to Mignet for details of the HM.350 but received back details of the new '360 and '380. Wishing to alter several aspects of the HM.380 he sought Mignet's advice. A very curt reaction came back; Mignet was far from happy so Lederlin set about his own design loosely based upon the basic wooden HM.380. He retained the spruce, plywood and fabric formula for the wings with box spars but used welded steel tube for the basis of the fuselage structure, covering this with light alloy at the nose and fabric at the rear. A spring steel landing gear, the same as used by Steve Wittman on his W.8 Tailwind two-seater in the USA, was incorporated, the tail was a fin and rudder made of wood with the rudder hinges coming from a Jodel. The engine was a Continental C90-14F with starter turning a McCauley 71/52 metal propeller.

Control for the Lederlin 380L is applied by varying the incidence of the whole front wing with a 0 to 12 degree range. There is a narrow flap on the trailing edge of the rear wing but used only for trim. However, Lederlin pointed out that it nonetheless has a very powerful action, enough to land safely in an emergency.

Lederlin 380L Ladybug, an original design by Grenoble-based François Lederlin based upon the Mignet HM.380.
(Geoffrey P. Jones)

The completed, two-seat aircraft weighed 800 lb (360 kg) dry, about 22 lb (9.9 kg) more than design weight, due to extra fuselage sound-proofing and the metal propeller. The centre of gravity was correct and no alterations were necessary to the rigging except for a small tab on the starboard wing to counteract torque at cruise speed – there are no ailerons so it is the only way!

The prototype, F-PMET, has been a familiar sight at European sport aviation events ever since its first flight on 14 September 1965, although it has now been put into semi-retirement as Lederlin has built himself a Rutan Vari-Eze. Plans for the 380L Ladybug were made available and although many sets were sold, only F-PMET has flown to date. Reflecting on the 380L after many hours of flight Lederlin praised the 'no-slip' aircraft in the air but had reservations about it in a strong cross-wind, near the ground. He proposed that the lateral motion of the stick be linked with spoilers on the outer front wing panels and the whole thing spring-loaded like the rudder pedals on a Jodel. 'Success in that respect certainly would put an end to the last valid argument remaining against Mignet's breed.'

At least one set of plans for the 380L crossed the English Channel. Jim Brayshaw of Harrogate, North Yorkshire, started construction under the aegis of the American Experimental Aircraft Association in October 1970. To have been powered by a Continental C90-14, construction of G-AYMR was suspended in 1979.

Other 'modern' Fleas keep appearing from homebuilders in France in the 1980s, particularly since the advent of the ULM 'revolution'. At Chatellerault, a blue and white version appearing to have the fuselage of the

A so far unknown Flea-type, seen in the hangars at Chatellerault in July 1987.
(Colin Giles)

There has been a series of 'new' designs going right back to basics and taking on very much the look of the HM.14. This VW powered version with cantilever undercarriage was to be seen at Brienne in 1981.
(Austin J. Brown)

The Turmeau HT-01 first appeared in 1984 and can be seen to follow strongly the HM.14 mould.
(Geoffrey P. Jones)

Landray Visa-Pou and the wings of the Belgian Butterfly, appeared in 1987, powered by a Volkswagen 1500 cc conversion. A few years before this, in 1981 a larger aircraft, an almost identical HM.14 with a Volkswagen and sturdy cantilever undercarriage was displayed at the RSA rally at Brienne. A similar, but different, aircraft was Hubert Turmeau's HT-01 F-PYLN that was one of the main Fleas at the RSA *Cinquantenaire* gathering at Brienne in 1984.

Monsieur O. Coutrot, a computer and data processing scientist by profession, is another builder with a Flea-formula ULM, based on the Landray Visa-Pou, which is a wood and fabric aircraft powered by a 844 cc Daf 44 converted motorcar engine. Coutrot paid 500 Francs for the engine, weighing 99 lb (45 kg) and modified the crankshaft, the intake and exchange pipes, and fitted two motorcycle carburettors in place of the original one. Net weight of his ULM Pou is only 308 lb (140 kg). When asked for the take off speed of his creation Coutrot answered, 'I don't know. I just look straight ahead and take off when the aircraft wants to!' Coutrot was given much help and encouragement with his Flea by Gilbert Landray.

Were Henri Mignet still alive he would have seen in Coutrot some of his own attitude to aviation and that *joie de vivre* for cheap, fun flying that he wanted to bring to the world through his HM.14. In France at least that spirit lives on prompting one to reflect on the verse of an inspired correspondent writing on the infection 'Poumania' in *The Aeroplane* for December 1935 following Stephen Appleby's successful crossing of the English Channel:

It isn't a plane it's not a balloon
And it's nothing that's found in the zoo
Makes a noise like a Peke that is baying at the moon
But we mustn't pooh-pooh the poor old Pou

FLYING FLEA PLANS

The following list is provided to help readers who wish to enquire further about Flea-type, plans, kits, etc. It is believed current at the time of going to press.

Avions Mignet HM.1000 Balerit
Société d'Exploitation des Aéronefs Henri Mignet (SEAHM), Logis de Pierrierres, Saint-Romain de Benet, 17600, Saujon, France.
Tel: 46.02.26.00.

Briffaud GB.10 Pou-Push
Georges Briffaud, 32 rue Pierre Curie, 78000 Versailles, France.

Croses Airplume
Yves Croses, 35 avenue de Saxe, 69006 Lyon, France.

Croses EC-6 Criquet
Emilien Croses, 63 Route de Davaye, 71000 Charnay les Macon, France.

Cuvelier/Lacroix Autoplan
Roland Cuvelier, Villers en Argonne, 51800 Ste Menehould, France.

Landray GL-1, GL-3, GL-4, GL-6
Gilbert Landray, 28 rue Remonteur, 91560 Crosne, France.

Lascaud Bifly and Butterfly
Établissements D. Lascaud, 41 rue de Crussol, 07500 Grange-les-Valence, France.
Tel: 75.44.47.02.

Lederlin 380L
François Lederlin, 2 rue Charles Péguy, 38100 Grenoble, France.

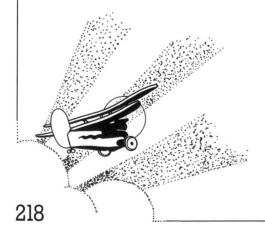

Mignet HM.14 Pou du Ciel

SEAHM (see the Avions Mignet HM.1000) stock the 1985 reprint of the famous Henri Mignet book *Le Sport de l'Air*. Greenhill Books published in 1988 a reprint of the English 1935 version in the Vintage Aviation Library series, entitled *The Flying Flea, How to Build and Fly it*.

Mignet HM.290E, HM.293, HM.297, HM.360, HM.380.
Chris Falconar, Falconar Aviation Ltd, 11343-104 Street, Edmonton, Alberta, Canada T5G 2K7.
Tel: (403) 479-3515.

Piel CP.150 Onyx

Aéropiel, 3 rue de Professeur Bordas, 19300 Egletons, France.
Tel: 93.09.79.

Notes: Many French suppliers of plans for homebuilds will only respond to requests for information if written to in French and if return postage is provided.

The authors of this book have provided the above information as a general guide. The inclusion of these details is not intended as an endorsement of these particular companies nor of their products. As a result the publishers and authors expressly disclaim responsibility for any unforeseen damage or injury resulting from the use or application of the above information and that contained in the main part of this book.

INDEX

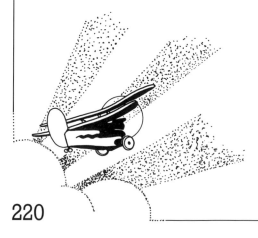